HISTORY OF RECONSTRUCTION IN LOUISIANA

SERIES XXVIII   NO. 1

JOHNS HOPKINS UNIVERSITY STUDIES
IN
HISTORICAL AND POLITICAL SCIENCE

Under the Direction of the

Departments of History, Political Economy, and
Political Science

———

HISTORY OF
RECONSTRUCTION IN LOUISIANA

(Through 1868)

BY

JOHN ROSE FICKLEN
Author of "Constitutional History of Louisiana."

———

GLOUCESTER, MASS.

PETER SMITH

1966

CONTENTS.

v

EDITORIAL NOTE.

The author of the present volume, John Rose Ficklen, son of Joseph Burwell Ficklen and Ann Eliza Fitzhugh, came of an old and sturdy family of Virginia, and the essentially fine qualities of the man were colored by that indefinable tint of gentility that is the precious heritage of such an ancestry. Born in Falmouth, Virginia, in 1858, he received at the University of Virginia that solid and yet broad cultural training that distinguished the old college, and after graduation he devoted himself at once to the pursuit of scholarship. After a short period of teaching at the Louisiana State University, Baton Rouge, Mr. Ficklen spent two years abroad, studying at the universities of Paris and Berlin. He was connected with the University of Louisiana, in New Orleans, before the foundation of Tulane University, and upon the merging of the two became professor of rhetoric and history. Mr. Ficklen grew with the newly created university, and soon began to devote himself to history, especially to the history of Louisiana. In 1893 he became professor of history and political science, and still held this position when, in the summer of 1907, his life was cut short by one of those accidents that seem the work of a blind fate.

In presenting to the public this last and most cherished fruit of his studies, I wish to turn aside for a moment to record my own impressions of Professor Ficklen as a man and as a teacher. I shall not soon forget the thoroughness of his method as an instructor, his innate refinement and unfailing courtesy in dealing with the student. In the class room, and when in later years I had the honor of becoming his colleague, Professor Ficklen was always the same helpful friend, unobtrusive yet ready in his counsel, generous, with no thought of making one who had been his pupil feel any condescension in his manner. It was this rare modesty and perfect frankness of attitude that was—I am confident other former pupils will bear me out—the most pleasantly remembered characteristic of the man.

For more than a decade before his death Professor Ficklen had been carefully collecting and digesting the materials for a history of the reconstruction period in Louisiana. The work was one requiring immense patience and tact, for the mists of party strife have not yet cleared away; many of the actors in the great contest for control of the State are still living; their accounts, as well as most of the documentary material for the work, even after they had once been secured, needed the most careful adjustment before it was possible to present a record at once clear and fair. Moreover, the work was frequently interrupted by other historical studies, and always made subordinate to the first duty of the academic instructor. But at the time of his death Professor Ficklen was proceeding rapidly in the synthesis of the scattered data he had collected, and the work now presented was completed by him in manuscript in something like the form he wished it to assume finally.

Since the manuscript, however, had not received his final revision, the editor has felt at liberty to revise, striving always to preserve the substance and the wording. There has been no alteration affecting matters of fact, no addition to or change in the deductions drawn from facts. Obvious errors have been corrected, a few passages of needless matter repeating facts stated elsewhere have been omitted, and the work has been divided into chapters. This has been done under the direction of Professor Charles M. Andrews, of the Johns Hopkins University, and under his direction the references have been verified and put into proper shape by Mr. Clarence P. Gould. The editor takes this occasion to acknowledge with gratitude the able assistance of Mr. William Beer, of the Howard Memorial Library, in verifying certain references.

In no state of the former Confederacy was the work of Reconstruction attended with greater difficulties than in Louisiana. The history of the period was marked by episodes that at the time attracted the attention of the nation, and that still echo in the press. It is a matter of deep regret that a student so well informed, so calm and judicious as Professor Ficklen did not live to complete in detail the account of the remarkable revolution whose beginnings he has presented with such clearness. Incomplete as it is, however, the present volume will prove a valuable contribution to the history of this most important period of southern history.

PIERCE BUTLER.

NEWCOMB COLLEGE,
  TULANE UNIVERSITY,
    February 19, 1910.

PREFACE.

It has been said by a northern historian that the story of the war between the States should be written by writers of the North because the victors can always afford to show, and will show, a more generous spirit in dealing with the facts than can be expected of the conquered, and also for the reason that the northern view is in the main correct. From this proposition the corollary has been drawn that the story of Reconstruction in the South should be told by writers of the South, for to the South was given the final victory in this conflict;[1] and it is beginning to be acknowledged by writers of the North that Reconstruction of the congressional type was a gigantic blunder—if not a political crime.

Whatever may be thought of the theories just mentioned, no one will deny that in the official records of the time we have the facts given in exasperating detail of the political progress of Reconstruction, innumerable investigations filling volumes, orders and statutes and decisions of court galore. For no other period is there so much sworn testimony, but of the life in the South at this period, of the thoughts and feelings of the mass of people who were disaffected to the Federal government, no adequate portrayal has been given for the South as a whole. Novelist and essayist have attempted it for particular States, but even here their attempts, however successful, have not given more than a partial view of life in the South during those days of storm and stress.

Such a book is not easy of execution. Those who lived through the time either do not care to write of their humiliation, or are so carried away by the intensity of their feelings that they present a distorted view of the period as a whole. The task must fall to the historian of the younger generation, but it demands a rarely sympathetic touch to draw

---

[1] David Y. Thomas, "The South and her History," Review of Reviews, October, 1902, p. 464.

forth from those who lived through this period the recollection that they would often rather conceal than reveal;
it requires much power of generalization not to lose oneself
in the infinite detail while drawing a picture that shall be
clear and distinct; and it requires a calmness and impartiality
of judgment, hitherto little shown by North or South, to
enter into the thoughts and feelings of that day and to
weigh its conflicting aims and purposes. To gather the
needed materials, to get into touch with those who can
speak with authority, will naturally be the task of southern
writers. Recognition of this fact has been constantly coming from the North itself, and the present writer has
received abundant encouragement from his northern friends
and colleagues in the arduous task of describing the reconstruction period in Louisiana since he set it before him
some five years ago.

It is not for the writer to arrogate to himself especial
qualifications for his task; but he might without presump-
tion urge that he has been accustomed for many years to
deal with historical problems in which the passions of men
were involved, and in this instance he was too young to
take any part in the events which he wishes to narrate, and
thus may escape some of the snares of partizanship. Actual
participants in a struggle are almost never the best narrators
of events. Their narratives are valuable for comparison
with the narratives of those who were opposed to them, but
generally those who participate are too near to see the
whole or to catch the proper perspective. Born in another
Southern State, the writer came to Louisiana just at the
close of the period of Reconstruction, and the best years of
his life have been passed among men who were active
participants in the work, and he numbers among his
acquaintances some of the prominent actors on both sides
of the great controversy. Upon these facts he bases his
hopes of a fairly unbiased judgment. He does not expect
nor wish, however, to produce a colorless narrative. He
proposes to comment freely on events and on the characters
of the men who figured therein.   JOHN R. FICKLEN.

HISTORY OF RECONSTRUCTION IN LOUISIANA (THROUGH 1868).

CHAPTER I.

ANTE-BELLUM HISTORY IN LOUISIANA.

There is a strong tendency in mankind to view the past through a golden haze—a tendency which is illustrated in history and literature from the times when the Homeric Nestor bewailed the fact that the young men were no longer so brave and strong as in his own youth down to our own day. Thus there are not lacking in Louisiana those who look back to the thirties and early forties with regret, and declare that at that period politics were pure, the office sought the man, and there was no rampant democracy to sue for the support of the proletariat and reduce all classes of voters to a level. These eulogists of the past would have us believe that in the years 1843 to 1846, when the old Whig party lost control of the State, and when not only was a Democratic governor elected but a Democratic constitution adopted abolishing the previous property qualification for the suffrage, Louisiana suffered a distinct deterioration in her political status and departed from the ideals she had held before her in the past. As democracy as a form of government is still on trial, it may not be possible to determine definitively whether the latter condition of Louisiana was better than the former; heredity and association will decide for most people whether they will take one side or the other. The fact remains, however, that the period mentioned records an important change in the dominant attitude of Louisiana toward political affairs. The State had for many years leaned toward the principles of the

Whigs. It is not to be expected that where towns are few and large plantations are numerous the seeds of democracy will find as favorable soil as in New England townships. Moreover, the Whig platform of protection to internal industries and of subsidies to internal improvements suited to perfection a State where each large plantation had invested much capital in the planting and manufacture of sugar and demanded protection, and where the numerous waterways needed the aid of the Federal government for their improvement.

But in the early forties the great mass of immigrants who had poured into the northern part of the State, where small farms contrasted with the plantations of the southern section, cared nothing for the theories of the Whigs, and their democratic sentiments were echoed by the foreign immigrants who took up their residence in New Orleans. Moreover, the Whigs began to lose popularity because of a new issue which had arisen like a storm cloud upon the horizon, and now began to overshadow ominously the question of protection to manufactures and internal improvements. This issue was the extension of slavery, violently opposed by the northern Whigs and strongly favored by the southern Democrats. Furthermore, the admission of Texas into the Union, which was already a national question, placed the Whigs of Louisiana in a quandary. As slave-owners themselves, they could not oppose the extension of slavery by the acquisition of Texas, but they feared the possible rivalry of Texas as a producer of Louisiana staples. In any case, in 1844 the State was carried for Polk and annexation by the political genius of John Slidell, who became the undisputed leader of the Democratic party, and who has never been equalled in Louisiana for skill in political strategy and for success in inspiring the blind devotion of political adherents. It is true that in 1848, in the national mix-up of politics, Louisiana, with five other Southern States, voted for Zachary Taylor, a Whig, but a resident of Louisiana and a slave-owner, in preference to Lewis Cass, the Democratic candidate, whose doctrine on the slavery question did not go far enough; but in all local affairs the Democrats held their own against the Whigs, and the spoils of office were theirs.

Many disgruntled Whigs went over to a new party which for a while exercised a great fascination over the minds of men in all sections of the country. The Know-Nothings, who derived their name from their invariable answer to all inquiries as to their platform that they " knew nothing in their principles contrary to the Constitution and the laws of the land," composed a gigantic secret society which appealed to many by its paraphernalia of signs, grips, and gradations of the initiated. Its principles seem to have included purification of elections, the exclusion of foreigners from public offices, and an insistence on the doctrine that the office must seek the man. We have the testimony of Charles Gayarré, the historian of Louisiana, who was an adherent of the new order, that not only the Whigs but the whole of Louisiana may truly be said to have rushed with enthusiastic precipitation into the arms of this seductive society. Soon, however, it began to be whispered about that the order was opposed to the Catholic religion and intended to proscribe all Catholics. The rumor was put to the test when, at a great convention in Philadelphia, a delegation of five Protestants and one Catholic presented themselves from Louisiana. The Catholic was refused admission,[1] and resenting this discrimination against a State in which half the population was Catholic, all the delegates withdrew. In vain the leaders of the movement agreed to make a discrimination on this point in favor of Louisiana; the order was doomed. In Louisiana its adherents fell away rapidly, and its secrecy and its religious intolerance, so opposed to the American spirit, precipitated its ruin everywhere.[2] In New Orleans, however, it did not die without a struggle. Such scenes of violence and intimida-

---

[1] This was Charles Gayarré himself.
[2] Gayarré, History of Louisiana, IV, 678.

tion occurred at an election for sheriff in 1853 that, though the Know-Nothings elected a sheriff named Hafty, he was removed from office by a formal act of legislature. The death-knell of Know-Nothingism had been sounded.

In Louisiana mutterings of the coming struggle between the States preceded actual hostilities by several years. As we read the messages of the governors of the State in the period before secession we catch more than one reflection of the deep unrest which filled the minds of Louisianians and of the defiant attitude which the utterances of the new or " Black " Republican party had aroused. " The irrepressible conflict between opposing and enduring forces," as Seward named it in 1858, had already been recognized as a reality by some of the wiser spirits of the time, and men had begun to take sides on the basis of the finer distinctions which the great controversy was bringing to light. A suspicion of heresy on the subject of the " peculiar institution " was sufficient to declare the ineligibility of any candidate for office ; nay, more, orthodoxy began to depend upon the correct attitude toward the doctrine of " Squatter Sovereignty " and the extreme view held as to Federal protection of slavery in the territories. It was even maintained that Slidell, the great leader of the Democracy, whose orthodoxy had been beyond reproach, was not above suspicion in regard to the extreme claims of his party, and that, being by birth a Northerner, he was not in full sympathy with Louisianians, but upheld the doctrines of Stephen A. Douglas.[1] Hence Pierre Soulé, a Frenchman by birth, but long a resident of Louisiana—a Prince Rupert of oratory—headed a factional fight against Slidell.[2]

When the Democratic convention met in Charleston in

---

[1] Soulé, who disliked Slidell, may have said this, but Senator Jonas says that there never was any truth in it; Slidell was always pro-southern.

[2] Soulé himself ended by becoming a Douglas man and a cooperationist, whether from conviction or from a desire to oppose Slidell does not seem clear. McCaleb says Soulé supported Douglas in 1856 and 1860: " Subsequently, to the surprise of his friends, he declared himself an opponent to the secession of Louisiana." The Louisiana Book, ed. by McCaleb, p. 137.

April, 1860, a strong opposition developed to the nomination of Douglas. On the question of the extension of slavery in the territories Douglas held the doctrine that the people of any territory in their territorial condition had the right to determine whether slavery should or should not exist there, and he denied the duty, or even the right, of Congress to protect persons or their property (slaves) in a territory against the will of a majority therein. This doctrine, that a territorial legislature was stronger than Congress itself and could determine the policy of a territory before it was ready to frame its constitution for statehood, was given full utterance by Douglas in his great debate with Lincoln in 1858, but it did not please the great majority of Southerners, who held that, according to the Dred Scott decision, Congress must protect slavery in a territory until the territory became a state.

In pushing his "Squatter Sovereignty" so far, Douglas lost, in a great measure, the adherence of the Southern States and forced them to choose a candidate who upheld their peculiar views. This candidate was John C. Breckenridge of Kentucky. The choice of Breckenridge produced a fatal schism; and, to make the situation still more desperate, some elements of the old Know-Nothing party and some new elements combined to nominate John Bell, of Tennessee, who conservatively held that the extreme views of Republicans and Democrats should be dropped and that the platform should be simply "The Constitution of the country, the union of the States, and the enforcement of the laws." Because of these Democratic divisions the Republicans carried their candidate, Abraham Lincoln, to victory on a platform which declared in favor of leaving alone the domestic institutions of the States and of keeping slavery out of the territories. The electoral vote for Lincoln was 180, and for all the other candidates 103; but the popular vote for the Democratic candidates was 2,823,741, while Lincoln received only 1,866,452. In Louisiana Breckenridge received 22,681 votes, Bell, 20,204, and Douglas,

7625. Slidell had organized his party so well that the State was carried for his candidate and Douglas was defeated; but it will be noted that the vote for Bell, representing the conservative view, was almost as large as the vote for Breckenridge.

In the meantime the messages of the governors of Louisiana to the General Assembly had shown evidence of the growing bitterness of feeling toward the North, and especially toward the Abolitionists. This party had indulged in unmeasured abuse of the South, and represented its whole industrial system as based upon sin and iniquity. It was a subject of special complaint on the part of the South that at least twenty Northern States had passed "personal liberty laws" intended to defeat the laws passed by Congress, in accordance with the Constitution, to secure the return of fugitive slaves. "Such acts," says Wilson, "were as plainly attempts to nullify the constitutional action of Congress as if they had spoken the language of the South Carolina ordinance of 1832."[1] Nor was this paying back the South in her own coin, for South Carolina at least maintained that her nullification ordinance was constitutional, while the North did not pretend to make any such claims for the "personal liberty" laws. Governor Chase openly declared that he would sustain by force, if necessary, the decision of the supreme court of Ohio against the decision of the Supreme Court of the United States, even if it resulted in a collision between state and general government.[2] Not at any time was nullification more rife in South Carolina than among Ohio Abolitionists.

Hence in 1856 we find Governor Hebert of Louisiana declaring in his valedictory message that "the wild spirit of fanaticism which has, for so many years, disturbed the peace of the country, has steadily increased in power and influence. It controls the councils of several states, nullifies the laws of Congress enacted for the protection of our property, and

---

[1] Division and Reunion, p. 208.
[2] S. S. Cox, Three Decades of Federal Legislation, p. 63.

resists the execution of them, even to the shedding of blood. It has grown so powerful that it now aspires to control the Federal Legislature. . . . The slave-holding States are warned in time. They should be prepared for the issue. *If it must come, the sooner the better.* The time for concessions on our part and compromises has past."[1] Again, Governor R. C. Wickliffe, who succeeded Hebert, in his inaugural address adopts a similar tone, and adds: "I do not wish to speak lightly of the Union. Next to the liberty of the citizen and the sovereignty of the States, I regard it as the 'primary object of patriotic desire.' It should be dear to us as a sentiment, and dearer to us for its real value. But it cannot have escaped observation, that the hold which the Union once had upon the affection of the South has been materially weakened, and that its dissolution is now frequently spoken of, if not with absolute levity, yet with positive indifference, and, occasionally, as desirable."[2] The election of Buchanan in 1856, however, came as a reassuring measure to the South, and the messages of the governors assumed a more hopeful tone; but in 1860 the rapid increase in numbers of the new Republican party aroused intense alarm, and the recent incursion of John Brown into Virginia summoned up the spectre of negro insurrection never entirely laid in the South.

No sooner was the election of Lincoln an assured fact than the legislature of Louisiana was called in extra session, and the governor's message expressed his belief that the election, "by a purely sectional vote, and in contempt of the earnest protest of the other section, . . . was to be considered as evidence of a deliberate design to pervert the powers of the Government to the immediate injury and ultimate destruction of the peculiar institution of the South." In accordance with a very general view in the South that action looking toward secession should be taken before the inauguration of Lincoln, the governor further advised the

[1] Gayarré, Louisiana, IV, 680.
[2] Ibid., 681.

legislature to issue a call for a convention " to meet *at once,* and determine *at once*" the attitude of Louisiana.   His own view of the matter the governor expressed in no uncertain tone: " I do not think it comports with the honor and self-respect of Louisiana, as a slave-holding State, to live under the government of a Black Republican President.   I will not dispute the fact that Mr. Lincoln is elected according to the forms of the Constitution, but the greatest outrages, both upon public and private rights, have been perpetrated under the forms of law.   This question rises high above ordinary political considerations.   It involves our present honor and our future existence as a free and independent people.   It may be said that, when this Union was formed, it was intended to be perpetual.   So it was, as far as such a term can be applied to anything human; but it was also intended to be administered in the same spirit in which it was made, with a scrupulous regard to the equality of the sovereignties composing it.   We certainly are not placed in the position of subjects of a European despotism, *whose only door of escape from tyranny is the right of revolution.*   I maintain the right of each State to secede from the Union, and, therefore, whatever course Louisiana may pursue now, if any attempt should be made by the Federal Government to coerce a sovereign State, and compel her to submission to an authority which she has ceased to recognize, I should unhesitatingly recommend that Louisiana assist her sister States with the same alacrity and courage with which the colonies assisted each other in their struggle against the despotism of the Old World."[1]

On January 7, when the election for members of the secession convention was held, the votes for the Southern Rights candidates is said to have been 20,448, and for their opponents 17,296.[2]   The policies of the opponents were

---

[1] Gayarré, Louisiana, IV, 689–90.

[2] J. F. Condon in Martin, History of Louisiana, p. 457; Lalor, Cyclopaedia of Political Science, subject " Secession." The present secretary of state for Louisiana (1903) informs the author that the returns of this election are not in his office, and that if they exist they are in Washington. No newspaper of the time published complete returns.

various, but the chief one was the cooperation[1] of the Southern States within the Union. The convention met at Baton Rouge, January 23, 1861, and adjourned two months later, Saturday, March 23. The message of the governor to the General Assembly, which met on the same day, was also read to the convention. The governor held that the recent election in relation to the convention "had confirmed the faith of their Representatives in the Legislative and Executive station that the undivided sentiment of the State was for immediate and effective resistance; and that there was not found within her limits any difference of sentiment, except as to minor points of expediency, in regard to the manner and time of making such resistance, so as to give it the most imposing form for dignity and success."[2]

After the convention was organized and Alexander Mouton elected president, J. A. Rozier, the spokesman of the cooperationists, proposed, as a substitute for immediate secession, the following: "That a Convention be called in Nashville, February 25, 1861, of all the slave-holding States, or as many as will unite therein to procure amendments to the Federal Constitution protecting the slave-holding States; and if these cannot be procured, it shall forthwith organize a separate Confederacy of slave-holding States." This motion, however, was lost by a vote of 106 to 24. James O. Fuqua, representing a somewhat different view, offered a motion providing that the coercion of any seceding State be regarded by Louisiana as an act of war on all slaveholding States, absolving any State from allegiance to the Federal government, and furnishing Louisiana with an opportunity to make common cause with the State attacked; Louisiana, however, should send delegates to Montgomery, February 24, 1861, and assist in the formation of a Federal union of slaveholding States. This hybrid motion was lost, 73 to 47.[3] The Slidell party, however, held that any plan for

---

[1] A cooperationist, according to the Century Dictionary, was "one who opposed secession unless carried out with the coöperation of other southern States."

[2] Gayarré, Louisiana, IV, 690.

[3] Journal of the Convention of 1861, pp. 11, 16.

cooperation within the Union was impossible of realization, as the army and the navy of the Federal government would have time to interfere before it could be executed.

Five States had already seceded, and on January 25, J. L. Manning, duly accredited commissioner of South Carolina, and John A. Winston, commissioner from Alabama, were conducted to the floor of the convention, and, showing their credentials like the ministers of foreign powers, addressed the convention on the wisdom of immediate secession. This appeal from sister States furthered the cause already strong in the convention. On the following day, January 26, the convention passed the Ordinance of Secession by a vote of 113 to 17. Eight of those who voted in the negative afterwards signed the ordinance, making the whole number of signers one hundred and twenty-one, only nine refusing. These nine were Roselius, Stocker, Rozier, Lewis of Orleans, Pierson, Taliaferro, Garrett, Hough, and Meredith.

The ordinance was as follows:—

"AN ORDINANCE

" To dissolve the union between the State of Louisiana and other States united with her, under the compact entitled ' The Constitution of the United States of America.'

" We, the people of the State of Louisiana, in Convention assembled, do declare and ordain, and it is hereby declared and ordained, That the Ordinance passed by us in Convention on the 22d day of November, in the year eighteen hundred and eleven whereby the Constitution of the United States of America, and the amendments of the said Constitution, were adopted; and all laws and ordinances by which the State of Louisiana became a member of the Federal Union, be and the same are hereby repealed and abrogated; and that the union now subsisting between Louisiana and the other States, under the name of ' The United States of America ', is hereby dissolved.

" We do further declare and ordain, That the State of Louisiana hereby resumes all rights and powers heretofore delegated to the Government of the United States of America; That her citizens are absolved from all allegiance to said government; and that she is in full possession and exercise of all those rights of sovereignty which appertain to a free and independent State.

" We do further declare and ordain, That all rights acquired and vested under the Constitution of the United States or any act of Congress, or treaty, or under any law of the State, and not incompatible with this Ordinance, shall remain in force, and have the same effect as if this Ordinance had not been passed." [1]

[1] Report of the Secretary of State of Louisiana, 1902, insert facing p. 112.

On the 18th of February, 1861, the Louisiana legislature passed the following joint resolutions:—

"1. *Be it resolved by the Senate and House of Representatives of the State of Louisiana, in General Assembly convened,* That the right of a sovereign State to secede or withdraw from the Government of the Federal Union, and resume her original sovereignty when in her judgment such act becomes necessary, is not prohibited by the Federal Constitution, but is reserved thereby to the several States, or people thereof, to be exercised, each for itself, without molestation.

"2. *Be it further resolved, etc.,* That any attempt to coerce or force a sovereign State to remain within the Federal Union, come from what quarter and under whatever pretense it may, will be viewed by the people of Louisiana, as well on her own account as of her sister Southern States, as a hostile invasion, and resisted to the utmost extent."

The States of South Carolina, December 20, Mississippi, January 9, Florida, January 10, Alabama, January 11, and Georgia, January 18, had already seceded; and now Louisiana, "with sublime imprudence," to use Gayarré's phrase, decided to cast in her lot with theirs. John Perkins, Alexander Decluet, Charles M. Conrad, Duncan F. Kenner, Henry Marshall, and Edward Sparrow were elected as delegates to the Southern Congress, to meet at Montgomery, February 4, 1861.[1]

When it was moved that the convention submit the Ordinance of Secession to the popular vote for ratification, the motion was defeated by a vote of 84 to 45. The constitution, modified in accordance with the new conditions, was to go into effect as the constitutions of the first States of the Union, except Massachusetts, went into effect—without popular ratification. There may have been other reasons for this, but the obvious and important one was that it was believed that there was no time to be lost in submitting to popular vote the action of the convention.[2]

---

[1] Crescent, February 4, 1861.

[2] Perkins of Madison argued against the idea of Roselius that the convention was irregular and unconstitutional because called by the legislature, and he proceeded to cite authorities to show the contrary. Nor was it necessary to refer the ordinance back to the people for approval. "Why submit it to the people when it was known it would be unanimously agreed to? Why refer it at a time when our Sister States are calling for action!! action! action!"

There is a widespread impression in the North that a popular vote would have carried Louisiana against secession and for the Union party. Nothing is further from the truth. However, as there is believed to be great virtue in mere majorities, it seems a pity that the Ordinance of Secession was not submitted to popular vote in Louisiana, as it was in Tennessee and Texas. It was carried by overwhelming majorities in both States,[1] and there is every reason to believe that it would have been carried by a substantial majority in Louisiana after the convention had decided almost unanimously that it was a wise measure. Six months before, the vote might have been against immediate secession, but one must beware of confounding August 1860 with January 1861.[2]

The fact that the ordinances were not submitted to popular vote except in two States has enabled northern writers to say that the South was hurried into secession by ambitious fire-eaters, who were really conspirators, afraid to consult their constituents. It is also claimed by northern writers that as the representatives in legislatures and conventions were apportioned according to representative population (i. e., three fifths of the slave population being counted in), the large slaveholding sections of each State had a disproportionate representation, and if the ordinances of secession had been submitted to the popular vote, the whole mass of white voters, who alone had the franchise, and the majority of whom had no slaves, would have voted down the ordinances, and thereby shown that the representatives in the conventions did not really represent the majority of white people.[3] The argument is plausible but by no means conclusive. It is flatly contradicted in the cases of Tennessee and Texas, and there seems to be no

Picayune, January 29, 1861. Some cooperationists now said that, whatever their previous convictions, they felt that the emergency called for straight-out secession.

[1] In Tennessee, 104,019 to 47,238; in Texas, 34,794 to 11,235.

[2] Senator Jonas says that he, though a Whig and a Bell man, would have signed the Ordinance of Secession.

[3] Lalor, Cyclopaedia, subject "Secession," p. 698.

reason to suppose that it would have met with a different answer in the other seceding States.

As there was no popular vote in Louisiana, let us consider what was the will of the voters as expressed in the election of the members to the secession convention. We have seen that out of 130 members 121 signed the Ordinance of Secession, though the vote for the cooperationist members was at least 17,256, while the secessionists claimed only 20,448. Nay, it was asserted by the newspapers of the time that the official returns of the election were suppressed. The Picayune of February 17, 1861, published a letter signed "C. B." which says, "I understand from a gentleman just from Baton Rouge that the popular vote in the recent election was in favor of the cooperationist ticket by a majority of 320." Again, the Picayune of March 19, 1861, says: "The Picayune has been accused by a contemporary of joining in the humbug cry of suppressing the popular vote, but last Saturday the Convention was asked by Mr. Bienvenu and Mr. Rozier to bring the election returns before that body, as it was necessary to know what the popular vote was on the cooperation and secession tickets. The Convention refused to suspend the rules and consider the question raised, by a vote of 72 to 23." Several years later it was a common thing for Republicans in Louisiana to maintain that the official returns were suppressed, and that the State "really voted against secession." A surviving member of the convention[1] writes the author on this point: "In regard to the letter published in the Picayune, February 17, 1861, alleging that the Co-operationists had a majority, but the correct returns had been suppressed in the Convention, I do not remember to have seen it, though I was a Co-operationist myself; but it is incredible that such strenuous and determined opponents as were Christian Roselius, J. A. Rozier—not to mention others—would have permitted such an outrage to have been perpetrated without raising a tempest long to be remem-

---

[1] Hon. S. S. Conner.

bered." Still the report that the cooperationists had been
elected by a majority of the votes was rife at the time and is
clearly stated in the diary of Mr. John Purcell, then a resident of New Orleans, under date of February 4, 1861;[1] and
the refusal of the convention to lay the returns before that
body brings out the fact that at least twenty-three cooperationists thought it worth while to demand the returns, even
after the majority of them had signed the Ordinance of
Secession three weeks before.

Even, however, if we should accept the theory that the
cooperationists had been elected by a majority vote, we must
avoid sharply the error of supposing that the majority of
the voters in Louisiana were opposed to the secession of the
State. This would be to misunderstand the general position
of the cooperationists. They were not battling against
secession. Their position is clearly stated in the motion of
J. A. Rozier, given above. Only a few members of the
convention seem to have agreed with James A. Taliaferro,
who declared that "the proper status of Louisiana is with
the border States with which nature has connected her by
the majestic river which flows through her limits; and an
alliance in a weak government with the Gulf States east of
her is unnatural and antagonistic to her obvious interests and
destiny." While he held the true theory from a commercial standpoint, he completely ignored the slavery question
—the great inciting cause of secession—which bound Louisiana most closely to the Gulf States. Moreover, it is clear
that both inside and outside the convention the illogical
character of the cooperationists' position became more apparent every day, and the cooperationist members of the
convention, except in a few cases where they had pledged
themselves to their constituents not to change, were won
over to their opponents' views and signed the ordinance.

The enthusiasts for immediate secession had begun, too,

---

[1] "It now appears that the popular vote in Louisiana is some 300
or 400 majority against secession, and yet the Secessionists are two
to one in the Convention." Purcell, MS. Diary. Lent the author by
Mr. Purcell.

to link the title of "Cooperationist" with that of "Sub-
missionist," and though Christian Roselius protested against
the confounding of two distinct things, the slur had an important influence on public opinion.   Already, on January 9,
the New Orleans Delta was quoting a letter recently written
by Senator Judah P. Benjamin in which he said: "The
North means war.   I trust our Convention will not hesitate
a moment about immediate secession.   *That* is Cooperation
now."   Among the newspapers the Picayune had rung the
changes on cooperation, but by January 12 the Picayune,
the Bulletin, the Crescent, the Bee, and the Delta were a
unit against every form of coercion;[1] and the Creole Bee,[2]
quoted in the Delta of January 8, had struck the true note
when it declared: "Whether the Cooperationists or Secessionists win in the elections now going on, it will not
strengthen the Union a tithe of a hair.   The destiny of
Louisiana is linked with that of her sisters of the South."
The formation of the immediate secession sentiment had
been hurried on by the logic of events.   The voice of
Roselius was "the voice of one crying in the wilderness."
It was the voice of a Whig when the Whigs had ceased to
exist.[3]   If any one, after considering the facts just mentioned, still doubts whether the majority of the white people
in Louisiana were ripe for secession in one form or another
in February, 1861, his doubts will vanish when he reads of
the wave of enthusiasm for separation from the Union
which swept over the whole State after the fall of Fort
Sumter, in April, 1861.   Not to follow Beauregard, a
favorite son of the State, in that momentous step was
treason to Louisiana. As early as January 29 even Mr. John
Purcell, a Unionist, and later a member of the Republican
convention of 1864, was writing in his diary, "I am myself
drifting into secession ideas."   Public opinion, halting at
first on account of the love of the Union, was rushing

---

[1] Delta, January 12, 1861.
[2] L'Abeille, published in French.
[3] Speech of May 30, 1860, in the Picayune of that date.

rapidly toward States' Rights doctrine in the late winter and early spring of 1861.

There seems to have been a general impression in Louisiana that the Federal government would not resist the withdrawal of the Southern States,[1] that " the erring sisters would be allowed to go in peace," but such was not the belief of Governor Moore. He believed coercion would be tried; and some days before the convention met he thought it would be wise to take possession of the United States military depot at Baton Rogue, and to occupy with state troops Fort Pike on the Rigolets and Forts Jackson and St. Philip on the Mississippi. In every case, he stated to the legislature, he had given receipts for the property found, in order to protect the officer dispossessed and to facilitate the future settlement with the Federal government. The South properly held that the forts and their stores belonged partly to the South, and to leave them to the North would be unfair.[2] On March 7 the convention passed an ordinance transferring the specie in the mint to the Confederate government. The amount was $536,000.[3]

The view taken by Governor Moore, that there was danger of coercion on the part of the North, was shared by Major P. G. T. Beauregard, of Louisiana, who returned to his native State from the North about this time. Beauregard had been appointed superintendent of the Military Academy at West Point in November, 1860, but he had announced that if Louisiana seceded, he would resign his position in the army. After he had discharged his duties as superintendent for a few days, in January, 1861, he was ordered back to New Orleans by the secretary of war. Here he found excitement and enthusiasm on every hand but a general feeling that there might be a peaceable withdrawal. Beauregard, fresh from the North, where he had

---

[1] Roman, Military Operations of General Beauregard, I, 16.
[2] The governor of Mississippi asked that the spoils of Baton Rouge be divided; and Louisiana sent him 8000 muskets, 1000 rifles, 6 twenty-four pound guns, and a considerable amount of ammunition. Garner, Reconstruction in Mississippi, p. 9.
[3] S. S. Cox, Three Decades, p. 115.

been able to gauge public opinion, expressed grave doubts as to such a possibility.[1]

Still, the South was prepared for the issue, whatever it might be. She failed to understand that the North was readier and stronger than she in every way, and that the spirit of the time was hostile to the continuance of slavery. Holding that slavery was justifiable in the eyes of God and man, she had been more and more exasperated, as the years passed, by what she regarded as the " holier than thou " attitude of the extremists on the other side of Mason and Dixon's line. How could the North assume the " holier than thou " attitude when she remembered that in 1833 Prudence Crandall had been prosecuted and imprisoned for teaching a school of colored children in Canterbury, Connecticut, and William Lloyd Garrison had received worse treatment in Boston from the best citizens there, as he stated, than he would have received in Charleston or New Orleans?[2] The Constitution protected slavery, and yet this great instrument, which had once more become a fetish in the South, had been declared by the followers of Garrison to be a " covenant with death and an agreement with Hell," and this because slavery existed in the South and wished to extend itself into the territories. Was the " higher law " to be flaunted in the face of the South as if that section could appreciate only the law of expediency?

The election of the Republican candidate, the South believed, meant the destruction of slavery. Benjamin had said the Republicans would not kill slavery but would gird it about and make it die. It is true that the Republican platform proposed to shut slavery out of only the territories, and in his inaugural address, on March 4, Lincoln was to say : " I have no purpose, directly or indirectly, to interfere with the institution of slavery in the States where it exists. I believe

---

[1] Roman, General Beauregard, I, 16.

[2] "Abolitionists were hunted by mobs; but they were not hunted so much because they were abolitionists as because the great body of people at that time believed that the agitation of the slavery question would jeopard the Union." Cox, Three Decades, p. 51. But was this true of Prudence Crandall?

I have no lawful right to do so; and I have no inclination to do so;" but Seward, in 1858, had spoken of the "irrepressible conflict," and Lincoln himself had declared that the country could not "remain one half slave and one half free, 'a house divided against itself'; it must become wholly slave or wholly free." Thus he had spoken in his great debate with Douglas, and the South took him at his word. His inaugural address, though not satisfactory to the Southern States, was more conservative than his utterances in the past had led them to expect; but when it was delivered seven States had already seceded, and the Congress of the Confederate States, on February 4, had met at Montgomery, and had elected Jefferson Davis and Alexander Stephens president and vice-president of a new confederacy.

As for Louisiana, on the very day that the Southern Congress met at Montgomery, the congressmen from Louisiana, Miles Taylor, Thomas J. Davidson, and John M. Landrum,[1] retired from the lower house and John Slidell and Judah P. Benjamin from the Senate. Both Slidell and Benjamin delivered stirring addresses in the august body of which they were members. As one reads these speeches, in the Congressional Globe of February 5, 1861, one may judge of the attitude of the Senate by the fact that Slidell used as the text of his farewell address the Ordinance of Secession recently passed in Louisiana, which he requested the secretary to read aloud. Slidell's address was temperate and well considered, though it sounded a note of defiance.[2] He said a new confederacy was to be formed, which would assume its proportion of the national debt and account for all the forts seized by the South in self-defence. "We offer you peace or war," he continued, "as you choose," and he humorously described the battle of Fontenoy in which the English Hay cried out to the French Guard to fire first, but the French refused to accept this courtesy, and when the

---

[1] John E. Bouligny did not retire, his action meeting with much disapproval.

[2] Blaine finds Slidell "aggressively insolent." Blaine, Twenty Years of Congress, I, 248.

English began the battle utterly defeated them. He also prophesied the destruction which awaited the commerce of the North at the hands of southern privateers.[1] Turning then to the causes of secession, he said it was the work of the people; that in the convention only four or five did not admit the necessity of separation. "We separate," he said, "because of the hostility of Lincoln to our institutions. . . . If he were inaugurated without our consent there would be slave insurrections in the South."

Benjamin combined logic and eloquence in his address, which followed that of Slidell. "It had been maintained," he said, "that Louisiana, having been purchased from France, had not the same right to secede as the 'original thirteen.'" He confuted this statement by quoting the treaty with France, and argued from it that once in the Union, Louisiana had the same rights as Virginia.[2] He ended with a burst of eloquence, declaring that the South was in rebellion, but it was a rebellion such as John Hampden led in England and George Washington in America. He was listened to with keen attention, not only on account of his eloquence, but because he was the exponent of the extreme southern view, and it was believed that to him was due the advanced position taken by the South in 1858 and 1859 against Douglas.[3] The New Orleans Daily Crescent of January 16, 1861, has a letter from a correspondent describing Benjamin as he made this speech. "He stood in a simple position between two desks, one foot crossed over the other, no attitude, no gesture . . . only his black eyes

---

[1] S. S. Cox says: "The writer heard his [Slidell's] savage and sneering threat to destroy the commerce of the North by privateers. As he delivered it, his manner was that of Mephistopheles, in one of his humors over some choice anticipated deviltry." Three Decades, p. 70.

[2] Charles Gayarré had used the same argument in the New Orleans Delta, January 10, 1861. The position taken by Benjamin is fiercely but unsuccessfully attacked by Blaine. Twenty Years, I, 249–253.

[3] Blaine, Twenty Years, I, 160. Schouler says, "Contemporaries had said at the outset that Toombs was the brain of this Confederacy; but that title, as events developed, belongs rather to Attorney-General Benjamin, the ablest, most versatile, and most constant of all Davis's civil counsellors." History of the United States, VI, 89.

showed the emotion he must have felt. They were elongated as Rachel's sometimes became, when at her stillest, most concentrated points of acting—the quiet curse of Camille, for example—scintillating with light, a faint smile, just a little scornful. He closed with, 'An enslaved and servile race you can never make of us, never, never, never.' This reiteration of the word 'never' was as free from emotion as if he had been insisting on some simple point of law which could not have been decided in a different way; but free from emotion as it was, it produced the greatest effect. The whole gallery on all sides burst out in one voice in uncontrollable applause."

Events now hurried on, and in April, 1861, when Beauregard of Louisiana fired the fatal shot at Fort Sumter—a shot which if it was not heard " round the world," at least reverberated through the United States—the North was aroused to coercion and the South to resistance, and the sections were solidified against each other. Lincoln's attitude on secession, if not on slavery, was clear: he would preserve the Union at all hazards. His call for seventy-five thousand volunteers electrified the North. Both sides prepared for a war which it was expected would last six months at the longest, but which proved to be one of the most fearful conflicts recorded in history, and which dragged its weary length along for four years.

It was Beauregard, a Louisianian, who opened fire on Fort Sumter, and Louisiana's rally to the support of her brilliant son has already been referred to. Her pride kept pace with her indignation. All writers of that day testify to the enthusiasm which swept over the State when Governor Moore called for volunteers "to resist invasion." Doubting Thomases disappeared. The feeling in the country parishes is illustrated by a letter from Baton Rouge, May 2, 1861. "From every quarter of the State the same enthusiastic cry 'to arms!' resounds, and no one remembers when such a whirlwind of united patriotic feeling has swept over Louisiana. . . . *Later*. A painful rumor is prevalent that the quota of troops required of Louisiana is filled to overflowing and that no more troops will be received. If this proves true, it will be a bitter disappointment to thousands throughout the State who were making their arrangements to leave."[1] The strongest rebels of course were the women, and the war could not have lasted long without the support of sympathy and sacrifice which they offered throughout the struggle. Mrs. Merrick[2] says that after the States seceded a Union woman could not be found in the entire South. Butler[3] declared that the loudest secessionists in Louisiana were people of northern birth and education. Several of the female teachers in public schools, among the most zealous in teaching their pupils to chant songs of secession and insult Union soldiers, were found to be natives of New England. "Renegades," he said, "are more zealous than the hereditary adherents of a bad cause."

There was no thought as yet that Louisiana herself might be invaded. All recognized that if "invasion" was to be resisted, the first battle-ground would be the border State, Virginia, and the Louisianians were hurried "to the front." The "Tigers" of the Pelican State won fame for themselves at Bull Run. The Louisiana Artillery—their mission consecrated, as they believed, by the most eloquent divine of New Orleans, Dr. Palmer—departed in May, 1861, amid the huzzas of thousands of enthusiastic spectators.[4] Eleven

---

[1] For an account of enthusiasm in New Orleans see Roman, Beauregard, I, 16.

[2] Merrick, Old Times in Dixie Land, p. 29.

[3] Parton, General Butler in New Orleans, p. 562.

[4] Dr. A. P. Dostie says that during the Breckenridge campaign unionism with such men as Randall Hunt, Christian Roselius, Thomas J. Durant, and Pierre Soulé, "assumed a bold front, and little fear was entertained for the State of Louisiana until the Rev. Dr. Palmer sacrilegiously preached disunionism from his pulpit. Then the parricides assumed a courage and confidence fearful in its influence for evil." Dr. Dostie was so pronounced in his Union sentiments that he was forced to go North. When a deputation called on him to announce his expulsion, he asked to see the writ by which he was expelled. They answered that the government had made up their minds to do nothing illegal, so they issued no illegal writs, and simply "intended to make him go of his own free will." Gen. D. E. Twiggs, major-general commanding, gave him a pass on August

months passed, the war raged at a distance from the Gulf, and the Confederate government failed to appreciate that New Orleans was the emporium of the South, the key of the great highway of the Mississippi Valley. If New Orleans were lost, would it be possible to hold the Mississippi? And if the control of the river were lost, could the Confederacy maintain itself?

The defences of New Orleans at this time consisted of some three thousand men under General Mansfield L. Lovell, encamped near the city, and some weak batteries at the Rigolets, Barataria Bay, and other inlets; but the safety of the city rested chiefly upon two strong forts, Fort Jackson and Fort St. Philip, about thirty miles above the mouth of the Mississippi. Above these forts, which had together one hundred guns, were eighteen war-vessels, and below was an obstruction of mastless vessels chained across the channel. In each fort were nearly seven hundred men. While the exigencies or the want of foresight of the Confederate government left the city inadequately protected, the Federal government, like the British government in 1814, saw the immense importance of capturing the southern metropolis, and expeditions were set on foot with that end in view during the spring of 1862. One was to come down the Mississippi and another was to ascend the river and meet it. No more important naval operation was undertaken during the war, and no more capable officer could have been placed

---

21, 1861: "Dr. A. P. Dostie . . . wishes to return to New York under the Alien Law. Allow him to pass through the Confederate States." Dostie writes that he left in August, 1861, and that before he left "a reign of terror was inaugurated; liberty of speech was proscribed. He was considered a bold and rash man who still advocated the cause of his country. . . . My assistant, Dr. Metcalf, from Kalamazoo, Michigan, was incarcerated in a loathsome prison as early as last April," for expressing Union sentiments. Reed, Life of Dostie, pp. 21–30. Dostie returned to New Orleans after the capture of the city, when it was once more safe for him, and played an important part as an incendiary orator on the radical side. He was killed in the riot of 1866.

C. P. Dimitry told the author that it was currently reported in New Orleans that Hannibal Hamlin was a negro. A merchant who offered for sale medals with likenesses of Lincoln and Hamlin was nearly mobbed. Bob Ogden saved him.

in charge of the principal one of these two expeditions than David G. Farragut.

It was on the 24th of April, 1862, that Farragut, having broken down the obstruction below, succeeded in running the gauntlet of forts and fleet alike. Though the feat was accomplished during the night, the peril of the passage is shown by the fact that his own flagship, the Hartford, was struck thirty-five times in hull and rigging, and was at one time set on fire by the burning rafts sent down by the Confederates. But nothing could check the onward sweep of the Federal fleet; within an hour the forts were passed amid a hail of shot and shell, the protecting fleet was scattered, and soon New Orleans lay at the mercy of the victorious Farragut. It is not proposed to describe the exciting scenes which followed the arrival of the Federal fleet and the withdrawal of Lovell. Angry and defiant at first, the city could do nothing but submit. A portion of Farragut's fleet, proceeding up the Mississippi, forced Baton Rouge, the capital of Louisiana, to surrender, and running the gauntlet of the batteries at Vicksburg, joined the Federal fleet which was descending the river. An attempt of the Confederates to recapture Baton Rouge ended in failure. Port Hudson, however, was fortified and held until the fall of Vicksburg in July, 1863. With the surrender of Vicksburg the Mississippi "flowed unvexed to the sea." It is hard to estimate the injury which this brilliant exploit inflicted upon the Confederate cause. New Orleans served as a point of departure throughout the war for the military expeditions fitted out by the Federals in the far South. The fatal weakness of the Confederacy is nowhere so clearly shown as in its inability to recapture this city.

In the meantime, the so-called Trans-Mississippi Department of the Confederacy, consisting of Missouri, Arkansas, Texas, Louisiana, and some of the territories, had been put under the charge of the Confederate Lieutenant-General E. Kirby Smith, in March, 1863. Under him was General Richard Taylor, son of General Zachary Taylor. General Taylor carried on a fairly successful campaign against the

Federals in southwestern Louisiana before the fall of Vicksburg, and even after that disaster he did not despair of holding western Louisiana. It was in the spring of 1864 that the Federals made up their minds to lead a strong force up the Red River, and, crushing all opposition, to march into Texas. This force consisted of seventeen gun-boats under Commander D. D. Porter, which ascended the Red River and protected 10,000 men under General A. J. Smith. Another Federal army under General Franklin, numbering 18,000 men, marched up the Teche to join General Smith at Alexandria. The commander-in-chief of this powerful army was General N. P. Banks, whom, if he was not a skillful general, we shall find to be a most astute politician.[1]

Taylor fell back before this strong force, but finally made a stand at Mansfield, April 8, 1864. Here his army consisted of 5000 horse, 3300 infantry, and 500 artillerymen. The first division of Banks's army that arrived on the scene consisted of 5000 men, but others came up rapidly. The Confederates succeeded in defeating each division as it arrived, and captured " 2,500 prisoners, 20 pieces of artillery, several stands of colors, many thousands of small arms, and 250 wagons."[2] On the following day, when the Federals occupied a strong position at Pleasant Hill with 18,000 men, another battle was fought. Both sides claimed a victory, but at nightfall the Confederates seem to have been in possession of the field, and the account of Admiral Porter declares that the whole expedition was for the Federals a complete failure. In any case, Banks retired to Alexandria, and finally crossed the Atchafalaya on May 20. Here the Confederates gave up the pursuit. There was no more fighting in Louisiana, but at the end of 1864 the Confederates were still so strong that there were three fourths of the State to which it was not safe for the Federals to send military supplies. Four months later General Lee surrendered at Appomattox, and the war was over.

---

[1] Annual Cyclopaedia, 1864, subject " Army Operations," p. 51.
[2] General Taylor's report. The Annual Cyclopaedia, 1864, gives Banks's force as 8000 and his loss as 2000 killed, wounded and missing. Subject " Army Operations," p. 53.

CHAPTER II.

From May 1 to December 14, 1862, New Orleans was under the control of General B. F. Butler, with a force of 15,000 men.[1] It was a comparatively short period, but Butler in this brief time contrived to make himself the best hated man in the South; and by one particular act he even won notoriety for himself in the English Parliament. It was, of course, a difficult task to govern wisely and tactfully a great city like New Orleans, which had been occupied by a victorious army, and which was inhabited by an exasperated people. In his civil as well as in his political administration Butler instituted the system of " thorough " which made Lord Strafford so unpopular in the reign of Charles I. In fact, his political administration, in its unbending severity and its total disregard of the feelings of those whom the chance of war had placed in his power, reflects methods of military occupation which had been obsolete for several centuries.

His civil administration has met with much encomium. It is claimed for him that he warded off starvation from the poorer classes,[2] cleaned the city thoroughly, established strict quarantine laws, and kept out the dreaded yellow

---

[1] In a speech at the North, Butler said he had 2500 soldiers to support him; so he does not seem to have kept the 15,000 in the city. Parton says Butler had an inadequate force to defend the city against an attack because of the strong garrisons necessary at Ship Island, Fort Jackson, Fort St. Philip, Baton Rouge, posts on the lake, and elsewhere. Butler in New Orleans, p. 436. Butler was major-general commanding the Department of the Gulf, with headquarters at New Orleans, while Major—afterwards General— George Foster Shepley, who was appointed military governor of Louisiana in June, 1862, and remained such until Hahn was elected, was evidently under Butler.

[2] He assessed rebels to aid the poor, and collected $340,000. In his farewell address he says he spent about a million which he had collected—doubtless by confiscation.

fever.[1] It is only proper, however, to state that great numbers of the inhabitants were absent in war, or as refugees,
and that the diminution of traffic in the city made the problem of cleanliness far easier than ever before; while the
embargo on foreign trade during his administration simpli-
fied greatly the problem of keeping out the fever. There
were two reported deaths under Butler, but who saved New
Orleans in 1861 when there was not one reported death or
case, and when blockaded New Orleans was occupied by
Lovell and his very many non-immune Confederate soldiers,
who enforced no preventives of any kind?[2] Moreover, it
has been noted by a competent critic that when Butler took
charge, " there had been no epidemic of yellow fever for
four years. The year of his domination was actually less
healthy than the year before, its death-rate being thirty-six,
against thirty-four for 1861."[3] Can it be that the cleansing
of New Orleans is inimical to the health of its people? However, Marion Southwood notes the fact that there was a
large number of unacclimated persons in New Orleans in
1862, and from inability to get away a greater proportion
of the population than usual remained through the summer;
she also says Butler " was the best scavenger we ever had
among us."[4]

But " thorough " in civil administration did not satisfy
Butler. Coarse by nature, and lacking totally the tact which
distinguished his successor, General Banks, he proceeded to
exercise a petty tyranny in the suppression of all disloyalty
of word or act. Although he permitted the municipal
authorities of New Orleans to continue their functions for a
while under strict surveillance, the city was practically under
martial law. The newspapers which had been too active in

---

[1] Butler said there was but one reported case of yellow fever in
New Orleans in 1862; " its mortality returns show it to be *the
most healthy city in the United States.*" Parton, Butler in New
Orleans, p. 401.
[2] Chaillé, " Yellow Fever," New Orleans Med. and Surg. Jour.,
July, 1870, pp. 563–598.
[3] Cable, Creoles of Louisiana, p. 306.
[4] Southwood, Beauty and Booty, p. 182.

reporting Federal losses were shut up until their columns promised to be entirely colorless. The Delta, "noted for the virulence of its treason," was seized and became Butler's own organ. The schools were reorganized after the model of Boston; all secession teachers and books were banished. Churches where the clergymen omitted to pray for the president of the United States were promptly closed; numerous arrests were made of those who, to avoid passing under the United States flag hanging over the banquettes, preferred to walk in the middle of the street; and some of the leading citizens were put in close confinement at Ship Island or at Fort Lafayette, New York. Finally, when some of his agents complained that the ladies of New Orleans insisted on playing secession airs on the piano, and even feigned nausea when Federal officers passed by, Butler, acting on his maxim that "the venom of the she-adder is as dangerous as that of the he-adder," issued his notorious Order No. 28.[1] This order was condemned in the British House of Peers as without a precedent in the annals of war; but Butler no less strenuously defended it on the ground that it effectually stopped all insults to his soldiers, and that no lady would be guilty of the misdemeanors which the order was intended to punish.

Butler's eulogist, Parton, praises Butler's honesty, his lofty sense of honor, and his splendidly efficient service in the city. His brother, according to Parton, made a fortune in New Orleans, but General Butler himself speculated only for the benefit of the United States government, whose

---

[1] The order was as follows:—
"Headquarters, Department of Gulf, New Orleans.
"As officers and soldiers of the United States have been subject to repeated insults from women, calling themselves ladies, of New Orleans, in return for the most scrupulous non-interference and courtesy on our part, it is ordered hereafter, when any female shall by mere gesture or movement, insult, or show contempt for any officers or soldiers of the United States, she shall be regarded and held liable to be treated as a woman about town plying her avocation."
Annual Cyclopaedia, 1862, subject "New Orleans," p. 647.

coffers were enriched by his sagacious seizure of commercial opportunities.[1] Denison, however, seems convinced that Butler speculated on his own account and obtained large profits from the sale of salt and other articles to the Confederates.[2] The better classes in New Orleans generally condemned him as a petty tyrant, who insulted ladies and gentlemen alike, and who even descended to the appropriation of silver spoons in order to increase his private fortune.[3] To them, his forcing the oath of allegiance on men and women alike was an act of oppression, and his general behavior to the inhabitants of the conquered city justified his soubriquet of " Beast Butler."[4]   The same view seems to be taken by a northern historian who says: " In one way or another Butler laid here [in New Orleans] the foundation of wealth which subserved his later ambition in politics. . . . Ill fitted for conqueror, he posed as avenger."[5]

No finer opportunity for the humiliation of rebels was ever vouchsafed to a northern general than was presented by the passage of the so-called confiscation act, and perhaps by none was it more thoroughly appreciated than by General Butler.   This act was passed by the Federal Congress against vigorous opposition, and was approved by the president July 12, 1862.[6] After declaring that the property of five classes of rebels—the various classes holding civil or military offices under the Confederate government—should be confiscated, the act goes on further to provide that the property should be seized of all those who " aiding, countenancing, or abetting the Rebellion should not return to their

---

[1] Butler in New Orleans, pp. 408–411.

[2] Diary and Correspondence of S. P. Chase, Ann. Rept. Amer. Hist. Assn., 1902, II, 320–327.

[3] The receipt given Butler for a box of silver deposited in the Citizens' Bank is still shown in Memorial Hall, New Orleans. It is related that when Butler left New Orleans, an old negro mammy shouted after him, " Good-bye, honey, you never stole nothing from me! "

[4] By means of the negroes Butler had " a spy in every house, behind every rebel's chair as he sat at table."   Parton, Butler in New Orleans, p. 493.

[5] Schouler, History of United States, VI, 259.

[6] Annual Cyclopaedia, 1862, subject " Congress, U. S.," pp. 349–374.

allegiance in sixty days."[1] As the belligerency of the Southern Confederacy was acknowledged in 1861 by several foreign nations and in many respects by the Federal government itself, the South resented bitterly any action that seemed to regard her as merely a rebellious section of the country.

In fact, before the passage of the confiscation act the feeling between the two sections had been exacerbated by two measures, adopted, one by the Federal and the other by the Confederate Congress. By act of August 3, 1861, the Federal government confiscated all property used in aid of the insurrection and declared that owners should forfeit all claims to slaves whose labor was used in any service against the United States. Crittenden, of Kentucky, opposed this measure, declaring that such a policy would only stimulate the adversary to still more desperate measures. In fact, retaliation followed quickly. Later in the same month the Confederate Congress passed an act declaring that all lands, goods, and credits owned by any alien enemy were sequestrated by the Confederate States, and held as an indemnity for all who should suffer under the Federal confiscation act.[2] This retaliatory act, though it could be justified by the rules of international law,[3] was regarded with great bitterness in the North; and, of course, Butler, when he was in com-

---

[1] Much international law can be quoted against this act; but except in ordinary operations in the field, the United States did not give the "States in rebellion" the benefit of international law. Cox says: "The confiscation acts of the Thirty-seventh Congress, and certain other acts, were in effect bills of attainder as the term is understood in the Constitution. The radicals sought by these acts, to impose pains and penalties on certain classes of the people of the South without previous ascertainment of criminal guilt in the judicial courts. . . . There must first be a criminal conviction as a foundation for confiscation. . . . The utmost extent of their vindictive policy was confined to seizure of property, and to proceeding *in rem* for its condemnation." Proceedings in rem require no jury. Three Decades, p. 249.

[2] Statutes at Large of the Provisional Government of the Confederate States, p. 201.

[3] Boyd's Wheaton condemns it, but the annotator is mistaken, it is not condemned by Wheaton himself. The custom is becoming obsolete, but "the right of the sovereign to confiscate debts is precisely the same with the right to confiscate other property." Wheaton, Elements of International Law (Boyd), p. 421.

mand in New Orleans, compelled the payment of all debts
due to Northerners.[1]

It has been maintained that perhaps in no part of the
South was the confiscation act so rigidly enforced as in
Louisiana.[2]   Even before the confiscation act of July 17,
1862, was passed by Congress, Butler ventured to sequester
the estates of such prominent rebels as Twiggs and
Slidell[3] on the ground that they were officers of the Confederate government.   He made himself free with such
private residences as he needed for his accommodation and
that of his staff; and he forced rich merchants in New
Orleans, who had contributed to the support of the Confederacy, to contribute a certain percentage of the same
amounts to the support of the poor and indigent in the
city.[4]

Finally, on September 24, 1862, the sixty days prescribed
in the congressional confiscation act having elapsed, Butler
issued an order that all persons, male or female, eighteen
years and over, must register, with a description of all
property owned.   This order included " all those who have
ever been citizens of the United States and have not renewed
their allegiance previously, or who now hold or pretend any

---

[1] Cox says that as early as May 21, 1861, all goods and credits
of citizens of the United States were sequestered by the Confederate
Congress.   Three Decades, p. 247.   Debts were not confiscated
May 21; the debtors were authorized to pay them into the Confederate treasury, which was to pay the debts after the war; but
August 8, 1861, the Confederate Congress passed an act not simply
to suspend payment during the war, but to seize said debts for
good.   This was held to be unjust.

[2] Cox, Three Decades, p. 434.   As a clause of the Federal Constitution was interpreted to declare that forfeited property could be held
only during the lifetime of the traitor or rebel, many of the Confederates on their return regained their real estate at a fair price
from the purchasers.

[3] Parton, Butler in New Orleans, p. 467.   The first act of the
Federal Congress authorizing the seizure of all property of rebels
after sixty days' notice was passed July 17, 1862.

[4] In order to give the inhabitants of New Orleans a visible re-
minder that the old hero of Chalmette would have condemned their
present attitude on secession, Butler sent workmen to Jackson
Square and caused to be engraved on the base of the statue the
famous toast of Jackson in 1830, " Our Federal Union; it must be
preserved."

allegiance or sympathy with the Confederacy." The latter class, on registering, were to receive certificates as claiming to be "enemies of the United States." Any person neglecting to register was to be subject to fine or to imprisonment at hard labor, or to both, and all his or her property confiscated by order, as punishment for such neglect.[1] Thus compelled, somewhat less than 4000[2] registered themselves as enemies, and many of these left the city, while 61,382 took the required oath of allegiance. To force women to take the oath or declare themselves enemies of the United States was regarded as a great outrage. Many persons refused to take any oath at all, but " many took it," says a lady who was present in New Orleans at the time, " contrary to every conviction of honor and right, and were led to embrace the doctrine that a compulsory oath was not binding—the morality of which, to say the least, is somewhat doubtful."[3] An Episcopal minister in the city wrote to Butler requesting him not to enforce the oath, as it was an inducement to perjury, but the commanding general refused to forego the right of insisting on the conscience test. A large amount of property belonging to persons who were absent in the Confederate army and who were thus unable to take or refuse the oath was promptly seized and sold.[4] Besides his con-

---

[1] W. L. Robinson was a registered enemy of the United States in 1862, and his house in New Orleans was assigned to Federal officers. He returned in 1865, took the oath, and applied for the return of his furniture. But General Canby refused, because he had no right to take the oath. He needed pardon. Times, October 21, 1865. Judge Seymour says that property of registered enemies was not confiscated because they were mostly young men and had none. This seems to show that, as Miss King says, the property of registered enemies was not confiscated, though Annual Cyclopaedia says, " Furniture, gold, and silver plate . . . from houses of rich absentees and registered enemies of the United States " were confiscated. 1865, subject " Louisiana," p. 515. Dr. Mercer, a prominent physician, asked to remain neutral, but Butler said " No," and Mercer registered as an " enemy of the United States."

[2] Parton, Butler in New Orleans, p. 474.

[3] Marion Southwood, Beauty and Booty, p. 159.

[4] The Rules of War drawn up by Francis Lieber, a distinguished jurist, and issued in 1863, left it to the discretion of the commanding general whether to require an oath of allegiance or not. Though this might still be required in cases of rebellion, for international warfare The Hague Peace Conference of 1899 drew up the fol-

fiscation in New Orleans, Butler sequestered, on November 9, 1862, all property in the so-called Lafourche district (all Louisiana west of the Mississippi except Plaquemines and Jefferson parishes) on the ground that disloyal persons there were trying to dispose of their property and thus defraud the United States. He ordered that all the personal property of this district should be brought to New Orleans and sold at auction. If there were any error as to loyalty and the " sheep were not properly distinguished from the goats," the sheep could make reclamation later.

What became of the large sums realized from the sale of confiscated property it seems impossible to say. Parton claims that the confiscation in Louisiana added $1,000,000 to the treasury of the United States;[1] but another authority says confiscations in New Orleans amounted to little in money. " The defaulting quarter-master here turned over $75 as the total net proceeds of the sales of all the splendid Paris-made furniture, gold and silver plate, . . . taken from the houses of rich absentees and registered enemies."[2] Judge Durell says: " The net proceeds of property adjudged to United States will be only $100,000. . . . Harpies who have done nothing but make money out of both parties during the war profit by confiscation; the government does not."[3]

During the summer of 1862, under the fostering care of General Butler, who was more of a politician than a warrior, at least one meeting of the so-called " Union Party " was held in New Orleans.[4] It is related of General N. P. Banks

---

lowing rule: " Any pressure on the population of occupied territory to take the oath to the hostile Power is prohibited." Scott, Hague Peace Conference, II, 135.

[1] Butler in New Orleans, p. 584. Butler says the same. Autobiography of Butler: Butler's Book, p. 522.

[2] Annual Cyclopaedia, 1865, subject " Louisiana," p. 515.

[3] Butler says there was " turned over to General Banks nearly eight hundred thousand dollars in cash and unsold property. . . . What was done with that money and property I have not found in any of the reports of General Banks." Butler's Book, p. 522. In 1864 the Freedmen's Bureau held some eighty plantations " liable to confiscation."

[4] As early as July 31, 1862, Lincoln wrote to August Belmont that

that when he occupied New Orleans in December, 1862, he said, " I could put all the Union men in New Orleans in one omnibus."[1] But this story is either apocryphal or Banks was densely ignorant of the conditions existing in the city. Many of the Douglas men were affiliated with Butler, and large numbers of the Irish laboring class and other foreigners declared for the Union as soon as Butler's coming made it safe. It was but natural, moreover, that many who had no love for the Union were won over to that side by the emoluments, perquisites, and favors showered on Union men and by the restrictions placed upon sympathizers with secession.[2] Dr. A. P. Dostie and J. Madison Day, both to be prominent at a later time, were the orators put forward to arouse Union sentiment.[3] By December 3, 1862, public sentiment for the Union had so far crystallized that on that date an election for two congressmen from New Orleans was held. The election was ordered by General Shepley, military governor of Louisiana. He acted with the permission of Lincoln, who insisted, however, that " to send a parcel of Northern men here as representatives, elected, as would be understood (and perhaps really so), at the point of the bayonet, would be disgusting and outrageous."[4] One secessionist, Dr. Thomas Cottman, came forward as a candidate; but Butler persuaded him to retire on the ground

---

he was anxious to have Louisiana " take her place in the Union as it was, barring the already broken eggs." Chase Correspondence, p. 297. Hence there is more than chronological connection between the preliminary proclamation of September 22 and the election of Hahn and Flanders.

[1] Merrick, Old Times in Dixie Land, p. 27.

[2] Parton, Butler in New Orleans, p. 596.

[3] G. S. Denison writes Chase that Flanders, Judge Heistand, Judge Howell and Fernandez undertook to arouse Union sentiments. Their families were slighted and themselves isolated, but they persevered. R. Hunt and Roselius held aloof, but Durant and Rozier helped. Chase Correspondence, p. 334.

[4] Lincoln's Works (Lapsley), VI, 172. As an inducement to participate in the election use was made of the promise in the preliminary proclamation of emancipation, issued in 1862, to deem the fact that a State was represented in Congress on January 1, 1863, as conclusive evidence that such State was not then in rebellion, and subject to the proclamation.

that however good a Union man he might be at present, he had signed the Ordinance of Secession in 1861. "It looked," added the general, "too much like Aaron Burr's attempt to run for Parliament after he went to England to avoid the complications in the Mexican affairs, or his duel with Hamilton."

The election resulted in the choice of B. F. Flanders and Michael Hahn (neither a native of Louisiana, but both long residents) as congressmen from the first and second districts respectively.[1] Thus was the first feeble step made in the reconstruction of Louisiana, and the success with which it met seemed a good augury for the future. Flanders received 2370 votes out of 2543, and Hahn 2581, which was a majority over all competitors. Parton, who gives these figures, adds that the whole number of votes cast in the city at this election exceeded the vote for secession by 1000. The result was certainly an evidence that the Union party was growing. Flanders and Hahn were both allowed to take their seats in Congress, but as the Thirty-seventh Congress expired March 4, 1863, they did not long enjoy their honors.[2] That Louisiana should have had two congressmen sitting in the House of Representatives in 1863 when it was unrepresented in the Senate and the greater part of the State was in the hands of the Confederates may be regarded as a foreshadowing of Lincoln's plan of reconstruction to be put into practice a year later.

Soon after the election General Butler's term as commander of the Department of the Gulf was cut short for reasons best known to the government,[3] and he was super-

---

[1] For sketch of Hahn, see p. 57.

[2] Cox has an amusing account of Hahn in Congress. Three Decades, p. 428. The vote admitting them was 92 to 44.

[3] Butler does not seem to have known why he was superseded, and he was much disgruntled. Rhodes thinks it was largely due to his famous order. Rhodes, History of the United States, IV, 93, note. Denison writes: "It is not certainly known why Gen. Butler was removed. Some say it is on account of demands of France—others that it is on account of speculations—others that it is owing to representations of Admiral Farragut." Chase Correspondence, p. 340.

seded on December 14, 1862, by General N. P. Banks. The policy of government adopted by General Banks showed a radical departure from that of his predecessor, and his clemency seems at first to have encouraged some disorder in New Orleans, thereby justifying in the eyes of many the severity of Butler.[1] In any case, he suspended until further orders all confiscation of property;[2] and after consulting with Butler he released a number of political prisoners whom Butler had incarcerated in the forts of Louisiana, among them Dr. Theodore Clapp, a distinguished and beloved minister of New Orleans, who had been confined at Fort Pike.

In his farewell address, which exhibited the general as a skillful rhetorician, Butler declared that his name would hereafter be indissolubly connected with New Orleans—apparently a true prophecy; that he had governed the city wisely and leniently in the interests of the poorer classes and adversely to the rich aristocrats who had precipitated rebellion, which is treason, and treason persisted in is death. "Any punishment short of that due a traitor," he continued, "gives so much clear gain to him from the clemency of the government." Such harshness as had been used had been exhibited to disloyal enemies. "I might have regaled you with the amenities of British civilization" (this is the retort courteous to the House of Lords for its criticism of his notorious order); "and yet been within the supposed rules of civilized warfare. You might have been smoked to death in caverns, as were the Covenanters of Scotland by command of a general of the royal house of England; or roasted, like the inhabitants of Algiers during the French campaign; your wives and daughters might have been given over to the ravisher, as were the unfortunate dames of Spain

[1] Denison writes Chase, "Gen. Banks is regarded by them [the rebels] as a gentleman. This is not a good sign. . . . They like to be conciliated." Chase Correspondence, p. 361.

[2] Denison says: "The military commission [for sequestered property]—a corrupt concern—has ceased its operations." Chase Correspondence, p. 341. But Butler says this commission was investigated three times, and found all right. Butler's Book, p. 522.

in the Peninsular war; or you might have been scalped and
tomahawked as our mothers were at Wyoming by the
savage allies of Great Britain in our own Revolution; your
property could have been turned over to indiscriminate
' loot ', like the palace of the Emperor of China; works of
art which adorned your buildings might have been sent
away, like the paintings of the Vatican; your sons might
have been blown from the mouths of cannon, like the Sepoys
at Delhi; and yet all this would have been within the rules of
civilized warfare as practised by the most polished and the
most hypocritical nations of Europe. For such acts the
records of the doings of some of the inhabitants of your
city towards the friends of the Union, before my coming,
were a sufficient provocative and justification."[1]   Thus did
the general in his farewell words attempt to soothe the
injured feelings of the disloyal inhabitants by a recital of
the dread punishments the infliction of which the arts of war
justified, but which his clemency had spared them.[2]   Butler's
eulogist, Parton, was so carried away by the " noble " sentiments contained in this address that he determined forthwith
to write a history of the general's sojourn in New Orleans.

---

[1] Parton, Butler in New Orleans, p. 602.
[2] Dr. Samuel Johnson used similar language in regard to the
American rebels of 1776.

CHAPTER III.

BANKS'S ADMINISTRATION—1862—RECONSTRUCTION UNDER
THE PRESIDENTIAL PLAN.

It was but natural that the election of Hahn and Flanders
as representatives to Congress from that part of Louisiana
lying within the Federal lines and their final acceptance at
Washington[1] should encourage the Unionists in New
Orleans to persevere in their efforts to secure still further
self-government. In this laudable desire they were supported both by the military governor, Shepley, and by the
new commanding general of the Department of the Gulf.
Banks in particular was a born politician, and delighted in
the holding of elections and the issuing of wordy proclamations marked by a certain eloquence. His deficiencies in the
field found complete compensation in the political arena.
But General Banks was not the only politician in Louisiana.
There were a number of prominent men who were anxious,
for one reason or another, to take part in any reorganization
that might take place. Some were seekers after the plums
of office; some were slaveholders who hoped that in spite
of the proclamation of emancipation means might be found
to protect the slaves of Unionists, original, or lately con-
verted; some were in both the above-mentioned categories;
while all the inhabitants of the city were desirous of escap-
ing from the incubus of martial law.

The first distinct party to enter the field was the so-called
Free State party, a radical association, which worked
through the Union clubs which had been formed in New
Orleans and in the neighboring parish of Jefferson. This
party, which began an active campaign in 1863, adopted as a
platform the general proposition that the state constitution

[1] Blaine says they were received "not without contention and
misgivings." Twenty Years, II, 36.

of 1852 had been superseded by the secession constitution
of 1861, and that the latter was null and void because the
convention had no constitutional right to frame it. As the
State had thus committed political suicide, this party held
that the proper method of procedure was for loyal citizens
to work out a new constitution in accordance with new conditions, calling on the Federal military government only for
such protection as might be necessary. With this end in
view, a registration was to be made by a civil commissioner
in each parish then under control of Federal arms, wherein
all those were to be registered who swore that they were
citizens of the United States and had resided six months in
the State and one month in the parish. After a " sufficient "
number of citizens had been registered and a " sufficient "
area embraced, the military governor should order an election for members of a convention to frame the new constitution. When this constitution had been adopted by such as
were made voters, under its provisions an election of state
officers was to be ordered.[1] While this party was in favor
of abolishing slavery, it declared that representation in the
convention should be based on a ratio of one delegate to
every twenty-five hundred of the white population. Their
objects in considering only the whites, they said, was to put
themselves on an equality with the slaveholders; for in the
first and second districts, where alone the Federal troops
exercised control, the slaves had not been emancipated by
Lincoln's proclamation of January 1, 1863, and thus slaveholders would be elected in disproportionate numbers unless
a white basis were adopted.[2]

Consequently, a Free State general committee was finally
appointed in the first half of 1863, its members consisting of
five delegates from each of the Union clubs of Orleans and
Jefferson. The Chairman was Thomas J. Durant and the

---

[1] Annual Cyclopaedia, 1863, subject " Louisiana," p. 589.
[2] As we have seen above, the rule for representation in Federal
affairs was that three fifths of the slaves should be counted. In
Louisiana, for state offices, representation was based on total population, including slaves.

secretary was James Graham. Durant was also appointed attorney-general and commissioner of registration by Governor Shepley, with power to appoint registrars in the parishes and to conduct a new registration of loyal citizens who wished to organize a loyal government in Louisiana.[1] Two things only seemed to militate against the success of this party. The first was that it represented too small a part of the State, a part which, by the aggressive action of the Confederates, was confined at the close of 1863 to New Orleans alone. As the Confederates controlled so large an area it was a dangerous undertaking to register for any such purpose in one of the country parishes. The second was that there soon arose another party, composed chiefly of planters, who, claiming as much loyalty to the Federal government as did the Free State party, were yet anxious to reorganize the State on a different and more conservative basis.

According to the latter party, secession was to be repudiated, but the constitution of 1852 was to be revived with all its slavery features. They believed that Lincoln had emancipated the slaves in the rebellious parts of the country as a war measure, and as slavery remained intact within the Federal lines except as to the return of fugitives,[2] it might be reinstated everywhere at the close of hostilities; or, in any case, compensation might be obtained by loyal citizens through a decision of the Supreme Court. The plans and views of this party may be found explained in an interesting speech delivered in New Orleans on October 13, 1864, by J. L. Riddell.[3] Riddell was a Union Democrat and a conservative, who, with Rozier, Fellows, Jerome, and others, favored the election of McClellan to the presidency in the autumn of 1864. In his address Riddell explained his position in 1863. He had cooperated with a large number of conservative Union men at that time to "loyalize" the

---

[1] Annual Cyclopaedia, 1863, subject "Louisiana," p. 589.
[2] An article of war forbade the return of fugitive slaves.
[3] New Orleans Times, October 21, 1864. Riddell was formerly Confederate postmaster. Chase Correspondence, p. 309.

entire States of Louisiana, Texas, Arkansas, and Mississippi, and to bring them squarely into their old places in the Union. In June, 1863, they asked Lincoln, through a committee composed of E. C. Mathiot, Bradish Johnston, and Thomas Cottman, to instruct Governor Shepley to permit the recurring biennial election to be held on November 3, 1863, under state laws (i. e., the constitution of 1852). Lincoln replied that since receiving this request, he had reliable information that a respectable portion of the people of Louisiana desired to amend the state constitution and contemplated holding a convention for the purpose. This fact was sufficient reason why the general government should not give the committee permission to act under the existing state constitution. " I may add," he continued, "that while I do not perceive how such a committee could facilitate our military operations in Louisiana, I really apprehend it might be so used as to embarrass them. As to an election to be held next November, there is abundant time, without any order or proclamation from me just now. The people of Louisiana shall not lack an opportunity for a fair election for both Federal and State officers by want of anything within my power to give them."[1]

In spite of this letter, which, though conciliatory, showed the president's strong leaning toward the plans of the more radical party, Riddell seems to have continued his efforts, for, a little later, consultations were held with Cottman and other leading men in northwestern and northern Louisiana, then under Confederate control, as well as with prominent men in Texas, western Mississippi, and Arkansas. In the month of July, Vicksburg and Port Hudson had fallen, and there had been growing a feeling of general distrust as to the success of the Confederate cause. The gentlemen consulted expressed their willingness to resume their place in the Union, with the laws and constitution as before secession, except as affected by Lincoln's emancipation proclamation, the legality of which they were willing to leave to the decision of

---

[1] Annual Cyclopaedia, 1863, subject " Louisiana," p. 590.

the Supreme Court. As the time for the election came first in Louisiana, it was agreed that Louisiana should lead the way, and if the movement should be favorably received by the Federal government,[1] the other States would follow.

Further details as to the plan to restore Louisiana to the Union while preserving the status of the negro as far as possible are to be found in the newspapers of the day. In October, 1863, the Daily Picayune contained an address to the loyal citizens of Louisiana signed by W. W. Pugh, president, E. Ames, vice-president, and J. Q. A. Fellows, secretary of the Executive Committee of Louisiana. This address urged the people on November 2 to vote for state and parish officers, members of Congress, and state legislature. "We think we can assure you," it ran, "that your action in this respect will meet with the approval of the National Government. The military will not interfere with you in the quiet exercise of your civil rights and duties. . . . Louisiana has always been at heart loyal to the United States. She never seceded by a majority vote. She was juggled and forced into the position of seeming rebellion, but in our opinion she was, and still is, one of the United States. Now that it is practicable, thanks to the gallant army and navy of the United States, her citizens desire to assume forthwith their old status and to replace the star of their State, with lustre bright as ever, on the glorious flag of our common country."

The collapse of the movement might have been predicted. The Free State committee, being invited to cooperate, refused on the ground that the constitution of 1852, as amended by the convention of 1861, was destroyed by the rebellion of the people of Louisiana, and that the present movement was consequently illegal and unjust. As General Shepley had estopped proceedings in the city, on November 3 elections were held in only the country parishes. On the 7th of November the Times (now radical) makes reference to this

---

[1] This seems to have been an appeal to Congress against the president.

election in a sarcastic article, and indicates that the movement, having but a small following, was arrogating too great importance to itself. A certain Colonel A. P. Field, who had " received 125 votes in one of the parishes, with two districts to hear from," and Dr. Cottman (said to have been a personal friend of Lincoln's) were elected to Congress. They stayed in Washington for a while, and even voted for the election of clerk of the House, but they were not recognized after the organization was effected.[1] Field, however, lingered on until Congress presented him with fifteen hundred dollars for his expenses and sent him home.[2] How the movers ever hoped to succeed in the face of the opposition of the president and the military governor, or to win the favor of Congress while they were unwilling to give up slavery, is hard to understand. The negro was becoming every day a more prominent feature in the great conflict. Even now he could not be ignored as a political factor, though he was not yet of decisive importance in this respect. When opportunity offered, as we shall see, he was not slow to urge his claims to equal rights.

The failure of the conservatives to secure recognition in Congress for their representatives seemed to open the way for the success of the Free State party. The party was all the time pushing on its work of reorganizing the State on what was termed " the fundamental principle of our government ' that all men are created free and equal,' "[3] a principle which the conservatives evidently did not accept. That the president was on their side seemed to be shown not only by his letter to the conservatives in June, 1863, but also by a later letter to Banks, August 5, 1863, in which he said: " Governor Shepley has informed me that Mr. Durant is now taking a registry, with a view to the election of a constitutional convention in Louisiana. This, to me, appears

---

[1] Annual Cyclopaedia, 1865, subject "Louisiana," p. 509.
[2] Reed, Life of Dostie, p. 126.
[3] This latter phrase is, of course, a misquotation of a phrase in the Declaration of Independence, which declares that " all men are created equal " (not free). It was borrowed by Jefferson from Locke's Essay on Government.

proper."[1]   It is true that in October, 1863, he told B. F.
Flanders, then in Washington, that the work of registration
was proceeding too slowly; and when Flanders showed how
necessary the delay was, the president is reported to have
said he would recognize and sustain a state government
organized by any part of the population then controlled by
the Federal power.[2]   Still, the Free State party found it so
difficult to win over adherents to its radical policy that registration by December, 1863, had not advanced far enough to
justify the plans of that party.   The registration was pushed
on, however, and plans were made to obtain permission from
Governor Shepley to hold an election on January 25, 1864,

---

[1] New Orleans Times, May 7, 1865.   Lincoln's letter of this date
is so interesting that it is quoted more fully:—
   "While I very well know what I would be glad for Louisiana
to do, it is quite a different thing for me to assume direction in the
matter.   I would be glad for her to make a new constitution, recognizing the emancipation proclamation, and adopting emancipation
in those parts of the State to which the proclamation does not
apply.   And while she is at it, I think it would not be objectionable
for her to adopt some practical system by which the two races
could gradually live themselves out of their old relation to each
other, and both come out better prepared for the new.   Education
for young blacks should be included in the plan.   After all, the
power or element of 'contract' may be sufficient for this proba-
tionary period, and by its simplicity and flexibility may be the better.
   "As an antislavery man, I have a motive to desire emancipation
which proslavery men do not have; but even they have strong
enough reason to thus place themselves again under the shield of the
Union, and to thus perpetually hedge against the recurrence of the
scenes through which we are now passing.
   "Governor Shepley has informed me that Mr. Durant is now taking
a registry, with a view to the election of a constitutional convention
in Louisiana.   This, to me, appears proper.   If such convention
were to ask my views, I could present little else than what I now
say to you.   I think the thing should be pushed forward, so that,
if possible, its mature work may reach here by the meeting of
Congress.
   "For my own part, I think I shall not, in any event, retract the
emancipation proclamation: nor, as executive, ever return to slavery
any person who is free by the terms of that proclamation, or by any
of the acts of Congress.
   "If Louisiana shall send members to Congress, their admission will
depend, as you know, upon the respective Houses, and not upon the
President.
Yours very truly,
A. Lincoln."
—Writings of Lincoln (Lapsley), VI, 374.
[2] Annual Cyclopaedia, 1863, subject "Louisiana," p. 591.

at which delegates should be chosen to a convention which should form a new constitution for the State.

In the meantime, Lincoln had been revolving in his own mind some feasible method of restoring the seceded States to their normal relations with the Federal government. There were two, or possibly three, theories held as to the status of seceded States. One was that by the act of secession a State placed itself entirely outside the pale of the Union and passed under the power of Congress as if it were a territory. Another theory was that a State might be " in rebellion " but that it could never, by its own act, be outside of the Union. In Congress, at a somewhat later period, there was a protracted discussion between the adherents of these two views; but Lincoln, with his strong leaning toward practical results, never formally gave his support to either of them. He regarded the discussion as metaphysical and impractical, and he used to say that at any rate both sides would agree—and this may be regarded as the third theory—that the relation of the seceded States with the Union had been so far disarranged that a readjustment was necessary before they could be recognized as in good standing. This view, while seeming to take a middle course, inclined strongly to the theory that the seceded States were still in the Union.[1]

As a cautious approach to the subject, Lincoln issued a proclamation on December 8, 1863, defining in a not very definite way what has been termed the executive mode of reconstruction. He held that, by a combination of disloyal persons in certain States—a kind of conspiracy—a rebellion had been undertaken, and now the time had come in some of those States to restore the government to the hands of the loyal element, which should be encouraged to come for-

---

[1] Cox says that Thaddeus Stevens hated " bitterly, some of his own party who would not follow his doctrine, and obliterate states in order to territorialize and terrorize them." Three Decades, p. 365. The South, following the States' Rights doctrine, held that a seceded State was out of the Union, but when it returned to its allegiance, it came not as a territory but with all its former rights and privileges.

ward and assume the responsibility of self-government.[1]
The steps in this restoration were to be, first, the taking of
an oath of allegiance to the United States government, as
follows: " I, —————, do solemnly swear, in the presence of Almighty God, that I will henceforth faithfully
support, protect, and defend the Constitution of the United
States and the Union of the States thereunder; and that I
will, in like manner, abide by and faithfully support all acts
of congress passed during the existing rebellion with reference to slaves, so long and so far as not repealed, modified,
or held void by congress, or by decision of the supreme
court; and that I will, in like manner, abide by and faithfully support all proclamations of the president made during
the existing rebellion having reference to slaves, so long and
so far as not modified or declared void by decision of the
supreme court. So help me God!" All persons taking this
oath voluntarily, except those having been civil or diplo-
matic officers of the so-called Confederate government, or
military officers thereof above the rank of colonel, or those
having left seats in the United States Congress or judicial
office under the United States, or having resigned commis-
sions in the army or navy of the United States, in order to
aid in rebellion, or those having treated colored persons
found in the United States service in any capacity, or white
persons in charge of same, in any other manner than as
prisoners of war,—all persons, with these exceptions, should
be regarded as having restored themselves to loyal citizenship. Second, whenever, in any of the States of Arkansas,
Texas, Louisiana, Mississippi, Tennessee, Alabama, Georgia,
Florida, South Carolina, and North Carolina, a number of
persons not less than one tenth in number of the votes cast
in each State at the presidential election of 1860, having
taken the oath and being qualified voters by law of the State

---

[1] As we shall see, the government based upon this plan pleased
neither the "rebels," who were designated as conspirators, nor the
radical Republicans, who thought it was too lenient. It was based
on the theory that secession was the act of a number of individual
rebels and not of States.

previous to secession, should reestablish a state government which should be republican and in no wise contravening said oath, such should be recognized as the true government of the State, and the United States should guarantee it all constitutional privileges. The president cautiously added that whether members sent to Congress from any State should be admitted rested exclusively, by the Constitution, with Congress and not with the executive. Third, "that, in constructing a loyal state government in any state, the name of the state, the boundary, the subdivisions, the constitution, and the general code of laws, as before the rebellion," should be maintained, "subject only to the modifications made necessary by the conditions hereinbefore stated, and such others, if any, not contravening said conditions, and which may be deemed expedient by those framing the new state government."[1]

The last clause allowed considerable latitude to an improvised government representing only one tenth of the voters, and the president brought upon himself much adverse criticism by deciding on so small a proportion of the population as a representative body. According to Lincoln himself, he chose one tenth because the "guarantee of a Republican form of government, which is imposed by the Federal Constitution, implies a feeble minority struggling against a hostile element."[2] However this may be, it should be said that the president's offer of one tenth showed far more consideration for the South in the midst of the war than did the policy substituted by Congress after the close of the war. It did not exclude the great mass of Confederate soldiers who owned the property of the South and who might wish at some time to return to their Federal allegiance, nor did it give the franchise to the emancipated slave.

---

[1] Proclamation of Amnesty, Dec. 8, 1863, Macdonald, Select Statutes, No. 35.

[2] "The delays caused by the inroads of the Confederate forces in the parishes around the city induced the President to consent to a reorganization of the state on a basis of less population than he had prescribed in his amnesty proclamation." Cox, Three Decades, p. 426. I think a further explanation is that Lincoln could not hope to obtain more than one tenth.

In the meantime, the Free State party had been pushing its registration, and was planning to obtain permission of Governor Shepley to hold an election on January 25, 1864, at which delegates should be chosen to a state convention which should frame an absolutely new constitution for the State of Louisiana. They had not, however, counted upon the strong fondness of General Banks for politics. To their astonishment, by his proclamation of January 8, Banks took matters into his own hands, and leaving both the existing parties in the lurch, announced his own plan for reconstructing Louisiana. He afterwards justified his action by declaring that in December the president had written to him of his dissatisfaction at the slow development of loyal sentiment in Louisiana, only two thousand having registered as voters. "I replied . . . ." said Banks, "that if he desired . . . a government organized, it could be done, and if he gave me directions I would do it immediately. I received a letter from him authorizing me to take such measures as I thought necessary to organize a loyal free State government by the people of the State."[1]

Banks now adopted from the president's proclamation the oath of allegiance prescribed as a qualification of voters, and instead of upholding the contention of the radicals or Free State party that nothing should be done toward establishing self-government until a new constitution was framed, he declared that an election should be held on February 22, 1864 (in honor of Washington), for the election of a governor, lieutenant-governor, secretary of state, treasurer, attorney-general, superintendent of education, and auditor. These officers, he declared, without a legislature and without a judiciary,[2] should constitute for the present the civil government of the State, and should be installed March 4. As a sop to the radicals, Banks further declared that an election of delegates to revise the constitution of 1852

---

[1] Louisiana Election Case, 38th Cong., 2d sess., H. Rept. No. 13, p. 17.
[2] As we shall see, Lincoln had established a provisional court with extraordinary powers.

should be held on the first Monday in April. In accordance
with the suggestion of the president, he declared that the
constitution of 1852 and the laws of the State should be
revived and should remain in force; but he went further on
his own responsibility in declaring that all laws upholding
slavery even within the Federal lines were null and void.
He added, however, that this proceeding was not intended
to ignore the rights existing prior to the rebellion or to
preclude the claim for compensation of loyal citizens for
losses sustained by enlistments or other authorized acts of
the government.[1] His proclamation concluded with the following burst of eloquence: "Louisiana, in the opening of
her history, sealed the integrity of the Union by conferring
upon its Government the Valley of the Mississippi.[2] In the
war for independence upon the sea, she crowned a glorious
struggle against the first maritime power of the world, by a
victory unsurpassed in the annals of war. Let her people
now announce to the world the coming restoration of the
Union, in which the ages that follow us have a deeper
interest than our own, by the organization of a free Government, and her fame will be immortal!"[3]

The conservatives were displeased by this bold step in
regard to slavery, while the radicals, who had been expecting
to work out the regeneration of Louisiana and choose from
their number such officials as might be needed in the civil
government of the State, were scandalized by the action
of the commanding general. When they recovered from
their surprise, they laid before Banks a protest in which
they called his attention to the fact that he had annulled
slavery[4] when the president's policy had left it untouched

---

[1] Era, January 31, 1864.

[2] The historical fact, however, is that the annexation of Louisiana
brought forth the strongest threats of secession from the New
England States.

[3] Annual Cyclopaedia, 1863, subject "Louisiana," p. 593.

[4] The St. Louis Democrat was quoted at the time as saying:
"Banks has gone further than Fremont or Hunter in making war
on the institution. The President reversed the action of Fremont
and Hunter. What will he do with Banks?" As a fact, the president did nothing. He had advanced beyond the period of Fremont
and Hunter. The whirligig of time was bringing in rapid changes.

within the Federal lines; that he had proclaimed to be in force a constitution which they held to be null and void; and that all this was an assertion of martial law dangerous to the liberties of the people, and was contrary to the proclamation of the president declaring that the state government must be established by one tenth of the voters of 1860.[1] Notwithstanding this able protest, Banks, strong with the authority of the president, proceeded to carry out his plans; and the two political factions of New Orleans, recognizing the inevitable, decided to take part in the election and to try to elect their respective candidates.

The administration candidate for governor, Michael Hahn, was born in Bavaria, but had lived in Louisiana for many years. He enjoyed the unbounded confidence of Banks, and received from him constant expressions of admiration.[2] It was believed from the beginning of the campaign that Hahn would be nominated by the Free State party. It was claimed for him that his qualifications were irresistible: he was the candidate of General Banks; he was going to run, nomination or no nomination; his principles were not fixed—he was neither slavery nor antislavery; if nominated on a Free State platform, it was believed that he would be true to it, but if not he would run on a "copperhead platform" and defeat the regular nominee.[3]

On February 1 the nominating convention met at Lyceum Hall, in New Orleans; but according to the newspapers of the following day pandemonium reigned supreme, and the "convention" adjourned to the rooms of the Free State committee, where B. F. Flanders and J. Madison Wells[4] were nominated for the offices of governor and lieutenant-

---

[1] Annual Cyclopaedia, 1863, subject "Louisiana," p. 593.

[2] Hahn (1830–1886) was graduated from the law department of the University of Louisiana in 1854. He was a Douglas man in 1860, and held the office of notary under the Confederacy, but omitted to take the oath of allegiance to that government, a fact said to have been winked at by the judge, T. W. Collens. In 1864 he edited the Delta, which supported Banks.

[3] Times, February 1, 1864.

[4] Wells was a repentant slaveholder who had been compelled to leave his home in western Louisiana by the secessionists.

governor. A part of the convention, however, called the "Rump" by some, continued in session at the Lyceum, and nominated Michael Hahn for governor and J. Madison Wells for lieutenant-governor. Thus Wells was given second place on both tickets. This would seem to indicate that the split was the result of a mere factional fight for office and that the differences were a matter of little moment.[1] Hahn's "Rump" adopted resolutions condemning slavery; and Hahn himself declared in the convention that he was a Union man, and that, if he could help it, there would be no slavery in Louisiana. This was also the platform of the adjourned convention; but if one reads between the lines, the real issue seems to have been what should be the treatment of the negro after he was emancipated. The Union, a newspaper said to be the organ of the colored population, supported Flanders, and this faction was openly accused of favoring negro equality. Moreover, at one of the Hahn meetings, Lombard of Plaquemines declared that he had been a friend of Flanders until a colored delegation was admitted to seats in the Lyceum on December 15, 1863, an admission for which Flanders had voted. In answer to such speeches the Flanders faction said that they had been opposed on the alleged ground that they favored "negro equality" when, in fact, they had never said anything about "negro equality." A few days before the election Flanders declared in a public speech that while he was in favor of abolishing slavery at once, he had never advocated negro suffrage and did not deem it practicable.[2]

Unless these utterances were the result of a secret understanding with the colored population, they must have borne dismay to their hearts. Already in the preceding November the free men of color had held a meeting and drawn up a strong appeal to Governor Shepley asking to be allowed to

---

[1] Denison says, "The only distinction I feel able to make is that one is a Banks and the other an anti-Banks party." Chase Correspondence, p. 430. Judge Seymour said that the Flanders party was in the majority, and so bolted.

[2] Times, February 14, 1864.

register and vote. They reviewed their services under Jackson, who called them "my fellow-citizens" just after the battle of New Orleans, and they declared their present loyalty to the Union. For "forty-nine years," the petition ran, "they have never ceased to be peaceable citizens, paying their taxes on assessments of more than nine millions of dollars."[1] But however strongly this petition appealed to Shepley, it was manifestly impossible to grant it at this time. The interests of the several parties were sufficiently conflicting without introducing the disturbing element of negro suffrage. Moreover, if the free men of color were to vote, could the suffrage be refused to the slaves who had been practically emancipated by the advance of the Federal army? As far as is known, Shepley returned no answer to the appeal; for in the following January the so-called Union Radical Association (colored) sent a committee to call on Shepley requesting him to recognize the "rights" of the free colored population to the franchise. Shepley, unwilling and unable to assume such responsibility, referred the committee to General Banks, but the latter gave them no definite reply. Accordingly, the committee sent P. M. Tourné to Washington to advocate their claims before the president and his cabinet.[2] What the result was is not known, though this appeal may have influenced Lincoln in a letter he wrote to Governor Hahn suggesting the extension of the suffrage to the more intelligent of the negroes. At this time he seems to have contented himself with sending to New Orleans a certain McKay, who was instructed to inquire into the condition of the colored people.[3]

As the election of February 22 drew near, the success of the administration candidate seemed assured. The Flanders faction, becoming frightened, made an appeal to the Hahn faction to unite; but the latter now felt themselves strong

---

[1] Annual Cyclopaedia, 1863, subject "Louisiana," p. 591. The free men of color had either never been slaves or had been free for several generations.

[2] Times, January 20, 1864.

[3] Times, February 9, 1864.

enough not to recognize their opponents, and they tartly
answered that Hahn would not retire in favor of harmony
(for thus they pretended to understand the advances of their
opponents). They must have been provoked, moreover, by
a communication entitled " Exceptions from Amnesty," appearing in the Times of January 7 and evidently inspired by
the Flanders faction. It criticised Lincoln's policy adversely, declaring that the exceptions to general amnesty
would not cover over twelve hundred, that is, not more than
a thousandth part of those participating in the great " crime."
" A large guilty class is omitted. What say you, faithful
and suffering loyalist of Louisiana, of seeing Thos. O. Moore
put upon the same footing with the unwilling conscript
whom his tyranny has forced to fight against the Union?
And so of Moise, Manning & Co., the regency who really
engineered the treason and ruin of Louisiana." Because of
this opposition to the president and for other reasons the
Flanders faction lost popularity, and did not even poll so
large a vote as did J. Q. A. Fellows, nominated by the Conservative Union party to take the place of the distinguished
lawyer, Christian Roselius, who had refused the position.
The platform of this faction was " compensation to loyal
men for slave property lost by war." As such compensation was included in Banks's proclamation, this faction
superficially did not differ from the Hahn faction, though
popularly believed to be wedded to the old order of things
in the matter of slavery. The Times represented them as
" bewailing " that institution, and Roselius, in a speech of
February 4, advocated leaving " the slavery question to be
decided by each State." They spoke of themselves as " inhabiting the temperate zone of politics." Some of them had
even balked at Lincoln's oath of allegiance. Roselius asked
to be relieved from taking an oath " to support all acts
passed by Congress," and declared that the necessity of
taking such an oath would cut down the vote in Louisiana.[1]

---

[1] Denison thought that Fellows would probably have been elected
if Banks had not demanded the proclamation oath. Chase Correspondence, p. 431.

But Banks was unrelenting on this point. He even declared that there should be no stay-at-home-vote, speaking in no uncertain terms on this subject in his proclamation of February 3, 1864. " Men," he said, " who refuse to defend their country with the ballot box or cartridge box have no just claim to the benefits of liberty regulated by law. All people not exempt by the law of nations . . . . are called upon to take the oath of allegiance." " Indifference will be treated as a crime, and faction as treason." Briefly speaking, his order was " Vote, fight or leave ! "[1]   This raised the indignation of many who proposed to remain neutral in the controversy, and who now loudly proclaimed that " to say *when* men shall vote is as much tyranny as to say *how* they shall vote." But Banks had unwittingly adopted the provisions of Solon's famous sedition law which declared that he who refused to take sides in the political controversies of the state should be deprived of his citizenship, that is, the protection of the government and participation in its offices. In this course, Banks was warmly supported by the New York Tribune,[2] but he found it necessary later to defend his action against the majority in Congress by denying that he had enforced his own regulations or had said, " You must vote or leave." Probably the principal reason for his insistence was that it was necessary for at least one tenth of the number of voters of 1860 to participate in order to make the election valid in the eyes of Lincoln, but whether that be true or not it is difficult to see why Banks should be blamed for his procedure. He certainly did not compel any one to vote for any special candidate.[3]

---

[1] Times, February 5, 1864.
[2] Times, March 3, 1864.
[3] The three tickets were :—

Ticket:	Administration:	Flanders:	Conservatives:
Governor	Michael Hahn	B. F. Flanders	J. Q. A. Fellows
Lieut. Gov.	J. M. Wells	J. M. Wells	J. M. Pelton
Sec. of State	A. Wrotnowski	Jona C. White	George S. Lacey
Treasurer	J. G. Belden	Dr. A. Shelly	John Gauche
Atty. Gen'l.	B. F. Lynch	Chas. W. Hornor	J. Ad. Rozier
Auditor	A. P. Dostie	Wm. M. Abbott	Julian Neville
Supt. of Ed'cn.	Jno. McNair	B. L. Brown	Denis Cronan, Jr.

The members of the first ticket, with the exception of Wells, were natives either of foreign countries or of the Northern States.

Nor did Banks attempt to include colored voters. He had abolished slavery within the Federal lines as far as lay within his power, but the constitution of 1852, the validity of which in other respects he claimed to acknowledge, did not authorize negro suffrage, and he did not think it expedient to ignore that constitution on this point. Accordingly, he declared the electors to be " every free white male, twenty-one years of age, who has been resident in the State twelve months, and in the parish six months, who shall be a citizen of the United States, and shall have taken the oath prescribed by the President in December, 1863." It is said that 10,000 citizens took the oath and registered previous to the election. The total vote on February 22 was 11,355, of which Hahn received 6171, Fellows, 2959, and Flanders, 2225, giving a majority to Hahn. Election returns came in from Orleans, Baton Rouge, Algiers, Lockport, Port Hudson, Carrollton, Donaldsonville, Franklin, Fort McComb, Fort Jackson, Buras, and even Barancas, Florida. Wherever it was possible Louisiana soldiers in the Federal army voted, but only to the number of 808 in all.[1] The conservatives declared that the existing suffrage laws had been violated and that consequently the election of Hahn was no election at all, while " A Free State Man " published in the Times a letter asserting that if the officers elected presumed to exercise the functions of their offices, they would be deemed by the mass of people in Louisiana to be usurpers and intruders. Little attention, however, was paid to these disgruntled losers. More than one tenth of the voting population of 1860[2] had voted, and this was all that Banks wished. His enemies kept asking where was his legislature, and whether the few officers he had elected constituted a state government. But the commanding general believed that he had made a good beginning, and that as yet it was

---

[1] Banks's letter to Senator Lane. Published as a pamphlet entitled " The Reconstruction of States." New York, 1865. There is a copy in the Howard Library, New Orleans.

[2] The vote of Louisiana in the presidential election of 1860 was 49,510. Blaine says it was 50,510. Twenty Years, II, 40.

premature to elect a legislature which could represent only a small portion of the State. Was he not already anticipating the conquest of the whole State in his campaign of March and April, 1864,[1] and the full restoration of Louisiana to the Union? And if his military talents had equalled his political talents, he might well have succeeded in his plans.

On the 4th of March Governor Hahn was inaugurated with imposing ceremonies. There were addresses by the new governor and by General Banks. " Thirty thousand voices (!) joined in singing America."[2] Around the walls of the hall, which were draped with flags, were such inscriptions as " Farragut, the bravest of the brave," " Major-General N. P. Banks, the hero of Port Gibson and of Freedom in Louisiana." At a great ball which followed at the Opera House a shield was placed between the proscenium boxes bearing the inscription, " Louisiana, first of the erring sisters, keeps step to the music of the Union." About ten days later President Lincoln invested Hahn with the powers hitherto exercised by General Shepley, the military governor of Louisiana, thus adding to his authority as civil governor while indicating his subordination to the Federal government.

In a personal note to the new governor the president said : " I congratulate you on having fixed your name in history as the first Free-State Governor of Louisiana. . . . Now you are about to have a convention which among other things will probably define the elective franchise. I barely suggest for your private consideration whether some of the colored people may not be let in, as for instance the very intelligent and especially those who have fought gallantly in our ranks. They would probably help in some trying time in the future to keep the jewel of Liberty in the family of Freedom."[3] Two years later Hahn was prepared to advocate the same policy; but at this time he seems to have regarded it as unwise, for the Era of February 15 had contained an " Ap-

---

[1] See page 32.
[2] Times, March 5, 1864.
[3] Blaine, Twenty Years, II, 39.

peal to Conservatives " in which it was stated that Hahn was
opposed to negro suffrage while Flanders was in favor of it.
This letter of Lincoln, says Blaine, was " of deep and almost
prophetic significance. It was probably the earliest proposition from any authentic source to endow the negro with the
right of suffrage."[1] We may recognize now that had
Lincoln's advice been followed the South would doubtless
have been spared the horrors of congressional reconstruction; but it was asking too much of Louisiana, or of any
other Southern State at this time, to expect her to open the
door to negro suffrage when that door was firmly closed in
many of the Northern States.[2] We shall see that the new
constitution shortly to be framed in Louisiana did not
confer the ballot on the negroes, but did go so far as to
authorize the new legislature to extend the right of suffrage
to citizens of the United States (without distinction of
color) in consideration of military service, payment of taxes,
and intellectual fitness. But this shifting of the responsibility was not a success. The gracious permission was
ignored by the legislature, and only after a period of bitter
dissension and even bloodshed was the suffrage extended to
the negro.

It may be added that General Banks would have been
glad to leave the door ajar for negro suffrage but he believed
the difficulties too great at that time to be overcome. " As
the negroes were in the majority " (within the Federal

---

[1] Twenty Years, II, 40.

[2] Lincoln himself had held a different view in 1858, for in September of that year he spoke as follows at Charleston, Illinois:—

" I will say, then, that I am not, nor ever have been, in favor of
bringing about in any way the social and political equality of the
white and black races; that I am not, nor ever have been, in favor
of making voters or jurors of negroes, nor of qualifying them to
hold office, nor to intermarry with white people; and I will say, in
addition to this, that there is a physical difference between the
white and black races which I believe will forever forbid the two
races living together on terms of social and political equality. And
inasmuch as they cannot so live, while they do remain together
there must be the position of superior and inferior, and I as much
as any other man am in favor of having the superior position
assigned to the white man." Writings of Lincoln (Lapsley), IV, 2.

lines[1]), he afterwards explained, " I thought it unwise to give them the suffrage, as it would have created a negro constituency. The whites might give suffrage to the negroes, but if the negroes gave suffrage to the whites, it would result in the negroes losing it." " My idea was to get a decision from Judge Durell declaring a man with a major part of white blood should possess all the rights of a white man;[2] but I had a great deal to do, and a few men who wanted to break the bundle of sticks without loosening the band defeated it."

While these political matters were agitating that portion of Louisiana which was within the Federal lines, the Confederates kept up more than a semblance of government at Shreveport. Here the legislature met, and here the Confederate governor issued his proclamations to all who were loyal to the cause of secession. On November 21, 1863, an election was held, and without opposition Brigadier-General Henry W. Allen[3] was elected governor, with B. W. Pearce as lieutenant-governor, P. D. Hardy, secretary of state, F. S. Goode, attorney-general, H. Peralta, auditor, and B. L. Defreese, treasurer. The vote for members of the Confederate Congress was taken by general ticket, and seems to have resulted in the reelection of the former representatives, C. J. Villere, C. M. Conrad, D. F. Kenner, L. J. Dufour, Henry Marshall, and John Perkins, Jr.[4] The legislature, which also met at Shreveport, passed a number of acts, among the most important of which were these: (1) Every citizen (negroes were not citizens) should vote who had not forfeited his citizenship by electing to adhere to the govern-

---

[1] While the white population of 1860 was more numerous by 7256 than the black, the number of adult negroes was greater than the number of adult whites. The whites over twenty were 101,499, and the colored were 101,814. McPherson, Political Manual, 1866, p. 125. Senator Jonas says this was due to the fact that the Louisiana planters bought slaves from Virginia, and naturally preferred to buy adults rather than children.

[2] It was claimed that such a decision would have given the suffrage to 30,000 colored persons.

[3] Allen was a much beloved and gallant Confederate soldier.

[4] Times, January 7, 1864.

ment of the United States. (2) Five hundred thousand dollars were voted to pay for slaves lost by death or otherwise, while impressed on the public works of the State. (3) Any slave bearing arms against the inhabitants of the State or the Confederate States, or who should be engaged in any revolt or rebellion or insurrection, should suffer death.[1] Hence, in 1864, there were two capitals in Louisiana, and two governors, each claiming legitimacy. If a majority can determine such a question, the government at Shreveport could claim to be not only de facto but de jure.

---

[1] In this connection it may be added that in the latter part of 1864 Governor Allen favored the arming of the negroes in behalf of the Confederacy. In September he wrote to J. A. Seddon, secretary of war in the Confederate government: "The time has come to put into the Army every able-bodied negro as a soldier. The negro knows he cannot escape conscription if he goes to the enemy. He must play an important part in the war. He caused the fight, and he will have his portion of the burden to bear. . . . I would free all able to bear arms, and put them in the field at once." To offset this threat and free the slaves from any fear of conscription in case they chose to run away from their masters, Major-General E. R. S. Canby, then in command of the Department of the Gulf, issued a proclamation in October, saying: "The class of persons referred to [in Allen's letter] will not be conscripted into the armies of the United States. If they come within our lines, they will be freed and treated as refugees. They will be accepted as volunteers or will be employed in the public service and their families will be cared for until they are in a condition to care for them. If a draft should become necessary, no discrimination will be made against them." Times, October 13, 1864. Fortunately, the authorities of the Confederacy concluded not to support its waning fortunes by the emancipation and arming of the slaves. The ultimate result of the conflict would have been the same, and such a measure would only have embittered the war and prolonged it for a very brief period, if at all.

CHAPTER IV.

THE CONVENTION OF 1864.

In the meantime, on March 11, 1864, General Banks had issued a proclamation fixing an election to be held on March 28 for the choice of delegates to a convention which should revise and amend the constitution of 1852. It was confirmed a few days later by Governor Hahn, probably with the intention of softening its military character by bringing it under the authority of the state executive. The proclamation named the forty-eight parishes of the State, gave the white population of each in 1860 (aggregating 357,629), and assigned to each parish one delegate apparently for each 2000 of the white inhabitants. The colored population, which Banks at this time believed to be in the majority, was neither to vote nor to be represented. Banks afterwards explained[1] that while this white basis was a departure from the constitution of 1852, it was adopted to prevent the slave-holding planters from keeping the control they had exercised in the past and to give New Orleans the power she really possessed.[2] If the freedmen were not to vote, they should not be permitted to influence representation. As many of the parishes named were not within the Federal lines, it was provided that such parishes should be entitled to elect delegates at any time before the dissolution of the convention. The qualifications of electors were the same as in the February election. The vote must have been a great disappointment to General Banks. By strenuous exertions in the February election he had succeeded in polling a vote of more than 10,000, which was twice the required tenth of Lincoln's proclamation; but in the last election he

---

[1] Louisiana Election Case, 38th Cong., 2d sess., H. Rept. No. 13, p. 19.
[2] The constitution of 1852 based representation on total population.

was absent from the city, and his opponents (conservatives
and radicals) seem to have decided that the best way to
hamper his policy was to stay away from the polls. In any
case the result was that the total vote amounted to only
about 6400.[1]

In Liberty Hall,[2] which had been dedicated with solemn
ceremony to " religion and liberty," the delegates met on
April 6, 1864, and sat for seventy-eight days. On April 8,
as we have seen, Banks's army was defeated at Mansfield
in western Louisiana; and though the battle at Pleasant
Hill on the following day was drawn, the general thought it
wise to retire from the " Trans-Mississippi Department."
As western Louisiana was thus left in the hands of the
Confederates, the convention, in order to insure as far as
possible the validity of its actions, adopted seventy-six as its
quorum, which number, it was held, would have been a
quorum had every parish been represented (seventy-six out
of a possible one hundred and fifty). The total number of
parishes represented was only nineteen, leaving the residue
of the State, or twenty-nine parishes, unrepresented. The
parishes represented were Orleans, Assumption, Avoyelles,
East Baton Rouge, West Baton Rouge, Concordia, East
Feliciana, Jefferson, Lafourche, Madison, Rapides, St.
Bernard, St. James, St. John the Baptist, St. Mary, Terrebonne, Ascension, and, later, Plaquemines and Iberville.
From these parishes the largest number of delegates ever
on the roll of the convention was ninety-eight.[3] Of course
all the delegates were antisecessionists, but there was a
scattering of conservatives in the assembly who hoped to
secure compensation for the emancipated slaves. J. A.
Rozier (conservative), who " inhabited the temperate zone

---

[1] A member of the convention gives the total vote as 6355, of
which 3832 were in New Orleans. Debates in Convention, 1864, p.
408. Banks afterwards claimed that New Orleans was really the
State of Louisiana, but the minority report of the congressional
committee showed that the city in 1860 did not have one half the
population of the State.

[2] This was the top story of the present City Hall.

[3] Of these, New Orleans had 63, leaving the country parishes only
35. Debates in Convention, 1864, pp. 4, 370.

of politics," had refused to be a candidate on the ground that Banks had committed too many irregularities at the last election. The most prominent members were not natives of Louisiana, but many of them had long lived in the State. They were said to be Banks's party.[1] It was in no sense a representative body. In fact, one of the members declared that many of the delegates were not able to return to their respective homes on account of the extension of Confederate jurisdiction in the State.

Hardly had the convention assembled and elected Judge Durell as its presiding officer before the question was raised as to the political complexion of the members present. One of the members alleged that he had heard it stated that one half of the members were "copperheads,"[2] and he moved that all members be required to produce evidence that they had taken the iron-clad oath prescribed by Lincoln in December, 1863, or that they now take the oath before the president of the convention. This motion, though finally carried, met with some opposition for various reasons: it was alleged that it reflected on the convention and was unnecessary, and eleven members out of seventy-seven voted against it. It was especially opposed by the most distinguished member, Christian Roselius, the Nestor of the Louisiana bar. He declared that he had been a member of three previous conventions in Louisiana, and that no such oath had been required of him.[3] The majority, however, being now against him, he withdrew.

---

[1] Denison, who was connected with the custom house, and supported Chase for president, wrote on April 1, 1864, that "the character, ability and standing of the Delegates, is not such as could be wished. There are a few excellent men elected, like Judge Durell, Judge Howell, Dr. Bonzano and Mr. Brott. . . . This time I worked to the best of my ability with Mr. Flanders and his friends." Chase Correspondence, p. 435. He later writes, "What fools they [the members of the convention] are making of themselves—is a very common remark even among those who helped to elect them." Ibid., p. 439.

[2] "Copperheads" were southern sympathizers living in the North.

[3] Roselius had voted against secession in the convention of 1861, but he signed the constitution of 1861. Originally a redemptioner from Germany, he had risen to great prominence in Louisiana.

That the convention was not wholly in sympathy with the president is shown by the fact that when a motion to endorse his nomination for a second term was made, it was carried by a vote of 60 to 20, the minority doubtless representing those who inclined to the choice of General McClellan, the Democratic candidate. Still, all the members were bitterly opposed to secession, and sincerely believed they would be hanged with great promptness if the "Rebels" regained possession of New Orleans. The only points on which the members did not show harmony and homogeneity were three: (1) compensation of loyal slaveholders; (2) the education of freedmen at the expense of the whites and blacks together; (3) the granting of the suffrage to certain classes of negroes.

As we have seen, Banks had suspended all laws concerning slavery. A large majority of the convention were in favor of immediate emancipation by constitutional enactment. When the provision came up on its third reading, that "slavery and involuntary servitude, except as a punishment for crime, whereof the party shall have been duly convicted," should be forever abolished and prohibited throughout the State, and the legislature should make no law recognizing the right of property in man, it was adopted by a vote of 72 to 13. Of those voting against emancipation one member moved as a substitute that all legislation hereafter to be had on the subject of slavery should look to the amelioration of the condition of the slaves with a view to their final emancipation on the first of January, 1900, as offered by the government of the United States through the president. The rest of the minority, however, seem to have voted "nay" on the ground that the convention should pass some provisos touching the questions of compensation and the suffrage, and they wished to hold up the question of emancipation until these important matters were settled.

As to compensation, the great majority of the members were in favor of first emancipating and then seeking compensation for loyal owners, which last, some one suggested, might best be accomplished by taxing the property of rebels. For, argued one member, the slaveholders outside the Federal lines, in spite of the president's proclamation, still owned their slaves and were getting rich from them, while slaves within the lines had been set free. Hence, if the loyal owners were not compensated, they would suffer injustice. Wishing to pacify as far as possible the members demanding compensation, the convention finally adopted a report recommending an appeal to Congress on the following grounds: (1) that the loyalists would be impoverished by emancipation; (2) that Great Britain, in 1832, in abolishing slavery, gave £20,000,000 for the compensation of slaveholders,[1] and that the United States government had likewise given compensation in the District of Columbia. Moreover, Louisiana was still more deserving because she had abolished slavery voluntarily. To carry out this resolution, a committee was appointed to correspond with members of Congress, but though the appeal, to the unprejudiced mind, seems to have been a just one, no favorable answer was ever received from the Federal government. Loyal and disloyal slaveholders were to be treated alike in the matter of compensation.

As to the suffrage, there seems to have been, in the early stage of the work of the convention, a strong sentiment against granting it to the negro. In fact, on May 10 that body adopted a resolution declaring that the legislature should never pass any act authorizing free negroes to vote. But as time passed pressure from without[2] and a consequent change of policy within induced the convention to throw the burden of responsibility on the legislature that was to meet in the autumn. Accordingly, on June 23 a member named Gorlinski moved that "the Legislature shall have power to pass laws extending the right of suffrage to such persons,

[1] It was also urged that Great Britain in her colonies had established an apprenticeship of four years before emancipation; and this compensated the owners for the care of the aged and infirm, who, in Louisiana, must be supported at public expense.

[2] Denison says that nearly forty votes were changed by the influence of Banks and Hahn. Chase Correspondence, p. 452.

citizens of the United States, as by military service, by taxation to support the government, or by intellectual fitness,
may be deemed entitled thereto." When this seemingly innocent resolution[1] was first offered, it was doubtless not
clear to many of the members what was its true intention.
The word "negro" was not in it, but Sullivan, of Orleans,
jumped to his feet to denounce it as a "nigger resolution,"
and moved to lay it on the table.[2] In spite of this protest
it passed the convention without further discussion by a vote
of 48 to 32. Subsequently one of the delegates (Bailey)
resigned, giving as his reason the passage of Gorlinski's
resolution.

As to the status of the slaves, Banks's proclamation, as we
have seen, had declared that all laws upholding slavery were
null and void within Federal lines, though the claim for
compensation on the part of loyal owners was not ignored.
In the convention this act of Banks was regarded by some
as abolishing slavery de jure and de facto wherever it was
left untouched by Lincoln's proclamation but by others as
merely suspending the laws on this subject.[3] But even after
the convention had passed the ordinance of emancipation
that body was astonished one morning by the news that
W. W. Handlin, a judge of the third district court and a
bitter opponent of slavery and secession, had virtually
decided, by dismissing the suit of a negro woman brought
against her master, that slavery still existed in New Orleans.
In a lower court, judgment had been given in favor of the
woman, and an appeal had been taken to Handlin's court.
The defence was that the plaintiff, being a slave, had no
rights in the court, that she could neither sue nor be sued.
Handlin, sustaining the objection, dismissed the case and
overruled the motion for a new trial. This news created
great excitement in the convention, and the following resolu-

---

[1] It was not generally admitted that the negro was a "citizen of
the United States."
[2] Debates in Convention, 1864, p. 450.
[3] Banks later said his action left slavery existing de jure but not
de facto.

tion was offered: "That all decisions of the courts of the State that declare slavery exists in the State, are contrary to the fundamental laws of the State, and are contempts of the emancipation ordinance passed by this Convention."[1] In the discussion of this resolution the president, Durell, gave it as his opinion that all blacks in New Orleans were free. " Go out into the street," said he, "and order your slave to perform your work: will he obey? Is there any means by which you can make him obey? The military has declared slavery no longer existent in Louisiana, and as all the Courts have been organized by military order, they must obey. There is not a District Judge in the City that doesn't sit as a military Judge." One of the delegates, Mr. Abell, in answer declared that Banks had no power to abolish slavery and the present constitution had not yet been ratified by the people. Finally, however, it was agreed by a vote of 58 to 21 to drop that part of the resolution declaring such decisions of the courts to be " contempts " and to pass the rest.

In the meantime, Governor Hahn had revoked the commission of Judge Handlin,[2] which caused the resignation of Howell, another judge of the civil courts. It would seem, therefore, that the courts held that slavery still existed in New Orleans, the decision of the commanding general to the contrary notwithstanding; but we hear of no more rulings to that effect. The function of the convention was simply to make permanent what was temporary under

---

[1] Debates in Convention, 1864, p. 540. The attorney-general of the State, B. F. Lynch, had previously given his opinion that all slaves in Louisiana were free, de facto and de jure, and hence could testify in court.

[2] Roselius sarcastically remarked that Handlin had been removed on account of the only correct decision he had ever rendered. Handlin, some years later, brought suit against the State for salary on account of illegal removal. The case reached the United States Supreme Court on appeal. The opinion of the court, given by Justice Chase, was that Hahn had the right as military governor to remove Handlin, a military appointee, "though the reasons assigned for the removal are not approved by the Court." It is not recorded that Handlin derived much satisfaction from the sop thrown to him at the end of the decision. Cf. 12 Wallace, p. 175.

Banks's proclamation. The action of Hahn showed that he regarded the State within Federal lines as strictly under martial law, for no sensible person could maintain that the provision for the emancipation of slaves incorporated in the pending constitution was binding on the courts before that constitution had been ratified by the people; the convention itself had decided that such ratification was necessary.

That the government of Louisiana was military was still further shown by a general order issued on March 22, 1864, before the assembling of the convention. General Banks, on his own responsibility, had made provision for the establishment of schools for freedmen. He appointed a board of education of three persons, and granted it large powers. It was to establish one or more common schools in every school district defined by the provost-marshal; to acquire by purchase or otherwise lands for school sites; to erect schoolhouses and employ teachers (as far as practicable among the loyal citizens of Louisiana); to furnish books; to provide each adult freedman with a library costing two dollars and fifty cents, this amount to be deducted from the wages of said freedman; and, finally, to levy for these purposes a school tax on real and personal property in every school district.

In the convention this order of Banks was discussed. Mr. Abell moved to declare it unconstitutional on the ground that it had been imposed without the consent of the people, but the convention approved it by a vote of 72 to 9. When, however, the question of providing for the education of the negro came before the convention, that body showed much diversity of opinion as to ways and means, and its final action on the subject was much more liberal toward the negro than the position at first taken, for at an early stage of the proceedings it was decided to establish schools for the whites to be supported by taxation of whites, and for the colored to be supported, in like manner, by taxation of colored persons. If this measure were not adopted, argued Abell, " whites and blacks might be com-

pelled to attend the same schools." This was not a necessary corollary, but, as we shall see, it was what naturally
resulted under radical rule. In any case the friends of the
freedman feared that he would suffer by separate taxation,
and Dr. Dostie wrote a letter to Abell urging that the word
" colored " be dropped from the educational and the militia
bills. For this or some other reason the mover of the previous resolution, Terry, moved some three weeks later that
there should be no separate taxation of the races, and that
the legislature should provide for the education of all children between the ages of six and eighteen by the maintenance, by taxation or otherwise, of free public schools. This
provision, being adopted by a vote of 53 to 27, was incorporated in the constitution. It was the first constitutional
provision for the education of the negro in Louisiana.[1]

Some members were bitterly opposed to the very presence
of the negro in Louisiana. One speaker urged that all
negroes should be "pushed off the soil of America;"
another, that they should all be sent to Massachusetts,
" where the philanthropists come from." It was answered,
however, with some force, that the negroes in the Federal
army were at that very moment defending the convention.
Negrophilists and negrophobists were both applauded.[2]

There was, however, much discussion in the convention as
to the proper status of persons in whose veins there was
only a small admixture of negro blood. It was stated that
there were rich planters living on the Mississippi who, in
spite of the known fact that they were not entirely white,
had yet been recognized as citizens of Louisiana and had
always enjoyed full rights as such. An effort was now
made to have the convention declare what degree of negro
blood should constitute a colored person. Henderson quoted

---

[1] Previous to the Civil War, when abolition sentiments were active
in the North, there was a law in Louisiana forbidding any one to
teach a slave to read and write. It is certain, however, that many
slaves could read.

[2] If there were any members in favor of negro equality in any
form except by granting the suffrage to certain classes, through
legislative enactment, they did not venture to express their views,
though the contrary opinion did find voice.

a passage from Edwards's West Indies declaring that in the Spanish and French West Indies there was no degradation of color beyond the quadroons, for beyond these the colored could not be distinguished from the white either by color or feature. It was further stated that, according to the laws of all the slave States except South Carolina and Louisiana, a person was held to be white after the fourth degree.[1] But the convention, not wishing to involve itself in the intricacies of a question which sometimes produced duels and street fights, voted down the resolution by a vote of 47 to 23.[2] General Banks, as we have seen, was worrying over the same problem, and found the solution equally difficult.

The expenses of the convention proved to be no small item. The first appropriation made by the convention for the per diem of members, for mileage, and for salaries of officers was $100,000, but as these items amounted to more than $1000 a day, and there was also a heavy outlay for "contingents," it was found necessary to appropriate $25,-000 additional. The New Orleans Times, which was antagonistic to the work of the convention, though it was at the same time strongly antirebel, published on November 4, 1864, with sarcastic comments, the auditor's account of the contingent expenses of the convention. They included:—

Ice	$ 414.50
Liquors and cigars	9421.55
Dinner at Galpin's	65.00
Fitting up of Liberty Hall	9150.25
Goblets, wine glasses	791.60
One pen case presented to General Banks	150.00
Daily papers	4237.50
Police duty	1904.00
Stationery	8111.55
Carriage hire, etc.	4304.25
Sundry items	236.35
Bill for printing	7000.00
Amounts for which no vouchers obtainable	608.70

[1] As a fact, however, in Virginia a colored person was one who had one fourth or more of African blood, and in South Carolina the line was drawn at octoroons. Stephenson, "Race Distinctions in American Law," Amer. Law Rev., Jan., 1909, p. 39. In Louisiana it was held that "the law does not contemplate that any number of crosses between the negro and the white shall emancipate the off-spring of the slave." Morrison vs. White, 16 La. Annual, 100.

[2] Debates in Convention, 1864, pp. 547, 548.

It will be seen that the convention paid without question for liquors and cigars consumed at a free bar the sum of $9421.55 in seventy-eight days, or $120 a day—all at the expense of the taxpayers, who were spoken of in the convention as groaning under the burdens of taxation. A thousand dollars was also distributed among the chaplains who had officiated in the convention. The Times headed its account of these heavy expenses for contingents with the appropriate words of Falstaff: "Rob me the exchequer, the first thing thou doest." And it is certain that the free bar established by this convention set an example of extravagance (to use no stronger term) which the later reconstruction legislative assemblies were not slow to follow. The legislature that met in the autumn investigated the disbursements of the convention, and discovered that the sergeant-at-arms had vouched for brandy as costing $23 per gallon which really cost only $8. A similar fraud was discovered as to the stationery. The sergeant-at-arms was arrested and presumably punished. As we sum up the expenses of this body it seems a pity that its work, which cost the State so dear, should have found no favor in the eyes of Congress and should finally have been ruthlessly rejected.

On one occasion a strange scene had been witnessed in the convention. On the 22d of July the New Orleans Times, whose editor was Thomas P. May, described the proceedings in the convention of the preceding day as "sickening and disgusting." Members, it said, had declared the president drunk and a d—— fool, and pandemonium had reigned. The debates show that on the day in question there was a great deal of confusion in the convention. Durell, the president, ordered one member under arrest, and amid loud cries of "No adjournment" declared the house adjourned and left the chair. When, however, the article from the Times was brought before the convention, it was denounced by Durell himself as a most infamous libel upon himself and the convention. A resolu-

tion was offered that the sergeant-at-arms should be ordered
to take possession of the paper, and that its publication
should be suspended until its responsible editor (Thomas P.
May) should appear before the convention and purge himself of the libel. When the motion was under discussion,
one of the members declared it to be his private opinion that
one of the editors of the paper was an adherent of S. P.
Chase, ex-secretary of the treasury and a rival of Lincoln in
1860 for the presidency,[1] hence its opposition to the work
of the convention. Abell came forward nobly to the
defence of Durell by declaring that he knew the statement of
the paper as to intoxication to be false. " I walked to an
art gallery," he said, " with the president yesterday after
adjournment, and if there had been anything unusual in his
condition, I should have noticed it." However, Abell was
not in favor of prosecuting the paper, as such a course would
give it too much distinction. Another speaker said that
such articles in the papers arose from the advance of the
rebels. " The nearer the rebels come to this city," he said,
" the prouder the copperheads become."

On the 23d of July Editor May appeared before the convention under orders of General Banks, and was asked what
he had to say. He defied the convention, saying that he
appeared in obedience to the orders of General Banks and
not in obedience to the resolution of the convention. At
the proper time and place, and in pursuance of the forms of
law, he would answer any charges against him or his paper.
This defiant answer coming instead of an expected apology
was regarded as an additional contempt, and a member
(Cutler) declared that there was only one thing to do—
" Send Thomas P. May to jail! Let him know that he lives
in a land of liberty! "[2] This extraordinary utterance was

---

[1] This was true of Denison, who owned the largest interest in the
paper and controlled its policy. Chase Correspondence, p. 413.

[2] In the debates are found the words, " but must not abuse that
liberty." The writer, however, is assured that Cutler added these
words to the report of the proceedings to avoid the conspicuous
" bull." One is reminded of the stocks in the old English monas-
tery, which were kept up " pro servanda libertate," libertas being
used with the peculiar sense of privilege.

received with shouts of applause, and no one of the members seems to have commented on the absurdity. May was condemned to the parish prison for ten days, unless the convention should sooner adjourn. At the same time the military authorities were requested to suppress the newspaper, and the president of the United States was to be requested to remove the offender from the office which he held of assistant treasurer of the United States. General Banks, not seeming clearly to understand why a man should be put in jail to enable him to appreciate the fact that he lived in a land of liberty, or for some other reason, set May free, and the latter boasted in his newspaper of his immunity.

A few days later the convention adopted the constitution by a vote of 67 to 16. This constitution, signed by seventy-nine members, is a brief document, occupying only ten pages of the printed proceedings, and really amounts to nothing more than a revised and amended copy of the constitution of 1852. Its chief features may be summed up as follows: (1) It abolished slavery in Louisiana. (2) It gave suffrage only to male whites of twenty-one years, but it granted the legislature the power to extend the suffrage to such other persons (negroes) as by military service, by taxation to support the government, or by intellectual fitness, should be deemed entitled to it. (3) State senators should be elected for four years and members of the lower house for two. (4) The legislature was authorized to license lotteries and gambling saloons. (5) The capital of the State was located at New Orleans. (6) Education was given to all, white and black, between six and eighteen, with no discrimination in the matter of taxation. (7) The governor should issue a proclamation for the election of a general assembly to meet October 1, 1864. (8) The constitution was to be submitted to popular vote on the first Monday in September. This constitution is of special interest as showing the sentiments of Union men in the South at this early period,[1] and it will

---

[1] It was afterwards shown by Durant that the constitution was

be noticed that their attitude, particularly with reference to negro suffrage, was marked by great caution.

Just before adjournment it was resolved " That when this Convention adjourns, it shall be at the call of the president, whose duty it shall be to reconvoke the Convention for any cause, or in case the constitution should not be ratified, for the purpose of taking such measures as may be necessary for the formation of a civil government for the State of Louisiana. . . . In case of the ratification of the constitution, it shall be in the power of the Legislature of the State, at its first session, to reconvoke the Convention, in like manner, in case it should be deemed expedient or necessary, for the purpose of making amendments or additions to the Constitution that may, in the opinion of the Legislature, require a reassembling of the Convention."[1] A careful perusal of this resolution will discover the fact that it left indefinite, and hence large, powers in the hands of the president in regard to reconvoking. The whole provision was opposed by Abell, who argued that the convention had done its duty and should adjourn sine die; if the constitution was rejected, he said, the present convention would only misrepresent the people. His view, however, was voted down; and no one was prophet enough to see that the power of reconvoking was fraught with disaster for Louisiana and the whole South—nay, that it was to be the main occasion for the drastic reconstruction legislation which harassed the South for ten years.

The convention adjourned in August, 1864, and at the appointed time the constitution was submitted to the popular vote within the Federal lines, and was adopted by a vote

---

adopted by the votes of parishes that were not represented in the convention. Denison gives the following letter from Lincoln to Banks: " I have just seen the new Constitution adopted by the Convention of Louisiana and I am anxious that it shall be ratified by the people. I will thank you to let the civil officers in Louisiana, holding under me, know that this is my wish, and to let me know at once who of them openly declares for the Constitution, and who of them, if any, decline to so declare." Chase Correspondence, p. 447.

[1] Debates in Convention, 1864, p. 623.

of 6836 to 1566,[1] which was a larger vote than had been polled for the delegates to the convention, and was well within the limits of the one tenth prescribed by Lincoln. Before the constitution was submitted to the people, however, it had become apparent that Lincoln's plan of reconstruction was to meet with much opposition among the radical adherents of the Republican party, both in Congress and in Louisiana itself. Strong as was Lincoln's place in the affections of his party and of the northern people in general, Congress in 1864 was coming to take a more radical view of the situation, and soon showed itself dissatisfied with the idea of admitting to its floors senators or representatives from what were called satirically the president's "ten per cent. States" and later "the spawn of presidential usurpation." A good occasion for the assumption of this position was offered when two senators from the "reconstructed State of Arkansas," who had been elected in April, 1864, arrived in Washington, and knocked at the doors of the Senate, presenting, so to speak, Lincoln's card as a note of introduction. Congress, led by Charles Sumner, promptly decided that a vote of both houses was necessary to admit representatives from "rebel States."

A bill of July 4, 1864, while the Louisiana convention was still in session, announced the congressional plan of reconstruction. This required (1) that, instead of one tenth, the majority of citizens of the United States in each rebellious State, having sworn allegiance to the Federal government, should elect delegates to a convention for the framing of a new constitution; (2) that Congress had the right to abolish slavery in the said States (as if they were territories); (3) that those who had held office under the Confederacy or who should hold any in the future should not vote; (4) that when a new constitution had been drafted, ratified by a majority of the voters, and approved by Congress, then the president, after obtaining the consent of Congress, should proclaim the new government established as the constitu-

---

[1] The parish of Orleans gave 5551, and the rest of the State 2951. Voting took place in only twenty parishes.

tional government of the State. Whereupon the reconstructed State might proceed to the election of Federal
senators and representatives. Lincoln, it is true, promptly
pocket-vetoed this bill, and as Congress adjourned within ten
days it failed to become a law.

But some days later Lincoln went further by issuing a
proclamation in which he doubted the competency of Congress to abolish slavery in the rebellious States without a
constitutional amendment, and practically refused to give
up the governments recently established in Arkansas and
Louisiana, though he was willing that the other States should
adopt the congressional plan. This brought out the famous
public protest from Senator Wade of Ohio and Congress-
man Henry W. Davis of Maryland in which the congressional
plan was upheld and Lincoln was warned that " he must
confine himself to his executive duties." The reelection of
Lincoln in the autumn seemed to leave the victory in his
hands; but the difference of opinion between him and Congress as to whether he or that body should take the initiative in reorganizing rebellious States boded no good for the
success of the new Louisiana constitution. Just before his
death, in the last speech he ever made (April 11, 1865),
Lincoln urged in a characteristic manner the acceptance of
his view. Referring to the twelve thousand men who had
organized the government of Louisiana, he said: " If we reject and spurn them, we do our utmost to disorganize and
disperse them.... Concede that the new government of Louisiana is only to what it should be as the egg is to the fowl, we
shall sooner have the fowl by hatching the egg than by
smashing it." But this homely, though happy, simile had
little effect upon the majority of Republicans in Congress,
and Blaine asserts that certain members even insinuated
that the president had a secret understanding with certain
rebels who, as soon as the president's hand was withdrawn,
would turn the State over to an unrepentant Democracy.[1]

In any case the protest of Wade and Davis met with the
entire approval of the radical faction in Louisiana. This

---

[1] Blaine, Twenty Years, II, 48.

faction was headed by Thomas J. Durant, who had been accused in the convention—whether justly or not does not appear—with receiving large sums of money from the North to further the election of B. F. Flanders to the governorship. Two years before he had fallen under the disapproval of Lincoln himself,[1] and now he did not enjoy any great popularity among the members of the convention. He had taken part in the election of February, 1864, but his radical candidate having been defeated, he was now determined to overthrow the Lincoln-Banks party. Falling in with the opponents of the president, he published in the New Orleans Times of August 18, 1864, a letter which he had written to Henry W. Davis. In this letter he held that the president's appointment of Hahn to take the place of the military governor, Shepley, was illegal; that the president had no right to make such appointments without the consent of the Senate; and that Banks had acted illegally in declaring the constitution of 1852 to be in force. The convention and Governor Hahn, he said, were both opposed to "that principle which in Louisiana can alone establish justice and insure domestic tranquility—equality of all men before the law." By this last phrase Durant doubtless meant that the ballot had not been granted to the freedman; for otherwise there was no inequality before the law. He concluded with the hope that Congress would reject the results of the convention recently adjourned.

Banks, grieved to see the legitimacy of his foster child thus questioned, wrote a defence of his work in Louisiana, which, if not convincing, is at least ingenious.[2] His avowed object was to show how closely the people of Louisiana had followed the provisions of the reconstruction bill in the reorganization of their government in 1864.[3] The conven-

---

[1] In 1862 Durant had been censured by Lincoln for expressing anxiety for the fate of the Union and not being willing to do anything to save it. Blaine, Twenty Years, II, 36.

[2] Letter to Senator Lane of September 24, 1864. Pamphlet, New York, 1865.

[3] In May, 1864, Banks had been supplanted by General R. G. Canby, but he returned later.

tion, he says, was elected in due form. Either the oath of
allegiance prescribed by the act of Congress in 1862 or the
"iron-clad" oath of the president's proclamation of December 8, 1863, was administered to every voter; in most
cases, both. The delegates were chosen by "white male
citizens of the United States, twenty-one years of age, who
had the qualifications required by law." Soldiers from
Louisiana were allowed to vote when in the State. So far
as was known, no person who had held office under the
Confederate government or who had borne arms against the
United States had participated in the elections. The new
constitution abolished slavery, prohibited involuntary servitude except for crime, and made all men equal before the
law. There was no liability for the rebel debt. It did
not deny the elective franchise to men who had borne arms
against the United States. "The Convention would have
readily adopted this measure, but it was impracticable for
Louisiana to overthrow the policy of the general government in this respect. The principal officer of the treasury
in New Orleans once held a commission in the rebel army."[1]
It had been held that the eleven parishes at the late election
had 233,185 inhabitants, and the residue of the State
565,617. But, argues Banks, this is regarding the population of the State as it was in 1860, while of the 331,726
slaves in 1860, nearly one fourth have died or left the State.
The mortality of the black population in the commencement
of the struggle until furnished with employment and comfortable homes was appalling. The reduction of the white
population is nearly equal to the loss among the blacks. Of
the 708,000 whites and blacks inhabiting the State in 1860
there are now not more than 451,000[2] within its borders, two

---

[1] This was Thomas May, editor of the Times; but May claimed
that his service in the Confederacy lasted only four weeks, and
that this service was compulsory.

[2] That Banks largely underestimated the population of the State
in 1864 is shown by the fact that the census of 1870 gave Louisiana
a population of 726,915, an increase which, supposing Banks's estimate to be correct, cannot be accounted for by natural increase or
by the return of the natives.

thirds of which are in the lines of our army. Almost the
entire negro population, not only of Louisiana but of the
surrounding States, has taken refuge here, together with
numerous white families. It is probable that the number
qualified to vote by the laws of the State is not over 25,000,
and there are from 15,000 to 17,000 voters registered within
the lines of the army.[1] Moreover, the constitution just
framed had authorized the legislature to extend the suffrage
to citizens of the United States without distinction of color
in cases of military service, payment of taxes, or intellectual
fitness, and the said constitution had been ratified by the
people. Hahn had been called the dictator of Louisiana, but
he had been designated by the people at a formal, free
election as the man they wished for governor, and the president had then designated him as military governor. In view,
therefore, of the close compliance which the State had made
with the requirements of Congress, Banks[2] urges that Louisiana be restored to her place in the Union. And it will be
noticed that his letter was written six months before the
surrender of General Lee.

In October of the same year Durant wrote another letter
to his patron, Henry W. Davis, in which he makes a search-
ing analysis of the defence offered by General Banks. This
letter[3] doubtless furnished the radicals in Congress with the
thunder bolts hurled against the president's policy. The
president, says this document, pretends to the right, in his
military character as commander-in-chief, to organize state

---

[1] In support of Banks's statement the registrar swore, on November 21, 1864, that there were 13,000 voters in New Orleans alone.
He had registered 8000, and 5000 registered before the war had
taken the oath.

[2] In his testimony in 1866 Banks declared that he believed it was
proper to reconvoke the convention in 1866 because the constitution
of 1864 was merely provisional for the following reasons: " It only
represented a portion, about three-fifths, I believe, of the parishes.
It could not be regarded as complete until formally accepted by all
the parishes, and until recognized by the government of the United
States." Report of the Select Committee on New Orleans Riots,
39th Cong., 2d sess., H. Rept. No. 16, testimony, p. 516.

[3] Published as a pamphlet, New Orleans, 1864. Copy in the
Howard Library, New Orleans.

governments designed to survive the war and, in the meantime, to possess the right to participate in the government
by sending senators and representatives to Congress and to
cast votes in a presidential election, a right which both the
Constitution and the courts have declared belongs to Congress.   General Banks had adopted in the fullest extent the
presidential idea: " No declaration of war without the consent of Congress, but once waged by its order, The President,
as commander-in-chief, cannot be restricted in his action."
This Durant conceives to be an error.   As to what was
actually done in Louisiana, there was no real compliance
either with the act of Congress or with the existing laws of
the State.   Military resistance had not ceased in one half
the State; and the whole political movement, while pretending to be civil, was purely military throughout.   Banks
ordered everything, dominated everything.   He pretended
to follow the law of the State, except as to slavery; but he
had based representation in the convention on white population when the existing constitution required it to be based on
the total population.   He had given sixty-three delegates to
New Orleans, though that city was entitled to only twenty-
six.   The new constitution had been adopted in convention
by a vote of 66 to 16, which was ten less than the quorum
fixed.   Moreover, when submitted to the people, it had been
ratified in some parishes which had no representatives in the
convention.   General Banks had estimated the population to
be for the most part within Federal lines, but his estimates
were only guesswork.   Whatever the number of voters
registered, the smallness of the vote cast showed that
Banks's action was not supported by the majority of the
loyal vote of the State.   Finally, Banks claimed that
" equality before the law " had been granted to all citizens,
but neither the " right " to vote nor to hold office had been
granted the negro.   If Banks had called only negroes into
his convention, would this have been regarded as granting
" equal rights " to the whites?

This letter was a powerful arraignment of Banks's work

in Louisiana; and, as we have seen, it fell in with the humor of the majority in Congress. Even the final argument that the " right " to hold office and to vote had been denied the negro was soon to gain force among the radicals; for, though States of the North and West denied these rights to the colored citizens, there was a growing feeling that the rebel States should be compelled to grant them. Moreover, the returning Confederates in 1865 rejected the convention's work as based on fraud and corruption. Only a small faction supported it.

CHAPTER V.

GOVERNMENT DURING THE WAR.

As provided in the new constitution, the state government was completed on September 5 by the election of a general assembly. It was alleged that the vote cast at this election was 9830; but the enemies of the legislature maintained that the registration had not been conducted in accordance with the constitution, or was otherwise illegal, and that over 5000 votes "bore no traces of legality." It was also maintained that many colored persons had been registered. The new legislature met October 3. It seems to have represented the State about as fully as the constitutional convention had done. At the opening session there were twenty-three senators and sixty or more representatives.[1] Some of these had been members of the convention, and the same sentiments toward political issues prevailed as in that body. No acts of any great importance were passed by this legislature. It was more noteworthy for what it failed to do than for what it did. Its negative attitude is perhaps excusable when we remember that its status was dubious; it was surrounded by hostile factions denying its legality, and it was by no means sure of its recognition in the halls of Congress.

The general belief is that this legislature refused by a large majority to grant the suffrage to the negro,[2] but an examination of the proceedings shows that no vote was ever taken on this subject. Governor Hahn in his message did not suggest that the legislature should avail itself of the constitutional provision; and when he resigned the office of governor in February, 1865, to accept the office of United States senator, he declared that "universal suffrage will be

---

[1] Twenty-five parishes claimed representation. Journal of the House of Representatives, 1864, p. 4.

[2] Annual Cyclopaedia, 1864, subject "Louisiana," p. 479.

granted whenever it is deemed wise and timely.[1] Louisiana has already done more than three fourths of the Northern States." His attitude doubtless determined the action of the general assembly. In the proceedings of the lower house there are very few references to the negro question. Marie introduced a bill to repeal article 95 of the civil code and to permit marriages between blacks and whites. It was voted down, 58 to 4. Later, a member gave notice that he would introduce a bill to submit the question of negro suffrage to the people of the State, but no further reference to this impracticable scheme is to be found. In the senate a bill declaring white every person having not more than one fourth negro blood was laid on the table by a vote of 20 to 4. The reasons assigned for this action were various. It was declared that a prominent journal had opposed such a bill on the ground that it was an unjust, incomplete, and partial method of treating the suffrage, which should be based on military service, intellectual fitness, or property qualification. A full-blooded negro, for example, had fought with bravery in the Union army at Port Gibson. Others said that the motion was premature. Later in the session a petition was introduced from five thousand negroes, "many, if not the majority" of whom were in the Federal army, asking for the suffrage, but no action was taken. One member, apparently expressing the general sentiment, said: "It will be time enough to grant this petition when all the other free States grant it and set us the example. When this State grants it, I shall go to China."[2]

Nor was the attitude of the senate toward the rebels marked by any decisive action. A bill was introduced to pardon Confederates under the grade of colonel who should take the oath of allegiance to Louisiana and the United States, but to institute proceedings against Thomas J. Semmes, E. W. Moise, J. P. Benjamin, John Slidell, Henry M. Hyams, and others, for treason and perjury, their prop-

[1] In the summer of 1865 he advocated negro suffrage vigorously.
[2] Debates of the Senate, 1864, p. 65.

erty to be seized and sold for the benefit of loyalists and refugees. This attractive program was voted down by the narrow margin of 3 in a vote of 21.

On two questions this legislature did reach an agreement. The thirteenth amendment to the Federal Constitution abolishing slavery in the United States was unanimously adopted in both houses,[1] and subsequently (December 18, 1865) Louisiana was mentioned as one of the States ratifying the same. The legislature also elected two United States senators. They were R. King Cutler[2] to fill the unexpired term of the "rebel," John Slidell,[3] and Charles Smith for the unexpired term of J. P. Benjamin. As Smith's term would expire March 4, 1865, the same legislature in February of that year elected Governor Hahn to succeed him.

When Cutler and Smith applied for admission to the United States Senate, their claims were considered by the Judiciary Committee, which reported, on February 18, 1865, that the government of Louisiana had been inaugurated in a manner that was not free from objection, but that it was as good a government as could be expected and fairly repre-

---

[1] It was readopted by the Democratic legislature of 1865–1866, which was fully representative of the State.

[2] Later, the legislature elected Henry Boyce, and began his term on March 4, 1861, the end of Slidell's. Hence Cutler was illegally elected. Slidell's term had really expired in 1861. Denison writes that Cutler is "an unprincipled demagogue. . . . In secession times he organized and was Captain of a Confederate Company called the King Cutler Guards. . . . Gov. Hahn intended that Judge Durell and another person (Bullitt) should be elected Senators, but the Legislature took the bit in their teeth, and refusing to mind the reins, elected Cutler and Smith." Chase Correspondence, p. 453.

[3] The Times, unfavorable to both Cutler and Slidell, published, on November 7, satirical epigrams at their expense :—

"A dealer sly was old John Slidell;
 Shuffle the cards—make the sly deal tell;
 John's highest aim is his pocket's weal,
 And in dealing slyly, he beats the de'il.

"A cutler keen is our R. K. C.,
 No barber can shave you as closely as he;
 He has brass for brains, and in woe or weal,
 He is never the man that objects to *steel.*"

sented a majority of loyal votes. Louisiana, however, according to the report, was still in a state of insurrection against the United States government, and Cutler and Smith could not be admitted until both houses of Congress had recognized an existing state government. But the Senate took no action on this report, and the Louisianians were never admitted to seats.

Louisiana's claims to representation fared no better in the House than in the Senate. Although it had been intended to elect five congressmen when the legislature was elected in September, it was found possible to hold elections for only two—F. Bonzano in the first district and A. P. Field in the second. When these two presented themselves for admission to Congress, the committee disagreed as to the validity of their claims, and submitted two reports to the House. The majority report was favorable to the applicants; it declared that they had been elected "by the loyal people of Louisiana and that these loyal people constitute a majority of the people of the State." The minority report contradicted that of the majority in every particular; it might have been written by Durant himself. The House consoled the applicants by paying their expenses, but practically rejected their claims by postponing action on the report until the next session. As the war was still waging, it was thought that no fixed plan of action could wisely be decided on.

A joint resolution recognizing the state government adopted in Louisiana met the same fate. It was introduced into the Senate along with the report of the Judiciary Committee and gave rise to a warm discussion. Sumner of Massachusetts championed the cause of the negro, stating that Louisiana should not be admitted unless upon the fundamental condition that suffrage be not denied on account of race. General Wadsworth, he said, had talked with a planter of Lafourche parish who said that his hope and expectation was that slavery would be restored in some form, and that if the North withdrew from the South, the arms of negro soldiers would be taken away. Although

Reverdy Johnson had prophesied that even if Louisiana were admitted on condition of negro suffrage, the State could not be estopped later from excluding the blacks, Sumner was persuaded that the best protection for the negro was the ballot. As to the existing government in Louisiana, he described it with bitter sarcasm as " a mere seven-months' abortion, begotten by the bayonet in criminal conjunction with the spirit of caste, and born before its time, rickety, unformed, unfinished—whose continued existence will be a burden, a reproach, and a wrong."[1] This startling metaphor seems to have put an end to all discussion for the time, and no definite action was ever taken on this resolution.

Such was the status of Louisiana up to the death of Lincoln in April, 1865. It seemed a favorable sign that the committees in both houses of Congress had reported in favor of recognizing the government established under the president's policy; but it was an equally unfavorable sign that Congress as a whole did not commit itself to such a policy. It is true that Louisiana's ratification of the thirteenth amendment was accepted, but this was the only sign of recognition. Even the electoral vote of the State for president, which was sent to Washington in January, 1865, was rejected, the two houses declaring that States in rebellion were not entitled to be represented in the electoral college.[2]

To the brief history just given of the government of Louisiana in its executive and legislative aspects during the Civil War should be added a still briefer description of the judiciary so far as it was established by the Federal authorities. This phase of military rule in Louisiana was not without its peculiar and interesting features.

After the occupation of New Orleans in 1862 the sessions

---

[1] Annual Cyclopaedia, 1865, pp. 287, 289.

[2] Some effort was made to except Louisiana from this ruling on the ground that the State had been reorganized, but it was successfully opposed, a member urging that no one was sure about Louisiana. The motion was lost by a vote of 15 to 22. The Chicago Tribune ridiculed Louisiana for appointing presidential electors, as an absurdity in a State the larger portion of which was dominated by the rebel army. Times, December 9, 1864. Cox, Three Decades, p. 342.

of the existing courts of the old régime ceased. Some of
the judges took refuge within the Confederate lines, and at
least one who remained refused to act. The general in
command, therefore, appointed military officers to hold
courts. In June, 1862, progress was made by the institution of a provost court—a military court which, in default
of any better, was charged with the trial of criminal cases
and, finally, even of civil matters. Though this court was
continued until August, 1863, it was so entirely inadequate
that under General Shepley an attempt was made to give
regular courts to the State. The old courts were opened
with a somewhat changed jurisdiction, and appointments
were made to take the places of the judges who had disappeared. The second district courts of New Orleans thus
came into existence with such "loyal" men as J. G.
Whitaker and Rufus K. Howell as judges.[1] Later, the first
and third district courts were also opened, with two
recorder's courts.

The most extraordinary court of this or any other period
of American history was the "Provisional Court" established by President Lincoln. Seeing the importance of having a higher court of justice in a city as large as New
Orleans, the president, on October 20, 1862, issued the following order: "The insurrection which has for some time
prevailed in several of the States of this Union, including
Louisiana, having temporarily subverted and swept away the
civil institutions of that State, including the judiciary and
the judicial authorities of the Union, so that it has become
necessary to hold the State in military occupation; and it
being indispensably necessary that there shall be some
judicial tribunal existing there capable of maintaining
justice, I have, therefore, thought it proper to appoint, and I
do hereby constitute a Provisional Court, which shall be a
Court of Record for the State of Louisiana, and I do hereby
appoint Charles A. Peabody, of New York, to be a Provisional Judge to hold said Court, with authority to hear,

---

[1] Annual Cyclopaedia, 1863, subject "Louisiana," p. 586.

try, and determine all causes, civil and criminal, including causes in law, equity, revenue, and admiralty, and particularly all such powers and jurisdiction as belong to the District and Circuit Courts of the United States, conforming his proceeding, so far as possible, to the course of proceedings and practice which has been customary in the Courts of the United States and Louisiana—his judgment to be final and conclusive." The said judge was to establish rules and to appoint a prosecuting attorney, a marshal, and other officers, but these appointments were not to extend beyond the military occupation of New Orleans. The salary of the judge was fixed at $3500 a year, his salary and that of the other officers being ordered to be paid out of the contingent fund of the War Department. Judge Peabody accompanied Banks's expedition to New Orleans in the latter part of 1862, and his court was opened in that city in the month of January, 1863. It followed the laws of Louisiana in criminal matters, and, as far as altered conditions would permit, all other laws of the State. Being a military court, it was required to regard as paramount all orders of the general of the department.[1]

It seems to have been thought in Louisiana that the president had established this court to pass upon the confiscated property of rebels,[2] and that it had failed to do its duty. It was urged that fifty or sixty libels had been brought before it, and that the court had not acted upon them. The truth is that the court had seen proper to limit its own jurisdiction. As it had been created not by the Constitution and laws of the United States but by the executive exercising powers conferred on him by the law of nations, it held that it had no jurisdiction in prize cases, and it seems to have held that there was a similar lack of jurisdiction in cases of confiscation. The latter question was argued before the court, but before a decision was reached the United States

---

[1] Annual Cyclopaedia, 1863, subject " Provisional Court for Louisiana," p. 770.

[2] Debates in Convention, 1864, p. 519.

district court was established in New Orleans (1863), and to it were transferred all the confiscation cases.[1]

The chief reason for the establishment of the court, however, was to decide controversies in which foreign residents of New Orleans were concerned, and which were likely to bring about international complications. In these matters it was so successful as to prevent all complaints of the foreign population of the city from reaching the State Department. Moreover, in several capital cases that were brought before it convictions were obtained, which were held at the time to be rare occurrences in New Orleans.

Its power was naturally questioned. Its deputy marshal once served a process at Morganza with a force of a thousand cavalry.[2] Secretary Seward once said, half jokingly, that the provisional court of Louisiana exercised more powers than the Supreme Court of the United States.[3] Nor did the great powers of this court escape adverse criticism in Louisiana. The New Orleans Times, July 9, 1864, in an editorial, declared that if the judge had not asserted less authority than his commission vested him with, much disorder would have crept into judicial affairs. As it was, many anomalous proceedings not within the cognizance of Louisiana law or practice had taken place. The court, it continued, was not a desideratum, and if the views of the convention (then sitting) had any weight with the military authorities, it had probably reached its end.

In 1864 Judge Peabody, in answer to criticisms of his authority, gave out a defence of the court over which he presided. He argued that his court was legal in international law because the president of the United States, as commander-in-chief, had conquered Louisiana, and in conquered territory such a court could lawfully be established. Though he admitted that some kind of civil government had been reestablished in the State, his court would continue to

---

[1] Annual Cyclopaedia, 1863, subject " Provisional Court for Louisiana," p. 775.

[2] Judge Peabody, " Provisional Court for Louisiana," International Review, May, 1878, p. 319.

[3] Ibid., p. 322, note.

exist until disestablished by the Federal government. In support of his position he cited the establishment of similar courts in California and elsewhere.[1] The validity of this remarkable tribunal was afterwards fully sustained by the Supreme Court of the United States.[2] At the end of the Civil War Judge Peabody resigned and returned to New York. By act of Congress, of July 28, 1866, the provisional court was formally abolished, all proceedings therein being transferred to the United States district court for the eastern district of Louisiana.

In April, 1863, though the provisional court had been in session for more than two months, Military Governor Shepley decided to reorganize the supreme court of Louisiana.[3] To the office of chief justice he appointed Judge Peabody, who had agreed to attend at the provisional court an hour earlier in the morning and adjourn in time for the supreme court. But as the associate justices appointed seem to have declined, the latter court never existed except in name. While the constitutional convention of 1864 was in session, the state auditor reported to that body that Chief Justice Peabody had been allowed to draw $3541.66 in salary from the State, for which he had rendered no service. This report excited some indignation in the convention, and it was proposed to bring suit against Peabody for the amount. Another member, however, urged that the judge should not be condemned unheard, and nothing further seems to have been done in the matter. The constitution of 1864 having provided for a complete judiciary, Governor Wells, in March, 1865, appointed a full bench, consisting of W. B. Hyman, chief justice, with Zenon Lebauve, R. K. Howell, John H. Ilsley, and R. B. Jones[4] as

---

[1] Annual Cyclopaedia, 1864, subject "Louisiana," pp. 480–485.
[2] 9 Wallace, 129; 22 Wallace, 297.
[3] The New Orleans Times of February 21 demanded the reorganization of this court.
[4] Judge Jones died of cholera in 1865, and was succeeded by J. G. Taliaferro. Jones's qualifications for his high office were not generally recognized. It is related that when he asked to be "qualified," the judge to whom he applied said, "I will swear you in; all h— couldn't qualify you."

associates. This court rendered its first decisions in May, 1865.

The Confederate lawyers, who were now returning to the city, poor, needy, tired of war and politics, were enabled to practice in the state courts[1] under the general amnesty proclamation or the special pardons of President Johnson; but in the United States circuit and district courts they were still refused the privilege unless they took the iron-clad oath of 1862, which in 1865 had been extended by Congress to include practice in the United States courts. The large cotton cases in these courts furnished such heavy fees to the lawyers that some secessionists stretched their consciences and took the oath, while their more scrupulous colleagues had to content themselves with such scraps of business as fell to them in the state courts.[2]

---

[1] The supreme court was reorganized by the Democratic legislature by act approved March 13, 1866.

[2] Address of B. F. Jonas in Times Democrat, May 5, 1901.

CHAPTER VI.

RECONSTRUCTION IN LOUISIANA UNDER PRESIDENT JOHNSON.

We have seen that, in spite of the protest of prominent radicals in the summer of 1864 and the opposition of the majority of Congress in the winter of 1865, President Lincoln persisted in declaring that his policy for the reconstruction of Louisiana was both constitutional and wise and in urging on Congress its adoption. To him, rebellion in the South had not appeared as a secession of States, but as an insurrection of individuals, resulting from a conspiracy of the prominent leaders.[1] Holding this view, it seemed to him only natural that in exercise of the pardoning power granted him by the Constitution he should extend an amnesty to those who had been misled, and, as commander-in-chief, should aid them in reconstructing their civil government. Congress, he hoped, would aid him in this good work by accepting representatives from the seceded States as fast as they returned to their allegiance. Alas for his plans, the great president fell by the hand of the assassin only five days after General Lee had surrendered at Appomattox Court House.

It has been held by many northern writers and most southern ones that had the life of Lincoln been spared he would have been able, by virtue of his sound judgment and his immense popularity, to carry out the plan of reconstruction begun in Louisiana and to extend it to the rest of the South, thus saving that section from the horrors of congressional reconstruction. To the present writer, however, this view of the matter seems unsound. That Lincoln was far better suited by nature than his tactless successor, Johnson, to soften the asperities of radical legislation is un-

---

[1] The truth, however, is that the people carried the leaders into secession, and that Jefferson Davis himself was in favor of delay. Rhodes, History of the United States, III, 276.

doubtedly true. The great soul of the president was absolutely free from any feeling of bitterness toward the
southern people. While he was ready to combat to its final
destruction the theory of state sovereignty and the extension
of slavery, he had learned to view the attitude of the South
with that large charity which inspired the hearts of so many
officers who took part in the conflict on the northern side,
the same sentiment that was exhibited in the relations between Grant and Lee at Appomattox. But this sentiment
was not widely shared by the members of the national legislature, who were not fighting but were making laws for the
Union. That Lincoln would have been permitted by the
Congress that met in December, 1865, to recognize state
governments established on the one-tenth basis and to make
easy the road for the return of "rebels" seems highly im-
probable. Is it likely, moreover, that he could have prevented the Southern States at the close of the war from
exasperating the feelings of the Republican majority in
Congress by unwise vagrant laws, and by premature attempts
to restore "rebels" to a participation in state and Federal
legislation? Or could he have persuaded this Congress to
relinquish its determination to deny the suffrage to the
"rebel" for his punishment, and to grant it to the freedman
for his protection and for the perpetuation of party
supremacy? Such influence would doubtless have been
beyond the power even of Lincoln's greatness.

If this view is correct, it is not surprising that Lincoln's
successor should have found the task impossible. Its difficulty had been enormously increased by the coming of
peace. The return of the Confederates to their homes complicated the problem of establishing civil government in the
seceded States, while at the same time the executive ceased
to exercise the great powers granted him in time of actual
war.[1]

---

[1] It is to be noted, however, that under Johnson's policy Texas
did not reconstruct itself until February, 1866, and the rebellion was
not officially declared to be ended until April 6, 1866. Cambridge
Modern History, VII, 626. On April 2 Johnson declared insurrec-

President Johnson, though a Union Democrat, had been reared in a slaveholding State, and one would suppose that he could have suggested a policy to which both the North and the South would lend their support. But Johnson had risen from the ranks of the proletariat;[1] and in spite of his honesty of purpose and the logical reasoning which he always displayed, he had brought up with him a certain coarseness of fibre and an extraordinary lack of good taste which ruined his influence with the ruling faction in Congress. At the same time, he had a deep dislike of the southern aristocrats, who, he believed, had been guilty of treason in bringing on the war. He had been opposed to the mild terms conceded to General Lee by General Grant at Appomattox, and had wished Lee and his army to be held as prisoners. Soon after he had become president, he had declared treason to be the blackest of crimes. He expressed a desire to force into exile or hang Jefferson Davis, Toombs, Slidell, Benjamin, and other prominent rebels.[2] As late as February, 1866, Johnson said, "I know there has been a great deal said about the exercise of the pardoning power as regards the executive; and there is no one who has labored harder than I to have the principals, the intelligent and conscious offenders, brought to Justice; and have the principle vindicated that Treason is a crime."[3]

tion at an end except in Texas, and on August 20, 1866, he gave official notice of its cessation in Texas. Burgess, Reconstruction and the Constitution, p. 103. The Supreme Court has accepted these dates as the legal close of the war. The Protector, 12 Wallace, 700.

[1] He was a tailor by trade, and, it is said, was taught to read by his wife.

[2] Blaine, Twenty Years, II, 3–9.

[3] In 1866 Congress voted to try Jefferson Davis for treason. There seemed "no way to write an indictment of a whole people," to borrow the words of Burke, but at least the arch offender might be punished. Accordingly, it is said that Attorney-General Speed, Judge Clifford of Massachusetts, William M. Evarts, and a half a dozen other prominent lawyers assembled at Washington to discuss the question. But the prosecution was abandoned, and Judge Clifford declared, "The laws of the United States, remarkable as it may appear, are not so constructed as to afford any certainty of punishing high treason or rebellion." Indictment for treason was finally brought against Davis, but on a writ of habeas corpus he was released on one hundred thousand dollars bail. Horace Greeley was

While, therefore, President Johnson went further than Lincoln in his desire to punish southern leaders and thus aligned himself more closely with the extreme Republicans, he did not satisfy that party in the measures which he took for the reconstruction of the South. Here he followed too closely the policy outlined by Lincoln. On May 29, 1865, he proclaimed a general amnesty to those taking an oath of allegiance, with the exception of certain classes which had taken a prominent part in the rebellion. Even these could return to their allegiance by seeking a special pardon from the president.[1] Later, each rebellious State was permitted, if it had not already done so, to frame its own government under a provisional governor. This act of amnesty surprised those who had heard Johnson's earlier fulminations against traitors, and it was maintained that there had been a change of attitude on the part of the president, due partly to the fact that the southern leaders flattered him, and partly to the persuasive tongue of Secretary Seward, who favored a conservative policy toward the South. A recent biographer of Seward, however, maintains that these views are " chiefly assumption and imagination and tend to conceal the facts." " No one ever produced evidence," says the writer, " showing that Johnson needed to be convinced that the work of reconstruction could be best directed by the executive department of the government. And before Seward was able to talk[2] without great pain Johnson had begun to follow the course Lincoln had laid out for himself."[3] Whatever may be the truth as to this contention, Johnson showed himself, according to the Republicans, too indulgent toward the South

the first surety. The government nolle prossed the case. Horace Greeley writes, May 31, 1866, that " Messrs. O'Conor and Shea, counsel for Jefferson Davis, will appear in Richmond on Monday next, at the opening of the U. S. Circuit Court there, expressly to urge on the trial of their client." Chase Correspondence, p. 514.

[1] By March, 1867, Johnson had issued three hundred and fifty special pardons to inhabitants of Louisiana who were in the excepted classes.

[2] Seward had been dangerously wounded by an assassin on the night when Lincoln was murdered.

[3] Bancroft, Life of Seward, II, 447, note.

and too anxious to assume the powers of recognition that
were claimed by Congress. If anything more was needed
to alienate the sympathy of the radicals it was found in the
fact that Johnson, like all persons of his social class in the
South, disliked the negro, and had no real desire to give him
either political or social equality. Herein he held distinctly
less advanced views than Lincoln, and was far behind the
extreme views of the radicals.

The political status of Louisiana during the first half of
the year 1865 was not clearly defined. Both Lincoln and
Johnson had recognized the state government as organized
by General Banks, but Congress failed fully to recognize the
State as restored to her place in the Union. A partial
recognition, however, was given by accepting the ratification
of the thirteenth amendment by Louisiana, and by permitting
a draft of soldiers within the Federal lines and assigning
quotas to the various parishes.[1]

Louisiana had suffered severely from the operations of the
hostile armies which had occupied her soil, and it was no
easy task to rehabilitate the prosperity of the State. The
demoralization incident to such a war as had been waging
was intensified by the fact that a portion of the State had
been held by Federal troops throughout a great part of the
conflict, and thousands of negroes had taken advantage of
their opportunity to leave the plantations and take refuge
within the Federal lines. They had also to a great extent
taken up the idea that emancipation from slavery meant that
the government which had freed them would present to
each freedman as a Christmas gift in the following December a mule and forty acres of land, confiscated from
the estates of the former masters.[2] No arguments of the
Federal officers could persuade them that this Utopian
scheme was not to be realized.

Major-General Hurlbut of the Federal army in an address
painted in vivid colors the condition of the State within

---

[1] Annual Cyclopaedia, 1865, subject "Louisiana," p. 508.
[2] Fleming, "Forty Acres and a Mule," North American Review,
May, 1906.

the Federal lines. "Let me call your attention," he said, "to this fact: the resources of this State are infinitely reduced by the casualties of war. The commerce, whose innumerable wheels used to vex the turbid current of the Mississippi, has passed away—the result of war. Plantations which used to bloom through your entire land, until the coast of Louisiana was a sort of repetition of the garden of Eden, are now dismantled and broken down. Trade, commerce, everything, crippled. . . . With all these things, this newly organized State of Louisiana has to confront difficulties such as never beset any community of men before. You have to create almost out of nothing. You have to make revenues where the taxable property of the State is reduced almost two-thirds. You have to hold the appliances and surroundings of government, and maintain them. All this you have to do out of a circumscribed territory and a broken-down country. Hence there is eminent practical wisdom in the suggestion contained in the address you have just heard, that the most rigid and self-denying economy should be exercised in all these relations which you hold to your fellow-citizens. Gentlemen, let me give you a few facts. The United States supports today 14,600 poor people here in the city of New Orleans. The same United States . . . is maintaining and keeping up to a great extent nearly every charity which belongs to the city or State. The levées, on which the life of your country depends, which from local causes cannot be repaired by the civil authorities, must be attended to by the United States, and the sum of $160,000 is being laid out now by the United States for the purpose of preventing this delta of the Mississippi from being subject to overflow. Now, in view of this state of things, if you desire to take these matters off the hands of the General Government, look to it well that you have the means to carry out the necessities of the times, and the power to compel observance."[1]

The Confederates, who after the surrender of Lee and other southern commanders came crowding back to the

---

[1] Annual Cyclopaedia, 1865, subject "Louisiana," p. 510.

State, showed a strong desire to take General Hurlbut at his word and to assume the burdens hitherto borne by the United States government. Both by self-interest and by the president's proclamation of amnesty they were encouraged to undertake the task of self-government, and to restore their broken fortunes.[1] Under the proclamation of amnesty those falling below certain ranks and possessing less than $20,000 worth of property were enabled, by taking an oath of allegiance, to be restored to citizenship; and many in the exempted class sought a special pardon of the president, and obtained it. Abandoned property, unless it had been condemned in the United States courts, was restored to those who had been pardoned. Where real estate had been confiscated and sold by the government the Confederates bought it back from the purchasers at a reasonable figure, being much aided by the resolution of Congress that "no punishment or proceedings under said act [Confiscation Act of July 17, 1862] should be so construed as to work a forfeiture of the real estate of the offender beyond his natural life."[2]

The Confederates were further aided by the attitude of Governor Wells, who, on March 4, 1865, on the election of Governor Hahn to the United States senatorship, had succeeded from lieutenant-governor to governor. Having been recognized by President Johnson as the legitimate governor of Louisiana, he was so far from showing any harsh feeling toward the returning rebels that he actually strove to win them over by every means in his power. He recommended to the president for executive pardon many who fell within the excepted classes. Offices were given them, and they were constantly called into consultation. All recollection of

---

[1] General Richard Taylor says that at the close of the war his plantation had been confiscated, and his property consisted of two horses, one of which was lame and unfit for service.

[2] The effect of this joint resolution was to give those purchasing the confiscated property of absent rebels the enjoyment of said property only during the lifetime of the rebels. Hence such purchasers, having only a precarious tenure, were willing to resell to the old owners.

the fact that he had been forced to flee his home on account of his Union proclivities seemed to have vanished from his mind. It afterwards became clear that Wells was merely seeking political advancement, and that he saw in the votes of the ex-Confederates the best chance of reelection to the gubernatorial office.

One of Wells's most important acts after his elevation to the governorship was to displace Captain Hoyt, the mayor of New Orleans, and to give that office to Dr. Hugh Kennedy. This action created somewhat of a sensation among the radicals and even among Banks's adherents, for Hoyt was an appointee of Banks and a supporter of Hahn, while Kennedy was regarded as an unregenerate pro-slavery man. Denison wrote on the day that Kennedy entered upon the duties of his office (March 21, 1865) that though the alleged reason for the appointment of Kennedy was that the office ought properly to be held by an old citizen, the real reason was that the mayor of New Orleans, through the police and other agencies, almost completely controlled the city elections, and through them the state elections.[1] Hence it was believed to be a clever move on the part of Wells to strengthen his own position.[2]

Governor Wells, however, now proceeded still further in opposition to the policy followed by General Banks. On May 3 he issued a proclamation rejecting the former registration of voters made under Banks, and ordering a new one for the elections that were to take place in the autumn. His plea was that the late register of voters in the city of New Orleans, J. Randall Terry, had made an official state-

---

[1] Chase Correspondence, p. 456. The official head in New Orleans after Monroe (1862) was first, G. F. Shepley, post commandant, then Godfrey Weitzel, Jonas H. French (provost-marshal acting mayor), Captain Miller, Captain Hoyt, and Hugh Kennedy. Kennedy was displaced later by S. Quincey, and then restored, and finally yielded to Monroe, elected 1866. Annual Cyclopaedia, 1866, subject "Louisiana," p. 449.

[2] Senator B. F. Jonas, however, says that his party soon came to regard Kennedy as a Union man and a scalawag, and were desirous of putting him out. He also says that his party soon became antagonistic to Wells because they wanted new elections over the State, while Wells wanted to keep his appointees in office.

ment under date of March 6, 1865, that nearly 5000 persons were registered as voters who did not possess the qualifications required by law.[1]   It was also maintained, though the governor did not refer to the matter, that many of those registered were negroes.[2]   General Banks, under whom the registration was made, was so anxious to secure a large vote for the ratification of his government that it is not surprising to find that many irregularities existed in the registration; and such irregularities naturally cast a shadow on the legality of the ratification of the constitution of 1864 and the elections held under it.   It was evidently not expected that the governor would take issue with General Banks on the subject of registration, for when his proclamation appeared it created quite a sensation in New Orleans.

In June the governor issued another proclamation—this time to the country parishes—urging them promptly to organize civil governments.   Until elections could be held for the formation of such governments, he said he would appoint sheriffs, recorders, police jurors, and other officers, but he would appoint only such capable men as the people of each parish might nominate.   Local organization, accordingly, was pushed forward energetically, and the newspapers nearly every day contained notices of fresh appointments by the governor.

The government of the State seemed to have become a government by proclamations; for on September 21 another proclamation appeared, announcing that on November 6 an election would be held in every parish in the State for the choice of a governor, lieutenant-governor, secretary of state, treasurer, attorney-general, superintendent of public education, representatives in the legislature, state senators in place of those whose term of office had expired, and representatives in Congress.   The qualifications of voters required by law were also given.   They embraced all male whites twenty-one years of age, who had been residents of the

---

[1] Page 88.

Annual Cyclopaedia, 1865, subject "Louisiana," p. 510.

State for the twelve months preceding the election, and who had taken either the iron-clad oath of December 8, 1863, or the amnesty oath of May 29, 1865. Those excepted from the amnesty must be pardoned by the president. Moreover, the governor ignored the constitution of 1864 so far as to declare that in all other respects the election would be conducted in accordance with the law, which was the same as under the constitution of 1852.[1]

There was great diversity of opinion among the voters of Louisiana as to the best platforms to be offered to the public for the coming elections, a diversity which reflected on a small scale the factions into which Congress itself was divided. As to the returning Confederates, they seem to have been for the most part desirous of renewing amicable relations with the state and the Federal government. They accepted in good faith the proclamation issued on June 2, 1865, by Governor H. W. Allen, which said, " The war is over, the contest is ended, the soldiers are disbanded and gone home, and now there is in Louisiana no opposition whatever to the Constitution and laws of the United States." Allen, moreover, had transferred to the Federal military authorities (Louisiana was still under martial law) all the important records of his government.[2] In his inaugural address a few years before he had said, " Give Louisiana to some foreign power rather than return into the Union;" but he had been a gallant leader in war and peace, and the Confederates were as ready to subscribe to his present sentiments of allegiance as they had been to follow him in the desperate venture of secession. The testimony of Governor Wells himself was that the soldiers returning to their homes were wiser and better men, frankly owning to the failure of their experiment, and all expressing a desire to atone for the

---

[1] In calling for a new election, however, the governor's action was based on the constitution of 1864, which provided for the election of new representatives to the legislature in November, 1865, as well as for the other officers mentioned in the governor's proclamation. Only half the state senators were to be chosen, the other half being elected for four years.

[2] *Annual Cyclopaedia*, 1865, subject " Louisiana," p. 510.

errors of the past by cheerful obedience to the government. In fact, as we shall see, the ex-Confederates were soon regarded by the radicals as somewhat over eager to be restored to proper relations with the Federal government and to offices under it; and when, in the winter of 1865, they came knocking at the doors of a Congress which a few short months before, it was remembered, they had wished to batter down, they met with a cold reception. Nor was the behavior of the Confederates anything but friendly toward the Banks party that had framed the constitution of 1864 during their absence; they even joked with the members of the convention on the results of their labors. The constitution, it is true, was regarded as a fraud, but under the favor of Governor Wells and the president they (the Confederates) hoped to change all that at an early day.

Many northern men, ex-officers in the Federal army, and others less worthy had found Louisiana an attractive place of residence, and had determined to cast in their fortunes with its people. Some question seems to have been raised as to how they should be treated by the returning natives. The popular attitude on this question was doubtless expressed by a Democratic paper which said: "We do not desire the newcomers to regulate our domestic institutions, furnish laws, or administer them. We have a sufficient number of competent men to do this."[1] However, the same paper, a few days later, hastened to say (rather inconsistently, declared a rival contemporary) "that in spite of much bigoted prattle, there was no design in any respectable class to regard with prejudice or suspicion, immigrants or settlers, bringing capital, energy, or talents." It is not impossible, however, to reconcile the two statements: capital, energy, and talents were desired, but the old inhabitants were not ready to surrender the reins of government to strangers, ignorant of the conditions and needs of the State. Especially was the prejudice strong against the radical Northerners, who had now come out decidedly in favor of negro suffrage.

---

[1] Picayune, July 2, 1865.

The Democrats in setting forth their principles declared strongly against negro suffrage. A meeting of Democrats was held in New Orleans on October 2, 1865, over which ex-Governor Wickliffe presided.[1] The resolutions adopted declared in favor of President Johnson's policy of reconstruction, but went on to say that " this is a government of white people, made and to be perpetuated for the exclusive benefit of the white race. In accordance with the constant adjudication of the Supreme Court of the United States, the people of African descent cannot be considered citizens of the United States, and there can in no event nor under any circumstances be any equality between white and other races." On October 14 there was another mass-meeting of Democrats at which ex-Confederates C. E. Fenner and B. F. Jonas spoke in praise of Johnson and Wells. Jonas declared that Wells had not only welcomed back the returning soldiers, but had avowed himself the champion of their rights. The Democrats, however, declared the constitution of 1864 to be the creation of fraud, violence, and corruption, but said it should be recognized as the de facto government of Louisiana until another could be organized; and they claimed the right to petition Congress for compensation for the slaves that had been emancipated. All Democrats were urged to join in opposition to the radical party " which wishes to consolidate government on the ruins of our State institutions." Governor Wells, having been recognized by the president,[2] was seen to be the safest candidate for governor, and accordingly he received the nomination of this party.[3]

---

[1] The vice-presidents were W. W. Pugh, O. N. Ogden, Leon Burthe, and the secretary was B. F. Jonas. Times, October 3 and 4, 1865.

[2] A letter of Wells, dated June 10, 1865, says he recently visited the president, and was assured that he would be sustained in all necessary and legal measures to organize and uphold civil government. Schurz's Report to President Johnson, 39th Cong., 1st sess., S. Ex. Doc. No. 2, p. 54.

[3] Previous to this time, in September, the National Democrats had advocated a return to the constitution of 1852, while another faction, the Conservative Democrats, had advocated the acceptance of the

In advocating Johnson's policy, it will be seen, the Democrats did not follow him in the more advanced position which he had assumed in the preceding August. Johnson had then become aware that it was unwise not to make some concessions to the radicals, and thus to cut the ground from under their feet. Accordingly, he had sent a despatch to Governor Sharkey, the provisional governor of Mississippi, saying: "If you could extend the elective franchise to all persons of color who can read the Constitution of the United States in English, and write their names, and to all persons of color who own real estate valued at not less than $250.00, and pay taxes thereon, you would completely disarm the adversary, and set an example the other States will follow. This you can do with perfect safety, and you thus place the Southern States in reference to free persons of color upon the same basis with the free States. I hope and trust your Convention will do this, and as a consequence the radicals who are wild upon negro franchise will be completely foiled in their attempt to keep the Southern States from renewing their relations to the Union by not accepting their Senators and Representatives." The president, in thus adopting a suggestion which Lincoln had made to Hahn in 1864 (though Lincoln's motive was a higher one), showed his political sagacity; and could the South have looked forward a few years into the future, this part of the president's policy might have been adopted in 1865. But at this time the South, feeling that the president had no real desire to extend the suffrage to the negro and suggested it merely as a matter of expediency, concluded to ignore the suggestion and not rashly to set the door ajar for the entrance of the negro to political rights. If we consider the question without doctrinaire prejudices, we shall see that it would have been a most extraordinary proceeding on the part of southern Democrats to confer the franchise on a class of

constitution of 1864 until the meeting of another convention. A month later the latter platform had been appropriated by the National Democrats. Annual Cyclopaedia, 1865, subject "Louisiana," p. 512.

persons who had just been emancipated from slavery, when nearly all the Northern and Western States at that time refused the suffrage even to negroes who had been born free. It was natural that they should expect to return to the Union without being required to make so radical a concession.

The Democratic platform proved unacceptable to the remains of the old Banks faction, now called the "National Conservative Union" party, which came forward to oppose what they alleged was a return to the constitution of 1852. Their platform did not favor negro suffrage, but it did not mention compensation for slaves. It upheld the constitution of 1864, repudiated the Confederate debt, and condemned secession. Its nominee for the office of governor was also Wells, but for the rest of the ticket its nominees were different.[1] Wells, wily politician that he was, gladly accepted both nominations, declaring that he did not see much difference between the two platforms, and that he was strictly a party candidate.[2]

But another faction, though few in numbers, were unable to accept Wells; they declared that the governor "was trying to carry water on both shoulders" and could not be trusted. Some of these, devoted friends of ex-Governor H. W. Allen, who was at this time in Mexico, determined upon him as their candidate for governor. This measure did not please those Democrats who had found it expedient to nominate Governor Wells; they declared that nothing could be

---

[1] The tickets were as follows:—

	Conservative Union.	National Democratic.
Governor	J. M. Wells	J. M. Wells
Lieut. Gov.	J. Q. Taliaferro	Albert Voorhies
Secty. of State	T. J. Edwards	J. H. Hardy
Treasurer	J. T. Michel	Adam Giffen
Auditor	C. M. Olivier	J. H. Peralta
Att'y-Gen'l.	Geo. S. Lally	A. S. Herron
Supt. Pub. Ed'cn.	R. C. Richardson	R. M. Lusher
Congress	Judge E. Abell	Louis St. Martin
	A. P. Field	Jacob Barker
	William Mithoff	R. C. Wickliffe
	Al. Duperier	John E. King
	John Ray	John S. Young

[2] *Times,* October 13, 1865.

more unwise than the nomination of a man who would be persona non grata to the authorities at Washington. Accordingly, E. W. Halsey and other prominent Democrats issued a circular withdrawing Allen's name;[1] but in spite of this fact he was so popular in the Red River country that he received a vote of 5497.

In the election Wells polled a vote of 22,312,[2] and the rest of the Democratic ticket was elected by a large majority. The returns showed how far the voting under Banks had failed to represent the State; it showed further the determination of the State to accept in good faith the executive plan of reconstruction.

In the meantime the radical Republicans had been holding meetings at which such speakers as Dostie, Warmoth, and Durell upheld the policy of Johnson in terms, but insisted that the leaders of the rebellion should be disfranchised forever, that the rank and file of the rebels should be permitted citizenship, and that all loyal men (white and black) should be "equal before the law." A committee of this party, calling itself the "Central Executive Committee of the Friends of Universal Suffrage," wrote to Wells in the early summer declaring that civil government in Louisiana on a limited suffrage had been a failure, and that as governor he possessed the discretion to order a registration of whites and blacks alike. Such a registration, they urged, should be made in the country as well as in the city. The governor answered that no registration had ever been made in the rural districts of any State. As to negro suffrage, he thought it neither wise nor expedient to grant it. If en-

---

[1] Allen afterwards thanked those of his friends who had tried to put down the movement that had been started in his favor. Dorsey, Recollections of Allen, p. 346.

[2] The vote for the chief officers was: Wells, 22,312; Allen, 5497; Voorhies, 23,664; Taliaferro, 5302; Hardy, 20,869; T. J. Edwards, 4181; Giffen, 21,667; Michel, 4773, etc. Journal of the Senate, 1865, pp. 25–27. The whole vote seems small when compared with the vote of 1860 (49,510), but it may be partly accounted for by the losses in the Confederacy. Of 15,000 men from Louisiana in Lee's army in Virginia, only 600 were reported as remaining. Annual Cyclopaedia, 1865, subject "Louisiana," pp. 513, 516.

dowed with the ballot, the freedmen would support their old masters, and Union men like himself and the committee would live by sufferance in the State.[1] It is impossible to say whether Wells really believed what he said;[2] certainly it was not believed by the radicals. It was declared by the Democrats that these radicals did not number two hundred whites in the State, but they were evidently determined not to allow the Democrats to carry things with a high hand without a protest. Adopting what was to be the view of the extreme radical element in Congress, they refused to recognize the existing government in Louisiana, declared that by secession the State had reduced itself to the status of a territory, and that as such it was entitled to elect a territorial delegate to Congress.[3] In accordance with this view they assembled and elected delegates to a convention, which met in New Orleans on September 27. After a session of several days this convention adopted a platform and fixed November 6 as election day (the official date).

To the great disgust and indignation of the Democrats the election was actually held. It resulted in the choice of Henry Clay Warmoth as delegate.[4] For the first time in the history of the State the negroes voted freely; and so delighted were they with this new privilege that they contributed of their means to defray the expenses of their delegate to Washington by depositing fifty cents or a dollar in a box at each polling place. The Democrats asserted that the negroes were assessed one dollar per capita, but the radicals denied that there was any assessment.[5]   War-

---

[1] Times, July 12, 1865.

[2] The New York Times, however, says, "Would not the negro vote with those on whom they are dependent?" July 8, 1865.

[3] Of course this view was not original with Warmoth; Sumner had adopted it two years before. Sumner, "Our Domestic Relations," Atlantic Monthly, October, 1863, p. 523.

[4] For his career, see National Cyclopedia of American Biography, X, 80.

[5] However, in the petition which he addressed to Congress on February 2, 1866, Warmoth claimed that the voluntary contributions of the voters at Napoleonville, amounting to eighty dollars, together with the ballot-box, had been seized by the sheriff and his posse. It is therefore certain that the negroes were persuaded to contribute to the expenses of their indigent delegate.

moth afterwards claimed that some of his polling places were closed by the military authorities; but certainly the governor was not responsible for this opposition, for he had announced that unless the negroes tried to vote at the official polls they must not be interfered with.[1] In any case, Warmoth, who had no opponent, claimed that the vote cast for him was 19,000.[2]

On November 13 the radicals held a mass-meeting in New Orleans at which speeches were made by Flanders, Waples, and Warmoth;[3] and resolutions were passed protesting against any attempts to substitute for slavery any system of serfdom or forced labor, and declaring that as the necessities of the nation had called the colored man into the public service in the most honorable of all duties—that of soldier, this fact, together with his loyalty, patience, and prudence, should assure Congress of the justice and safety of giving him a vote to protect his liberty.

In his special plea of February 2, 1866, Warmoth stated that the Democratic party had rejected the constitution of 1864 as fraudulent, which was exactly the position his party had taken. Louisiana had no valid civil government, and must depend on Congress to receive one delegate, like any other territory; for to the condition of a territory had it been reduced by its secession and rebellion. As to the existing government, he quoted Colonel A. P. Field as declaring that Governor Wells had received Confederate officers in his house when "their hands were still bloody with the blood of Union soldiers," and that Confederates had been registered without a pardon when they were worth over $20,000, and had not been twelve months in the State. Moreover, two men who had said that negroes must vote and that blood would be spilt in defence of this right had been

---

[1] True Delta, November 7, 1865.

[2] The Tribune says that Warmoth claimed 2500 white votes. December 12, 1865.

[3] Warmoth on this occasion said that he was going to get a Yankee to invent a machine that would pump out the black blood of negroes and pump in white blood, a statement which was received with great laughter and applause. Times, November 14, 1865.

arrested for seditious language, and bail had been refused on the ground that their offence was treason against the State of Louisiana.[1] Finally, threats had been made by Democrats that as soon as the Federal soldiers were removed from Louisiana, "all Union men and damned Yankees would have to go." The Times, a prominent newspaper, had said, moreover, that the attempt to deceive the negro by a solemn electoral farce was treason against the entire population, for it would sow the seed of bitterness between the two races; and that the charge of disloyalty was false, Louisiana being as loyal as Connecticut. The Southern Star, the organ of Wells, it said, had spoken in contemptuous terms of the radical meeting, saying: "The negro people—black and white—held a meeting last night (November 13). Some of the speakers will be taken in hand by the Grand Jury. As a matter of course we do not report the proceedings; no decent paper would."

With this extraordinary petition Warmoth presented himself at Washington, and took his place in the anteroom of the halls of Congress, with Randall Hunt and Henry Boyce, who had been elected senators by the Democratic legislature of Louisiana. But Congress, as we shall see, was not prepared to receive either the Democrats or such a radical member as the "delegate from the territory of Louisiana." It does not appear that Warmoth's claims were brought before Congress.[2] Perhaps he himself did not expect to be received after such an irregular election, but he is said to have got a great deal of amusement out of the campaign.

The legislature elected in November, 1865, represented the State as no other legislature had done since the beginning of the war. The senate consisted of twenty-seven members, part of whom, in accordance with the constitution of 1864, held office by virtue of the election of 1864.

---

[1] General Canby, the successor of Banks, released these two men.
[2] See Life of A. P. Dostie. The Tribune says that Warmoth presented his credentials to Clerk McPherson; and that Thaddeus Stevens told Warmoth that if Congress adopted the territorial form of government for the insurrectionary States, he (Warmoth) could claim his seat. December 9 and 13, 1865.

The lower house consisted of one hundred and six members,[1] and included such conspicuous names as B. F. Jonas, T. C. W. Ellis, Charles E. Fenner, James McConnell, John McEnery, and other prominent young lawyers just back from the battlefields of the Confederacy. The Democrats had carried every parish but one. This legislature met in extra session on November 23, 1865, in the old Mechanics' Institute, New Orleans. It sat until December 22. The extra session was called by the governor to consider the state debt, the labor question, and other local matters, but especially to elect two senators to be present in December at the opening meeting of the new Congress.

That Wells should counsel the choice of two senators when there were already two senators-elect, Hahn and Cutler, who had been chosen by a body over which Wells himself as president of the senate had presided, may seem remarkable; but it was plausibly argued that Hahn and Cutler had been rejected as not representing the State, and it was now time to try again with a reorganized State which ought not to fail of recognition. If Wells had desired the senatorship, he would have been elected; but he thought it wiser to hold on to the office he had. He received a complimentary vote; but the two candidates finally chosen were Randall Hunt[2] (term to begin March 4, 1865) and Henry Boyce (term beginning March 4, 1861).[3]   Charles Gayarré, the historian, was also a candidate.

Another question discussed by the legislature was that of calling a new constitutional convention. A committee was appointed the majority of whom reported in favor of submitting the question to the vote of the people, while the minority thought it would be wiser and cheaper to accept

---

[1] This was the number present by December 1.

[2] Hunt was a prominent lawyer, a native of South Carolina, who seems to have been a consistent Union man, while his brother, T. G. Hunt, fought for the Confederacy. In 1867 Randall Hunt was elected president of the University of Louisiana. He and Justice Chase married sisters.

[3] On February 19, 1861, the legislature paid $7000 to the representatives and senators. Acts of Legislature, 1866, p. 44.

the existing constitution, amending it so far as was found necessary. Both reports were laid over for consideration at the regular session of 1866. The most important matter considered was the labor question; but to understand the attitude of the legislature on this important subject it will be necessary to go back and consider, as briefly as possible, the economic status of the negro as it was during the Civil War and as it was affected by the close of hostilities.

In 1860 the slave population of Louisiana was 331,726, while the free persons of color numbered 18,647. According to this census, the white population had a majority of 7000; but when the summons of war came and thousands of the whites left the State to fight in Virginia and Tennessee, the colored population must have formed a large majority of those that were left.

No sooner had Butler assumed control of New Orleans and the surrounding districts than the question of what to do with the negro forced itself upon his attention. A year before, at Fortress Monroe, he had solved the question by an epigram. When some five hundred slaves took refuge in his camp, he refused to return them, and put them to work on his fortifications, declaring that they were "contraband of war." This witticism, winked at by the War Department at Washington, gave a new name to the slave; the North received it with applause.[1] Following the same view,

---

[1] The application of "contraband" to persons was not new. The diplomacy of the United States had already made the law of contraband apply to persons as well as to goods. Cox says military enemies found on a neutral ship are classed under "contraband" by the United States. Three Decades, p. 265. Of course, Butler's application was new, unless slaves be regarded as enemies' goods and chattels. Rhodes says Butler applied the term first to three slaves, and by July 30 he had nine hundred. "The application of this phrase had not, as Butler himself admits, high legal sanction." History of United States, III, 466, 467. Peirce says: "Contrabands appeared with their wives and children, dependents to whom the contraband theory could not be applied." The War Department, moreover, wrote to Butler that the military authorities could lay no claim to fugitives, and that he must not interfere with the slaves of peaceable citizens or prevent voluntary return of slaves. Peirce, Freedmen's Bureau, University of Iowa Studies in History, 1904, pp. 5, 6.

the government, by act of Congress of August 3, 1861, declared that all property used in the aid of insurrection should be confiscated, and that owners should forfeit all claims to slaves whose labor was used in any service against the United States.[1]   In the following year, moreover, the Confiscation Act of July 17, 1862, declared free the slaves of all persons in rebellion.[2]   In the same year the War Department forbade the restoration to their masters of any slaves that took refuge in the Federal lines.   Nothing further in the matter of regulations was done until the appearance of the emancipation proclamation, which, after due notice one hundred days before, was issued by Lincoln on January 1, 1863.

Enough, however, had been done to encourage many slaves, when the Federal camps were in their vicinity, to escape from the plantations and the toil of the fields and to throw themselves within the Federal lines, seeking at the hands of the army officers food, raiment, and a life of leisure. The exodus of slaves from the neighboring country parishes of the State into Baton Rouge, into Carrollton, and into New Orleans was so great as to strain the resources of the Federal authorities to support them. When the Federal army marched into a sugar parish, all was excitement among the negroes. It was like thrusting a walking stick into an ant hill, says Parton,[3] the negroes swarmed out, quit work, and became servants of the officers, or camp followers. Ten thousand poured into New Orleans alone, and Butler, although evidently pleased that they should run away from their masters, had to issue orders that no more should be received at the various posts. Some planters, unable to make their slaves work, and unwilling to support them in idleness, actually sent them within the Federal lines, hoping to reclaim them later. This Butler tried to stop by

[1] This act, as we have seen, caused much indignation in the South, and led to retaliatory acts on the part of the Confederate Congress in regard to the confiscation of debts. See page 37.
[2] Schouler, History of the United States, VI, 222, note.
[3] Butler in New Orleans, p. 489.

emancipating such slaves on his own responsibility, though he knew that Lincoln had revoked the orders emancipating slaves issued by Federal commanders in Missouri (1861)[1] and in South Carolina (1862).[2]

As the dark flood threatened to overwhelm the city, Butler's ingenuity devised a way out of the difficulty. He forestalled the method, which later was widely adopted, of seizing abandoned sugar plantations and working them for the benefit of the United States with the labor of "contrabands." His brother, Colonel Butler, who was making a large fortune by speculations under the patronage of the commanding general, had bought a standing crop for $25,-000, and now began to cultivate it with hired labor, white and black. Loyal planters in St. Bernard and Plaquemines were persuaded to enter into an agreement by which they were to pay wages—$10 a month for able-bodied males—to their former slaves, and the military authorities became the nominal employers and controlled the conduct of the employees. Insubordination among them was punished by the provost marshal, generally by imprisonment in darkness on bread and water. This experiment seems to have been successful. A visitor to Colonel Butler's plantation, which was some distance below the city, describes the employees as working admirably under the promise of wages.[3] In New Orleans the refugees were for the most part dependent on the bounty of the military authorities. Many of them became the servants of Butler and his officers; and as has already been noted, among the negro servants in New Orleans, to whom his door was always open, the commanding general had "a spy behind the chair of the master of every household."

In July, 1862, General Phelps, who was stationed at

---

[1] Fremont tried to free slaves only of those in rebellion, and Lincoln refused because he feared to lose Kentucky. Rhodes, History of United States, III, 470. Hunter went further; he declared free the slaves in Georgia, Florida, and South Carolina, and enlisted them. Peirce, Freedmen's Bureau, p. 4.

[2] Parton, Butler in New Orleans, p. 492.

[3] Chase Correspondence, pp. 378, 379, 380, 409.

Carrollton, decided to utilize the negroes that were crowding into his camp by organizing them into companies to
fight for the Union. He assigned as a reason for this action
that "Society in the South seemed to be on the point of
dissolution, and the best way to prevent the African from
becoming instrumental in a general state of anarchy was to
enlist him in the cause of the Republic. If his services were
rejected, any petty military chieftain, by offering him freedom, could engage the negro for the purpose of robbery
and plunder." Much to the indignation of General Phelps,
Butler informed him that organization of "contrabands"
into companies had not yet been authorized by the president,
but that as Congress had authorized the employment of
negroes in public service, Phelps might employ them in
cutting down trees and forming abatis. This suggestion
Phelps loftily rejected, saying that he was "no slave
driver."

A few months later, however, Butler himself decided to
carry "Africa into the War" by enlisting his friends, the
free men of color.[1]   Of the 28,000 colored persons in New
Orleans, 10,000 were of this class. Frequently owning
valuable property, and in many cases well educated, they
overwhelmed Butler with attentions, and he found pleasure
in dining at their tables. One of them, says Parton, gave
the commanding general a banquet, at which the seven
courses were served on silver plate. At another banquet
a colored orator thought to eulogize the general by pro-
posing as a toast: "Here's to General Butler. He has a
white face, but a black heart," a sentiment which excited
much amusement in the North as well as in the South.[2]

Butler recalled the fact that these men had fought with
bravery under General Jackson at the battle of New
Orleans, and though there was much dissatisfaction felt at
their enlistment, they had been publicly thanked by Jackson
for their services. Butler, moreover, was able to assign a

---

[1] Parton, Butler in New Orleans, pp. 505–507, 516.
[2] Cox, Three Decades, p. 425.

still stronger excuse for his action. The only body of negro soldiery organized in support of the Confederacy was composed of these free men of color from New Orleans. It is true that they never fought for the Confederacy, but in April, 1861, they had been accepted as part of the Louisiana state militia. In the following year,[1] when the state militia was reorganized (January 27, 1862), it was made up wholly of whites; but, a month before the fall of New Orleans, Governor Moore issued an order to the free men of color to maintain their organization and to be prepared to obey orders.[2] When the city was captured they did not retire with the regular troops; and when Butler called on them to enlist on the Union side, they eagerly accepted his invitation. Three regiments and two batteries of artillery, for the most part under white officers, were formed in a short time. It was the first colored contingent of the Federal army, as it had been the first and last such contingent of the Confederate army.[3] Their complexion, according to Butler, was "about that of Vice-President Hamlin, or the late Mr. Daniel Webster." In November, 1862, they served under General Weitzel in his expedition to the Lafourche district; and the general protested against their use, declaring that the presence of colored troops tended to stir up the slaves against the women and children in that region. Butler calmly replied that if there were any insurrection, the rebels had only themselves to blame; let them submit, and thus

---

[1] Times-Democrat, April 30, 1903.

[2] Charles W. Gibbons (colored) testified that he was in the Confederate service for two weeks, but that as soon as Butler arrived, he and other free men of color wrote him a petition asking authority to raise a company. He says that when the rebellion broke out, the Confederates called on all the free people to do something for the Confederacy, and if they did not, a committee was appointed to look after them, and they would be robbed of their property, if not killed. Gibbons was advised by a policeman to enlist under penalty of lynching. He enlisted in Captain Jourdan's company, but resigned as soon as possible. Others had to enlist to save themselves. Some free men of color did not enlist. Report of Select Committee on New Orleans Riots, 39th Cong., 2d sess., H. Rept. No. 16, testimony, p. 126.

[3] These free men of color were, of course, far superior in education and general enlightenment to the slaves.

obtain the protection of the Federal army against insurrection.   But Weitzel offered his resignation, and it was not
without much persuasion that he was induced to continue
in the service.[1]

Butler now went further.   Anticipating the later policy
of the Federal government, he began to enlist not only the
free men of color but also the freedmen who had been set
free by their owners or by the military courts, or had come
in from the enemies' lines.   In fact, if the fugitive negroes
were brave enough to enlist, the general forgot to ask
whether they were legally slaves or free.[2]   As the proclamation of emancipation made the Federal government responsible for ex-slaves, the enlistment of freedmen naturally
went on apace, and later General Banks maintained that the
number in the Federal army from Louisiana amounted to
15,000.   Many of them served with bravery at Port Hudson
in 1863, and their devotion to the cause of the Union on
that occasion and others was frequently urged at a later
period as entitling them to the suffrage at the hands of the
Federal government.

On the other hand, the Confederate authorities, recognizing the immense difference between the free men of color
and the lately emancipated slaves, never enlisted the latter
as soldiers, although it was suggested more than once that
the experiment should be tried in retaliation.   When the
Federal government first adopted the policy, indignation at
the South ran high.   It was regarded as a measure un-
authorized by the laws of civilized warfare, worse in its con-
sequences than the arming of savages by the English in the
Revolutionary War.   Accordingly, Jefferson Davis, hoping
to arrest the movement, issued a proclamation declaring
"that negro slaves captured in arms should not be treated
as prisoners of war, but should at once be delivered over to
the executive authorities of the respective States from
which they had been taken, to be dealt with according to

[1] O. G. Villard, "The Negro in the Regular Army," Atlantic
Monthly, June, 1903, p. 721.
[2] Chase Correspondence, p. 316.

the law of the said States."[1] This attitude of the Confederate authorities only exasperated the North, and called
forth threats of retaliatory measures; it did not stop the
enlistment of freedmen.[2] As the South refused to regard
them as soldiers or to exchange them, the North assigned
this as one of the reasons for stopping exchanges and leaving northern soldiers crowded in southern prisons. The
main reason, however, was that a failure to exchange
crippled the South more rapidly than the North; and General Grant decided to take advantage of this fact, declaring
that a soldier that died in a southern prison served his
country as well as one that died on the battlefield.[3]

The emancipation proclamation of January 1, 1863, as
is well known, emancipated the slaves only in those States
or parts of States then in rebellion. The president did not
believe that he had the right to free the slaves in loyal
States like Kentucky and Maryland, but in thus crippling
the South he held that he was doing " an act of justice
warranted by the Constitution upon military necessity."

---

[1] Just before the surrender of Lee, however, the Confederate
Congress, finding itself in desperate straits, decided to authorize
President Davis, at his discretion, to arm negroes and grant them
freedom, but it was already too late for this desperate venture.
Cox, Three Decades, p. 213; and Garner, Reconstruction in Mississippi, p. 28. T. N. Page says that a number of negro regiments
were enlisted in the Confederate army, one in Louisiana, and two
in Virginia; but he does not say they fought. He says that if it
had been permitted, more negroes would have enlisted in the
southern army than in the northern (186,097). Page, " The Negro,"
McClure's, March, 1904, pp. 552 (note), 553.

[2] It is interesting to note that in our Revolutionary War the Conti-
nental Congress in December, 1777, ordered that all loyalists taken
in arms in the British service should be sent to the States to which
they belonged to suffer the penalty inflicted by laws of such States
against traitors. Two prominent Quakers in Philadelphia, convicted of having assisted the English, were hanged. Lecky, England in 18th Century, IV, 108. The North maintained that at Fort
Pillow and elsewhere no quarter was given to negro soldiers; and
Grant told Lee that he would retaliate if negroes enlisted in the
Federal army were not treated like whites. This action seems to
have prevented the execution of negro prisoners according to state
law. At least no such cases are mentioned by Smith. Smith, Political History of Slavery, pp. 150, 151.

[3] Annual Cyclopaedia, 1865, subject " Congress, United States,"
pp. 228–230.

Though it is held that the president had no further object than to cripple rebellious States by freeing their slaves, it was but natural that in the excited state of public opinion at that time the South should regard it as intended to stir up an insurrection among the slaves.[1]   It is certainly extraordinary that such was not the effect.   An explanation of the phenomenon will be attempted later.[2]

As far as Louisiana was concerned, the effect of the proclamation was much complicated by the fact that a portion of the State was occupied by Federal troops.   All the slaves were declared to be free except those in the parishes of St. Bernard, Plaquemines, Jefferson, St. John the Baptist, St. Charles, St. James, Ascension, Assumption, Terrebonne, Lafourche, St. Mary, St. Martin, and Orleans (New Orleans).   These parishes, thirteen out of forty-eight, were assumed to be under Federal control, and consequently in them the existing slaves were left in a state of de jure slavery.[3]   What was the exact number of slaves in these parishes it is impossible to say.   According to the census of 1860 they numbered 87,812.   By January, 1863, this number may have been increased, for thousands of fugitive slaves had taken refuge within the Federal lines before this date, and these the proclamation evidently did not free.   On the other hand, the number may have been less if Banks was right in 1864 in declaring that one fourth of all the negroes in Louisiana had died or left the State.   Whether many of the planters in these parishes had emancipated their slaves of their own accord I have not been able to discover.   The newspapers of the day made much of the case of J. Madison Wells, afterwards the Union governor

---

[1] Nor did the proclamation satisfy foreign powers, if we may judge by the criticism of Lord John Russell, who declared that the proclamation " ' makes slavery at once legal and illegal.   There seems to be no declaration of a principle adverse to slavery. . . . It is a measure of war of a very questionable kind;' and he intimated that its object was not 'total and impartial freedom for the slave' but 'vengeance on the slave owner.'"   Rhodes, History of the United States, IV, 357.

[2] Page 127.

[3] Annual Cyclopaedia, 1863, subject "Louisiana," p. 594.

of the State, who freed his hundred and fifty slaves and conducted them within the Federal lines. Doubtless there were many other cases among loyal men who had been living in the exempted parishes.

The de facto status of the negroes within the Federal lines depended largely upon the attitude of the commanding general. We have seen that Butler made no deep scrutiny into the previous or present condition of servitude among those negroes that applied to him for service of any kind. He gave a particular welcome to those that had fled from rebel households; and as it was forbidden to return even those that fled from loyal masters, the condition of the ex-slave was one of practical freedom. A " rebel " who was in New Orleans at the time of its capture tells the writer that her slaves, as soon as they learned that the Federals were coming up the river, gave notice that they would work no longer. In 1864, however, slavery was still existent de jure within the Federal lines; but on the 8th of January of that year General Banks, upon his own responsibility, suspended all the laws concerning slavery existing in the old constitution or statutes of Louisiana. His explanation was that as the War Department had forbidden the return of fugitive slaves, and as the owners could not get them back without disturbing the public peace, the slavery laws could not be enforced; they were already a dead letter.[1]

The effect of the proclamation in the thirty-five parishes controlled by the Confederates is a much less complicated matter to consider. Of course, for Confederates the proclamation had no validity whatever. They looked to Davis and not to Lincoln for proclamations. But to the two hundred thousand or more slaves left in these parishes the proclamation was naturally an invitation to steal away in the night-time if the Federal lines were distant, or to walk boldly away in the daytime if those lines were near. In a New Orleans paper of June, 1864, I have

---

[1] It has been shown in a previous chapter that the courts of New Orleans refused to hold valid Banks's suspension, but that the constitution of 1864 declared slavery abolished in all Louisiana.

found a letter written from Covington, Louisiana, by a mother to her son in the Confederate army. "Nearly every negro on this side of the Lake," she tells him, "has run away and gone to the Yankees." Caroline Merrick[1] gives a similar account of nearly all the plantations in the Atchafalaya district, where she was living during the Civil War. A former professor of Grand Coteau College relates in his memoirs that after the proclamation the slaves of that neighborhood kept quiet for a while; but when the Federal army passed by, many followed it to New Orleans, where one fifth of them died of privation and disease.[2] Freedom from bondage, a surcease of toil, and a more or less hearty welcome on the part of the deliverer naturally proved to be an attractive program to the slave.

A large number of the plantations, however, were not deserted by the negroes. Some of the most valuable slaves had been sent by their masters into Texas and Alabama.[3] Many others remained on the plantations because they had always been well treated, and feared that if they decided to leave, their latter state would be worse than their former.[4] Still others, who wished to go, were induced to stay by their masters, who told them that they could be free where they were; that it was not necessary for them to leave their homes, their children, and their household effects. Their freedom, it was explained to them, was assured, and they could expect wages from their old masters. Many planters did not follow this plan; but Mrs. Merrick says, "Our slaves remained on the place, and many of them and their descendants are still in the employ of the family." In the parishes far removed from Federal headquarters the news of the proclamation did not reach the negroes until long

[1] Merrick, Old Times in Dixie Land, pp. 51–53.
[2] Memoirs of Rev. Father Widman. MS., Jesuits' College, New Orleans.
[3] Chase Correspondence, p. 399.
[4] Miles Taylor testified that slaves left a great many plantations; and although his own place was within six miles of Donaldsonville, which was occupied by the Federals again and again, yet not one of over one hundred slaves ran away from him. Report on New Orleans Riots, p. 307.

after it had been issued. Their masters did not tell them of
their freedom; for, among other reasons, they did not believe
that Lincoln had a right to free them.

It has often been remarked that throughout the four years
of terrible war there was no case of insurrection among the
slaves, nor, in fact, any of those awful crimes for which the
worst class of negroes are distinguished at the present day.
This seems all the more praiseworthy when we remember
that, in the great majority of cases, the master was far
away on the battlefield while his family on the plantation
was helpless amid a swarm of slaves. A southern paper,
remarking on this noteworthy phenomenon, attributed it
to the mildness and humanity of the master's rule in ante-
bellum days.[1] While, however, an inhumane master was
exceptional, there were a sufficient number of brutal overseers to create a feeling of revolt among the slaves in many
parts of the South, and there had been at least two dangerous insurrections in the history of Louisiana. The absence
of crimes against the whites should rather be attributed to
the unconscious appeal which unprotected women and children made to a simple race made conservative by the long
discipline of slavery, and more especially to the habit of
obedience which subordination had instilled into every fibre
of the slave's being. He looked upon the white race as
occupying a place far above his sphere; no dream of social
equality had come to distemper his brain.[2]

[1] Mobile Register quoted in New Orleans Times, June 23, 1865.
[2] Another view of the negro's good behavior during this period
has been offered to the writer by the Rev. Dr. Tucker, of Baton
Rouge, who has made a deep study of negro character during and
since the war. He says that throughout the Southern States, in
expectation of an uprising, patrols were kept ready to move to any
threatened place. It was the fear of quick vengeance, he maintains,
which kept the negro down. Carl Schurz says the great majority
of the slaves stayed with their masters. He also speaks of the
patrols which kept negroes from leaving the plantations. "Can
the South Solve the Negro Problem," McClure's, January, 1904, pp.
260, 261. T. N. Page discusses this question, and says that it was
a compliment to both races, and was due partly to the instinct of
command possessed by southern whites and partly to the peaceful
disposition of the negroes. He also says that in revolutionary times
the British offered freedom to the slaves in Virginia and the Caro-
linas, and it had no effect, except to exasperate the masters. Mc-
Clure's, March, 1904, p. 553.

Whatever may have been the reason, it is admitted that not only were there no uprisings against the whites, but there were a large number of cases in which the household slaves, or " family servants," showed a single-minded devotion and fidelity to their masters and their masters' families. Booker Washington was justified some years ago, when making an eloquent appeal in behalf of his race, in reminding a white audience of the faithful service which so many of that race performed in war times. Nor were the negro servants of Louisiana an exception. Many instances of devotion have been brought to the writer's attention. In one instance one of the slaves carried off his master's horses to Texas, and after keeping them there for two years brought them back in fine condition. A more interesting case is that of an old servant who, learning in the winter of 1903 that the present writer was seeking information about the conduct of the slave during the Civil War, wrote to his former mistress as follows: " I ask of you as a favor if you find any action of mine during those days worth mentioning, please do so. As I am getting old, and am bringing up a grandson, and trying to teach him how to get along in this world among all people, and especially the Southern people, who are our best friends, I would like to read something myself and have my grand-child to read something that his grandfather had done, even when he had the opportunity of being his own man." In answer to this appeal, his former mistress writes as follows: " Harry was bought in New Orleans when he was fully grown. He proved himself faithful; a trusted servant and friend, never having forfeited the confidence reposed in him. He served through the campaigns west of the Mississippi with Major W——— as body servant. He was frequently sent on important errands, which trust was never betrayed, though opportunity offered; and during the trying period after the war, when at times left as protector of the family, never wavered in his duty. As proof of Major ———'s attachment to him, he once risked his life to rescue him from drowning in Bayou

Vermillion, for which Harry always seemed to feel he owed a special debt of gratitude. He then began studying to educate himself, and afterwards located in Plaquemines Parish, from which he was sent as a representative to the legislature. An occasional letter informs us of his continued interest and affection for us, of his own welfare and prosperity, and the good will he has carried through life for our people." Governor H. W. Allen had a colored servant named Vallery[1] to whom he wrote in 1866 as follows: " I think of you very often, not only as my faithful servant in former days, but as my companion in arms, and on the battle-field. God bless you, Vallery. . . . If I am ever a rich man again, I will help you. . . . You were ever true to me, and I will never, never forget your services."

These instances of friendly, affectionate relations between master and servant—and they are only a few among hundreds—are worthy of remembrance as a pleasing contrast to the very hostile relations which Reconstruction was to produce. They serve also to show the falsity of the statements occasionally made by northern men in regard to the relations between the two races. Thus in the letters to Secretary Chase, so frequently quoted in these pages, Denison writes under date of October 8, 1864, that a law giving suffrage to negroes could not be sustained at that time in any State, county, or town throughout the whole South, and he then adds: " I do not think you appreciate or understand the intense antipathy with which Southerners regard negroes. It is the natural antipathy of races, developed and intensified by the servile, brutal condition of one—the insolent despotic position of the other. We used to hear much of the patriarchal character of the institution —of the fond attachment of the faithful sla —of the paternal and affectionate care of the kind masu —and Southerners used to profess a liking for the negro, never exhibited in the North. This was all gammon. They liked the negro as I like my horse—a convenient beast of

---

[1] Dorsey, Recollections of Allen, p. 352.

burden for my use and pleasure.   But that a negro should
have a voice or influence in Government, or any rights
which a white man is bound to respect—this is intolerable."[1]
While Denison is correct as to southern feeling at this time
toward negro suffrage and social equality, he might have
found the same sentiment wide-spread in the North.   But
his comparison of southern servants to " convenient beasts
of burden " should be contrasted with the instances of
genuine affection given in the foregoing pages.[2]

   The proclamation of emancipation naturally increased
rather than diminished the demoralization of the negroes
within the Federal lines.   The fittest of them, as we have
seen, were enlisted for a while into negro companies ; but
thousands of them still wandered from plantation to plantation, or forced their way into the camps to be supported by
their new friends.   Here, while much sympathy and good
will were expressed for them, they were found to be an
intolerable burden.   Such planters as were left in the lines
were glad to employ them and pay them wages if they
could thereby be certain of their continued services.   In this
new order of things they had the hearty cooperation of
General Banks, who was pondering the question of how to
manage the negroes on the abandoned and confiscated
plantations which the government was trying to cultivate.
The terms granted by the old masters varied on different
plantations.   Wages were from three dollars to ten dollars a
month, and rewards and punishments were fixed for good
and bad conduct respectively.   The punishments were, first,
fines, then the stocks, and lastly expulsion from the plantation.   No negro was allowed to quit a plantation without a written license.   If a hand left the place, or was
expelled, his back wages were forfeited to the hospital

---

[1] Chase Correspondence, pp. 449–450.
[2] A Confederate veteran was lately heard to say: "If I live to
get to the Confederate Reunion at New Orleans next month, I am
going to propose a monument.   It is to be of black marble and to
be erected in honor of the 'Confederate nigger.'" W. B. Hill, in
Report of Conference of Southern Educational Association, 1903,
p. 207.

funds, out of which the physicians and medicines were paid for. Stealing was punished by a fine of twice the value of the property stolen, one half to go to the hospital fund. Much to the relief of the commanding general these regulations seem to have drawn many negroes back to the plantations and to have resulted in a fair degree of success.[1]

In the early part of the year 1864 Banks took up again the herculean task of dealing with the negro as a laborer. In January, as we have seen, on his own responsibility, he suspended (not abolished) all the laws concerning slavery. He followed this act, February 3, 1864, by a general labor order for all plantations, public or private, during the current year. It was more detailed and more stringent than any previous war regulation: it forbade the enlistment of soldiers from plantations until further orders; plantation hands were not allowed to pass from one place to another except under such rules as might be established by the provost marshal of the parish; flogging and other cruel or unusual punishments were forbidden; all questions between employer and employee were to be decided by the provost marshal; the possession of arms or concealed weapons without authority should be punished by fine and imprisonment; laborers should render to their employers, between daylight and dark, ten hours in summer and nine hours in winter of respectful, honest, faithful labor, and receive therefor, in addition to just treatment, healthy rations, comfortable clothing, quarters, fuel, medical attendance, instruction for children, and wages according to the following scale: (1) first-class hands, $8 per month; (2) second-class hands, $6 per month; (3) third-class hands, $5 per month; (4) fourth-class hands, $3 per month. Wages might be commuted for one fourteenth of the net proceeds of the crop. Indolence, insolence, disobedience of orders, and crime were to be suppressed by forfeiture of pay and such punishments as were provided for similar offences by army regulations. Laborers were to be allowed to choose their employers; but

---

[1] Annual Cyclopaedia, 1863, subject "Louisiana," p. 594; Chase Correspondence, p. 377.

when the agreement was made, they were to be held to the engagement for the year under the protection of the government. In cases of attempted imposition by feigning sickness, or stubborn refusal of duty, employees were to be turned over to the provost marshal for labor upon public works, without pay. Arrangements were to be made by which hands could cultivate land on private account. A free-labor bank was to be established for safe deposits of the savings of the freedmen. As overseers, unlike the negro and the planter, had shown that they did not appreciate that anything new had occurred and still adhered to old customs, they were to be disciplined by reduced wages and mild punishments.[1] Labor was declared to be a public duty and vagrancy a crime. If, however, planters, without just reason, refused to cultivate, their estates should be temporarily forfeited to those that would.[2]

These regulations of General Banks were rigorous enough to bring order out of the existing chaos, and were condemned by northern philanthropists as oppressive of freedmen. It is said, however, that during the year 1864 some 15,000 plantations were worked with 50,000 freedmen. The Federal agent in charge reported that only on one per cent. of these plantations would the freedmen fail to get their full wages.[3] The newspapers of that day, however, are full of the letters of planters discussing the momentous question of free labor. Banks expected wonders of free labor, and prophesied that in two years the product of the State would be quadrupled by the change from slave to free labor. It is needless to say that he did not understand the newly emancipated freedman. Life in the South was too easy, emancipation had been too sudden, for any immediate conversion of the slave into a strenuous free laborer. The planter, accustomed to compulsory labor, doubtless expected too much of his ex-slave; and the letters in the newspapers

---

[1] Annual Cyclopaedia, 1863, subject "Louisiana," p. 595.
[2] Times, 1864, passim.
[3] Annual Cyclopaedia, 1865, subject "Louisiana," p. 515.

are full of the stealing, the neglect of work, and the mortality of the negro under the new conditions. Production fell off enormously. For the year 1861, for example, Terrebonne parish cultivated 80 plantations and produced 28,282 hogsheads of sugar, while in 1864 it cultivated 37 plantations and produced only 625 hogsheads. " Why do I not starve my hands into better behavior? " pathetically asks one planter, and then answers his own question: " Because a negro never starves where there is anything eatable to be obtained (by stealing)." In November, 1864, a meeting of planters was held of which Judge Joshua Baker, of Terrebonne, was elected chairman. This convention considered the labor question, and drew up regulations which, if accepted by the government, would have brought the freedmen again into bondage, in fact, if not in name; for they provided that insolence or contempt of superiors should be punished as " formerly." Obstinate cases were to be treated " with corporal punishment as in the army and navy of the United States."

In order to deal with the problem more thoroughly, Congress, on March 3, 1863, had authorized the secretary of the treasury, through his agents, to collect captured and abandoned property in the South.[1] In March, 1865, just about a month before the surrender of General Lee, a bureau for the relief of freedmen and refugees (called the " Freedmen's Bureau ") was established under the control of the War Department. It was to continue during the rebellion and for one year thereafter. This bureau had full charge of all matters relating to freedmen, especially the distribution among them of lands abandoned by their owners or confiscated by the United States government. Forty acres might be given for a term of three years to each freedman, who was to pay an annual rent on the same or purchase it. In case of purchase he was to receive such title as the United States could confer. As soon as the war was over the operation of the bureau was extended to

---

[1] Peirce, Freedmen's Bureau, pp. 22-23.

the whole of Louisiana. Aided by missionary and religious societies of the North, it doubtless helped the negro in making provision for himself in his new state of freedom; but its officials were mostly indiscreet army officers—often bent on making their own fortunes—who managed the work of the bureau in such an inefficient manner that the planters, especially those coming home from the war, found the bureau an intolerable nuisance, and longed to be rid of it. The planters complained of the bureau; the bureau complained of the planters; and the freedmen complained of both. It was confusion worse confounded.

It is not surprising that such a bureau was not conspicuously successful in this conflict of ignorance, passion, and self-interest, for the freedmen believed that as the Federal Congress had passed the thirteenth amendment setting them free, it was going to despoil their old masters of all their property and divide it among the ex-slaves as a Christmas gift. They dreamed already of riding in the white folks' carriages, and of enjoying a kind of saturnalia of freedom. "Where is de government, de forty acres of land and de mule?" they began to cry. In vain the agents of the bureau informed them that the government had no intention of giving gratuitously. Many of the freedmen would not believe that the war had been waged only to set them free. As to the Confederate planter returning from the war, they did not trust him at all; contracts with him might mean a renewal of slavery. "Shall I sign dat ar paper dat I can't read?" one old darky near Shreveport was heard to say; "I'm afraid it will bring me back to slavery." The planters, on the other hand, desperate at the thought of their crops not being gathered, and exasperated by the not unnatural attitude of their ex-slaves, sometimes resorted to extreme or unlawful measures to control them. The Shreveport Gazette of July, 1865, regrets that one or two persons in the vicinity have inflicted on some of their former slaves punishment which the law no longer regarded as excusable. Some planters drove away the helpless aged and infirm negroes, and promptly received orders from the bureau that they must take them back and make such contracts as would enable such persons to be properly supported. The town of Opelousas (and there were others) passed an ordinance that no negro or freedman should be allowed to rent or keep a house in the town, and that none should reside in the town who was not in the regular service of some white person or former owner; nor should any freedman barter, sell, or exchange within the town without a permit.[1] Last, but not least, in July, 1865, a negro at Shreveport brought in a paper which read as follows: "This boy Calvin has permit to hire to whom he pleases, but I shall hold him as my property until set free by Congress. Signed, E. V. Tully." It is needless to say that the Opelousas ordinance was abolished by the Freedmen's Bureau, while both it and the slave permit were forwarded to Washington by Carl Schurz, special agent of the president, who reported that some Louisiana planters refused to accept the proclamation of emancipation as valid in times of peace, while others wished to establish a system of peonage.

The thousands of destitute freedmen who came into the Federal lines were to be cared for and furnished with employment. To meet the difficulties of the situation the Bureau of Free Labor under Superintendent Conway established what were termed "home colonies." Of these there were four in Louisiana: the McHatton at Baton Rouge, the Rost and McCutcheon in St. Charles parish, the General Bragg in Lafourche parish, and the Sparks in Jefferson parish. The number of acres included in the "home colonies" was 9650. The number of dependents placed in them was 1902, of whom 609 were sick. The colonies were organized with a superintendent, a physician, a cultivator of land, and a clerk. On each were a school and, "where parties so desired," churches. The govern-

[1] Schurz's Report to President Johnson, 39th Cong., 1st sess., S. Ex. Doc. No. 2, p. 23.

ment was to receive one third of the crops on the lands cultivated.[1]

In March, 1865, General Hurlbut issued a general labor order which provided for the continuance of the home colonies and for the enforcement of all fair contracts through the military authorities and the superintendent of the bureau. No cruelty, inhumanity, or neglect of duty was to be allowed on the part of employers. Wages for time lost by sickness were to be deducted, and both wages and rations where sickness was feigned for the purpose of idleness. In cases of feigned sickness or refusal to work according to contract the offender was to be reported by the provost marshal to the superintendent and put at forced labor on the public works without pay.

Very interesting information as to the condition of the freedmen from the Republican standpoint is to be found in the final report of the Bureau of Free Labor, Department of the Gulf,[2] prior to its transfer to the " Bureau of Refugees, Freedmen, and Abandoned Lands," over which Major-General O. O. Howard presided. This report contains an account of the management of the Bureau of Free Labor up to July 1, 1865. The superintendent complains that the press of the State is almost universally opposed to the continuance of this bureau, and that there are bad men who have come from the free States who care nothing for humanity or religion, and " who are as ready to whip the freedmen, provided it will bring them gain, as they are to condemn the same conduct on the part of the men who formerly owned the freedmen." In accordance with the

---

[1] General Fullerton, who succeeded Conway, declared that he found these colonies " managed so miserably that he consolidated the four into one." Banks had established a board of education for freedmen, which met with some success. He was also the pioneer in laying a regular tax on the southern people for support of public schools. Peirce, Freedmen's Bureau, p. 20. J. T. Sprague, assistant commissioner for Florida, says that the colony in that State stole all the hogs and cattle in the neighborhood, and that the colonists would not work. Fleming, Documentary History of Reconstruction, I, 348.

[2] This is the report of Superintendent Thomas W. Conway, printed at New Orleans, 1865. In the collection of Gaspar Cusachs, Esq.

law of Congress of March 3, 1865, the superintendent says he is prepared to lease the abandoned and confiscated lands of Louisiana to freedmen and loyal refugees in lots of forty acres each, and some plantations have been already so leased. In conclusion, the superintendent declares that the people of the South have some noble qualities; but they are not yet fitted to be trusted with the defence of the liberty of the freedmen. He therefore recommends " that the work of the bureau be continued for three or four years, by which time the freedmen, having acquired lands and the suffrage, will be able to take care of themselves. If the freedmen are not protected in the liberty proclaimed to them, they will go away from the country, trusting to God."

In spite of the efforts of the bureau, which was not able to cope with the situation, there was a general demoralization of labor, which is reflected in the newspapers of the day. A planter in Terrebonne writes that " laborers are allowed to disregard agreements with the planters. The provost marshal says he has no adequate force to stop the evil. Our people are in great distress and want, from the fact that they made no crop last year, and will make nothing this year— and the tax collector knocking at the door and the levees broken down." A New Englander writes to the Times that he has come to Louisiana and hired a plantation of a thousand acres. He came South with the opinion that the negro was a much abused race, but of his lot of hogs, chickens, etc., nearly all had been stolen by his "hands."

It was but natural, therefore, that the planters, facing ruin, with the levees in a wretched condition and the crops ungarnered, should turn to the legislature for relief, as was done in a number of other Southern States when the war was over. The Freedmen's Bureau was regarded both as a failure and as an unwelcome agent between employer and employee. Accordingly, in September, 1865, the National Conservative Union men of Louisiana, in an address to the public, urged that " representatives to the General Assembly should be selected who favored the enactment of such laws for the regulation of labor as would induce the general government to relieve the State of that terrible incubus, the Freedmen's Bureau."

When the legislature met in extra session on November 23, 1865, it took up, as the governor had suggested in his proclamation, the all-important labor question. Blaine declares that among the Southern States which passed stringent labor laws at this time Louisiana perhaps " attained the worst eminence." " At the very moment," he says, " when the Thirty-ninth Congress was assembling [December, 1865] to consider the condition of the Southern States and the whole subject of their reconstruction, it was found that a bill was pending in the Legislature of Louisiana providing that ' every adult freed man or woman *shall furnish themselves with a comfortable home and visible means of support within twenty days after the passage of this Act,*' and that ' any freed man or woman failing to obtain a home and support as thus provided shall be immediately arrested by any sheriff or constable in any parish, or by the police officer in any city or town in said parish where said freedman may be, and by them delivered to the Recorder of the parish, and by him hired out, by public advertisement, to some citizen, being the highest bidder, for the remainder of the year.' And in case the laborer should leave his employer's service without his consent, ' he shall be arrested and assigned to labor on some public works without compensation until his employer reclaims him.' The laborers were not to be allowed to keep any live-stock, and all time spent from home without leave was to be charged against them at the rate of two dollars per day, and worked out at that rate."

" By a previous law," continues Blaine, " Louisiana had provided that all agricultural laborers should be compelled to ' make contracts for labor during the first ten days of January for the entire year.' With a demonstrative show of justice it was provided that ' wages due shall be a lien on the crop, one half to be paid at times agreed by the parties, the other half to be retained until the completion of the contract; but in case of sickness of the laborer, wages for the time shall be deducted, and where the sickness is supposed to be feigned for the purpose of idleness, double the amount shall be deducted; and should the refusal to work extend beyond three days, the negro shall be forced to labor on roads, levees, and public works without pay.' The master was permitted to make deductions from the laborer's wages for 'injuries done to animals or agricultural implements committed to his care, or for bad or negligent work,' he, of course, being the judge. 'For every act of disobedience a fine of one dollar shall be imposed upon the laborer'; and among the cases deemed to be disobedience were 'impudence, swearing, or using indecent language in the presence of the employer, his family, or his agent, or quarreling or fighting among one another.' "[1]

Upon these two sets of laws—the pending bill of December, 1865, and "the previous law for agricultural laborers" —Blaine naturally passes some severe strictures, maintaining that they violated the spirit, if not the letter, of the thirteenth amendment, which was ratified by this same legislature. Moreover, in the Congress that met in December, 1865, Senator Wilson of Massachusetts recited this same "pending bill" of the Louisiana legislature, and introduced a bill providing for the nullification of such peonage laws.[2]   It is a noteworthy fact, however, that neither of the bills mentioned by Blaine ever became law in Louisiana.   No such statutes appear in the acts of the legislature.   An examination of the journals of the two houses shows that "the pending bill" was never voted upon, nor even recorded in the minutes.[3]   The agricultural labor bill, however, introduced by Duncan F. Kenner, did pass both houses, but it was either never submitted to the governor or was pocket-vetoed by him.   The surviving members of the legislature

---

[1] Blaine, Twenty Years, II, 101, 102.
[2] Congressional Globe, 39th Cong., 1st sess., p. 39.
[3] It appears in the radical organ, the New Orleans Tribune, of December, 1865, but was doubtless lost in committee.

cannot recall what was the fate of this bill. It is very probable that, after passing both houses, it was suppressed on account of the commotion which it created when recited by Senator Wilson in Congress. Any odium that attaches to it, of course, rests upon the legislature that passed it.

Another law, however, which passed both houses, was approved by the governor, and was duly promulgated (December 20, 1865), excited much adverse criticism in Congress, and was exploited by the radicals within and without that body. This was the vagrant law, similar in character to existing laws in Northern States and to the vagrant laws passed by other Southern States at this time. This law adopted as a description of vagrant a definition to be found in the acts of 1855, as follows: " All idle persons who, not having visible means to maintain themselves, live without employment; all persons wandering abroad and lodging in groceries, taverns, beer-houses, market-places, sheds, barns, uninhabited buildings, or in the open air, and not giving a good account of themselves; all persons wandering abroad and begging, or who go about from door to door, or place themselves in the streets, highways, passages, or other public places, to beg or receive alms; habitual drunkards who shall abandon, neglect or refuse to aid in the support of their families, and who may be complained of by their families, shall be deemed vagrants."[1]   Adopting this definition, the law provides:

That upon complaint made on oath before a justice of the peace, mayor, or judge of the district court, or other proper officer, that any person is a vagrant within the description aforesaid, it shall be the duty of such justice, judge, mayor, or other officer, to issue his warrant to any sheriff, constable, policeman, or other peace officer, commanding him to arrest the party accused and bring him before such justice of the peace or other officer; and if the justice or other officer be satisfied by the confession of the offender, or by competent testimony, that he is a vagrant within the said description, he shall make a certificate of the same, which shall be filed with the clerk of the court of the parish, and in the city of New Orleans the certificate shall be filed in the office of one of the recorders; and the said justice or other officer shall require the party accused to enter into bond, payable to the Governor of Louisiana, or his

---

[1] Acts of Legislature, 1855, p. 149.

successors in office, in such sums as said justice or other officer shall prescribe, with security to be approved by said officer, for his good behavior and future industry, for the period of one year; and upon his failing or refusing to give such bond and security, the justice or other officer shall issue his warrant to the sheriff or other officer, directing him to detain and to hire out such vagrant for a period not exceeding twelve months, or to cause him to labor on the public works, roads and levees, under such regulations as shall be made by the municipal authorities;

Provided, That if the accused be a person who has abandoned his employer, before his contract expired, the preference shall be given to such employer of hiring the accused; and provided further, that in the city of New Orleans the accused may be committed to the workhouse for a time not exceeding six months, there to be kept at hard labor, or to be made to labor upon the public works, roads or levees. The proceeds of hire in the cases herein provided for, to be paid into the parish treasury for the benefit of paupers; and provided further, that the person hiring such vagrant shall be compelled to furnish such clothing, food and medical attention as they furnish their other laborers.[1]

It will be noticed that this vagrant law makes no discrimination of race, color, or previous condition of servitude. In this respect it was different from the law enacted about the same time in Mississippi, which declared that " all freemen, free negroes, and mulattoes in the State, over the age of eighteen years, found on the second Monday of January, 1866, or thereafter, with no lawful employment or business, or found unlawfully assembling together either in the day or night time, together with all white persons so assembling with them on terms of equality, or living in adultery or fornication with negro women, should be deemed vagrants." It was also shown at a later time that the Louisiana law was practically a copy of the Massachusetts vagrant law and that similar laws existed in Connecticut, New York, Maine, and other States of the North,[2] and that it was approved in Louisiana by a governor who had voluntarily emancipated his slaves and was a consistent Union man. Such laws, it was argued, were absolutely necessary in the South where emancipation had flooded the country with idle and possibly criminal freedmen; they were applicable to whites as well as to blacks.[3] Nothing, how-

---

[1] Acts of Legislature, extra session, 1865, p. 18.
[2] For these laws see Garner, Reconstruction in Mississippi, p. 119, note.
[3] These laws were repealed by the constitution of 1868.

ever, could still the outcry of the northern radicals against what they deemed a return to slavery. It was plausibly argued by the opponents of the South that, while in the North such laws could be enforced with wisdom and impartiality, the same laws in the South at this time would be enforced so as to discriminate against the ex-slaves, at whom the laws were really directed. The only result would be a practical return to slavery, especially when the negroes were denied that weapon of defense, the suffrage.

Surely the legislators of the South must have been blind to their best interests to suppose that Congress would permit such a return to the old régime.[1] Were they "Bourbons that learned nothing and forgot nothing?" Yet the writer has been assured by a member of the legislature of 1865 that this body never doubted that Congress would approve the vagrant law of this State, which appeared so clearly necessitated by the existing status of the freedman. It was not perceived by the members that in attempting to rid the State of the Freedmen's Bureau by legislating on the labor question they were really insuring the continuance of that incubus. So strong was the belief in the legislature that President Johnson would be able to carry out his policy in spite of the factious opposition of the radicals that no fears seem to have been felt for the future.

There was, however, in New Orleans at this time a very dangerous organ of opposition, which the conservatives rashly concluded to ignore. This was the New Orleans Tribune, an exponent of universal suffrage, vigorously edited in the interest of the negroes. This journal, a copy of which was sent to every member of Congress, carried on a relentless war upon the legislature. It printed every labor law proposed or passed by that body, and appealed

---

[1] The Chicago Tribune, of December 1, 1865, said, relative to the Mississippi laws, "We tell the white men of Mississippi that the men of the North will convert the state of Mississippi into a frog pond before they will allow any such laws to disgrace one foot of the soil in which the bones of our soldiers sleep and over which the flag of freedom waves." Quoted by Garner, Reconstruction in Mississippi, p. 115, note 3.

to the friends of the freedmen in the North and in Europe to say whether there was any free labor in Louisiana. It ridiculed the legislature for its attempts to pass labor laws which were promptly nullified by the counter regulations of the Freedmen's Bureau.[1] When the bureau recommended yearly contracts for labor, the Tribune declared that the freedmen should demand their wages every week, and that any kind of labor contract was disguised slavery. It maintained that wherever the Federal troops were withdrawn, persecution of the freedmen and of the loyalists either had followed or would follow. Alleged instances of this persecution in the country parishes were given. The only safety for the freedman was in the bestowal of the ballot. It urged upon Congress the rejection of southern representatives, and declared that if they were rejected "Mr. James Madison Trickster" (Wells) would soon "turn up as good a republican as of yore"[2]—a prophecy which was to be fulfilled exactly. It proclaimed to Congress that persecution of the negro was the dominant note of the legislature as well as of the planters. The influence of the Tribune at Washington, seconded by Warmoth and other disgruntled radicals, was immense. Its columns supplied the radical orators with the thunder which they launched against "the vicious legislation of Louisiana."

Before the adjournment of this special session (December 22), a bill was offered in the senate by Duvigneaud to define the civil status of the freedman: "The freedman was to have the same rights and privileges as were enjoyed by the free colored population previous to the Civil War; that they should be heard as witnesses in all the Courts of the State, and should sue and be sued in all the courts." This bill, however, having passed its first reading in the senate two days before adjournment, was dropped amid the pressure of

[1] The New Orleans Tribune of December 20, 1865, states that on the very day the legislature tried to regulate the relations between laborers and employers the bureau issued an order which reduced the regulation to nothing before it saw the light of day.

[2] New Orleans Tribune, December 20, 1865.

business at the close. It would have given the freedman every right except the suffrage. While, however, no law was passed granting rights and privileges to the freedman,[1] it was generally understood that, having been emancipated, he was thereby placed on the same footing as the free man of color. In fact, General Fullerton, a wise and sane superintendent, who succeeded Conway as agent of the Freedmen's Bureau, in making his report during the latter part of 1865[2] said that as all free persons under the new constitution as well as under the old code were admitted to the state courts, he had abolished the freedmen's courts and transferred the pending cases to the civil courts of the State.[3]

Yet, as we have seen, the laws actually promulgated by the legislature made no discrimination against the negro except in the matter of suffrage. In this cautious wording

---

[1] The Annual Cyclopaedia of 1865, page 514, says that the status of the negro was fixed at this session, but this statement is an error. It is true that at the regular session of this legislature in 1866 the same bill was taken up and approved by both houses, but it was not submitted to the governor, and hence it did not become a law. A committee of the senate reported on February 22, 1866, that such a law was unnecessary " in view of the humane provisions of the law of Louisiana which existed long anterior to the late war, and which extends to all free persons alike the right to hold property, testify in courts, acquire education, etc., in a word, the guarantees of law for life, liberty, and pursuit of happiness. In these respects, the laws of Louisiana are and have always been different and exceptional among those of other States, and these provisions apply as well to the recently emancipated as to any other class of free colored persons."

[2] New York Times, December 31, 1865.

[3] Whereupon the New Orleans Tribune, the organ of the negroes, declared that the confidence of the people of color had been terribly shaken in the bureau " since the delivery of the whole machinery into the hands of the rebels." December 14, 1865. Fullerton was disliked by the Tribune because he advocated Johnson's policy of reconstruction. Fullerton favored the contract system, and predicted that in five years, if no new element of discord intervened, the negroes would be as prosperous as any one could desire. It is noteworthy that he did not suggest the advisability of entrusting the ballot to negroes. One of the New Orleans papers, however, urged the legislature to deny the ballot to ignorant and incompetent whites and thus forestall any blame for not granting it to freedmen. This sound advice was unfortunately ignored. Even if there had been a wish to accept it, the framing of such a law would have presented many difficulties.

of statutes Louisiana differed from most of the other Southern States. In Mississippi, for example, the old penal laws applying to slaves were practically reenacted against the freedmen; and it was provided that "no freedman could rent or lease lands except in incorporated towns or cities" where the corporate authorities were empowered to control their privilege.[1]   While the Louisiana legislature did not deserve the odium attached to such laws by the North, it did not fail to put on record its belief that it lay with the State to determine the political and civil relations of the ex-slaves.   Accordingly, in readopting the thirteenth amendment to the Federal Constitution, the legislature added a clause declaring "that any attempt on the part of Congress to legislate otherwise [than is necessary for the prevention of slavery] upon the political *status* or civil relations of former slaves within any State, would be a violation of the Constitution of the United States."[2]

---

[1] Garner, Reconstruction in Mississippi, pp. 114–115.
[2] Annual Cyclopaedia, 1865, subject "Louisiana," p. 515.

CHAPTER VII.

THE SO-CALLED RIOT OF JULY 30, 1866.

The culminating point in the struggle between the Democrats and the radicals in Louisiana was the so-called riot of July 30, 1866. This important event in the history of Reconstruction, which gave the quietus to the constitution of 1864 and was a proximate cause of the severity of the reconstruction measures adopted by Congress in 1867, may best be understood by the consideration of three questions: (1) What was the attitude of the legislature of Louisiana toward the freedmen and the white radicals in the first half of the year 1866? (2) What was the attitude of Congress toward the South? (3) What was the attitude of the radicals in Louisiana toward the freedmen and the Democrats during the same period?

In answer to the first question it is to be noted that the harmony existing between the legislature and Governor Wells in the autumn of 1865 could not in the nature of things last indefinitely. Wells had hoped that Louisiana, as reconstructed by Lincoln and Johnson, would be readmitted by the Thirty-ninth Congress. He was disappointed. For some months he seems to have hoped that Johnson would be able to score a success over Congress; but when in the spring of 1866 all hope of this seemed to have vanished, Wells prepared to go over to the opposition. On the other hand, the Democrats, who dominated the legislature, had accepted Wells as governor because he seemed the most available candidate to meet the demands of President Johnson. His intense Unionism during the war, however, naturally prevented him from being persona grata to the mass of ex-Confederates. Moreover, many of his appointees to office had proved unsatisfactory. They were not radicals; but they were, for the most part, Unionists, and the legislature was now determined to restore the State to the control of the old office-holders. Far from conceding any share in the government to the freedmen and the radicals, the legislature felt itself strong enough to evict Unionists and to demand the restoration of pure democracy as represented by ex-Confederates. Wells was naturally opposed to the eviction of his appointees.

Accordingly, when the legislature, declaring that the present holders of offices were merely appointees, voted that new elections should be held in March for both municipal and parish offices, the governor vetoed the two bills embodying these provisions on the ground that one of them did not allow the usual time for a proclamation, and that a modification of the charter was necessary for a fair election, while the other was equally objectionable from a constitutional standpoint. The legislature, regarding these objections as trivial, promptly passed the bills over the veto, and then proceeded to make some concessions to the governor's views by making changes in the city charter and by deferring the parish elections until the month of May. Thereupon the governor, making the best of a situation which must have been very unsatisfactory to him, issued the necessary proclamations.[1] The Daily Crescent stated that the disagreement between the governor and the legislature was "due to a desperate attempt of interested and unpopular officials to hold on to the emoluments of office in utter defiance of an overwhelming public opinion."

The city election for mayor, comptroller, aldermen, and other city officials was held March 12, in accordance with the strict election laws in force in the autumn of 1865. This law provided that only male whites, twenty-one years of age, who were citizens of the United States and resident in the State for one year preceding the election, and who showed that they came under the provisions of the amnesty oath, should be allowed to vote. It seems to have been

---

[1] New Orleans Daily Crescent, March, 1866, passim.

agreed that there should be no deep scrutiny into the qualifications of Democratic voters.[1]   The radicals, recognizing
their weakness in the absence of negro suffrage, did not
take part in the election, and the Democrats carried all the
polls except in the case of a few aldermen elected by the
National Unionists.   The mayor-elect, John T. Monroe, and
one of the aldermen, J. O. Nixon, were promptly suspended
from the exercise of their functions by the commander of
the department, General E. R. S. Canby, on the ground that
they were not qualified under the oath of amnesty.   Monroe,
it was maintained, had " uttered rebellious language after
the City had been captured, and had refused the oath of
allegiance."   However, a special pardon was obtained from
President Johnson, the order of suspension was revoked,
and on May 15 Mayor Monroe entered upon his duties.[2]
The parish elections were duly held on the first Monday in
May.   The state government, as reorganized by the Democrats, was now in full operation.

Another matter of importance considered by the legislature was the advisability of calling a convention to frame
a new constitution for the State.   There was much difference of opinion.   Some members argued that it was unwise
to agitate the question at this time, while others held that
it was the duty of the legislature to provide for the framing
of a new constitution, as that of 1864 had not been adopted
by the majority of people in the State.   Finally, it was proposed to submit the question to the people at the election to
be held in May.   But before this proposal was finally
adopted, despatches were received from W. B. Egan, D. S.
Cage, and J. B. Eustis, who had been sent to Washington
to consult President Johnson in regard to the future of
Louisiana.   They reported that, after several agreeable
interviews with the president and the secretary of state, they
had become convinced that further agitation of the convention question would embarrass the president's policy of

---

[1] Annual Cyclopaedia, 1866, subject " Louisiana," p. 448.
[2] Mayor Kennedy protested against him.   Report on New Orleans
Riots, testimony, p. 518.

reconstruction, a policy which he (the president) was confident of bringing to a successful conclusion. Whereupon the legislature laid the bill on the table.[1] The True Delta,[2] commenting on these proceedings, said that the president's refusal to allow a new convention to be called showed that he approved of the policy of Governor Wells, and that the latter was evidently actuated by good motives.[3]

The second question which must be considered in order to gain a complete understanding of the New Orleans riots is the attitude of Congress toward the South. The New Orleans Crescent of March 1 announced: " War is now on between the radicals in Congress and President Johnson." In fact the situation had been becoming more and more strained ever since Congress met in December, 1865. The mild policy of the president was unpopular, and that body had the necessary two-thirds majority to override his veto.

The cause of the South, which the president advocated, was extremely weak for several reasons. These may be briefly stated as follows: (1) The Confederate States during the war had assumed the position of having withdrawn absolutely from the Union by action of the several States. Hence they could not admit that Lincoln and Johnson were right in regarding secession as a mere rebellion of individuals; hence they were estopped as secessionists from rejecting the radical platform that the rebellious States were out of the Union, and that Congress could prescribe measures for the readmission of their representatives. (2) Southern legislatures had in no case granted the suffrage to the negro. It would have been a remarkable concession if they had done so; but their refusal enabled the radicals to say that the three-fifths rule having been abolished, the South would be more largely represented in Congress than before the emancipation (which was true), and that southern Demo-

---

[1] Journal of House of Representatives, 1865, pp. 97–98. True Delta, March 10, 1866.

[2] The files of the radical organ, the New Orleans Tribune, for this period are unfortunately missing in the city archives.

[3] Wells says that Johnson telegraphed to him for his view, and that he opposed it. Report on New Orleans Riots, testimony, p. 439.

crats and northern Democrats could combine in Congress to control the destinies of the country (which was at best very doubtful). (3) Some of the Southern States had passed laws denying civil rights to the negro and discriminating against him in the holding of land, etc. (4) There was undue haste on the part of the South to send to Congress "ex-rebels." Alexander H. Stephens, vice-president of the Confederate States, was released from a Federal prison on October 11, 1865, and was elected United States senator in February, 1866. The reception of such men could not be cordial. It may be added that the cause of Louisiana was peculiarly weak because the constitution of 1864, which was recognized by Johnson and on which the State sought readmission, was not regarded as valid by the Democrats who had been elected under its provisions. These Democrats were willing to accept Sumner's lurid description of it. The recognition of such a constitution by the president was a serious handicap, both to the success of the president's general policy and to the reconstruction of Louisiana itself.

Nevertheless, there was in Congress much diversity of opinion, and the cause of the South found stronger defenders among northern and western Democrats than she herself could have furnished, for these defenders were able to urge that all acts of secession had been constitutionally null and void, and that a speedy recognition of the southern governments would be the proper confirmation of this fact —a plea which the South itself was unable to set up, but which the radicals could not logically reject. On many other points, also, there was so great a diversity of opinion that it is in some cases difficult to discover what was the attitude of Congress. Amid this clash of opposing views it was not unnatural for the South to hope that the policy of the president might still prevail. The principal questions discussed were three: (1) Had the president the constitutional right to recognize state governments in the rebellious States without the consent of Congress? (2) Were the rebellious States within or without the Union? (3) Should these States be forced to give the suffrage to the negroes before their representatives were received by Congress?

As to the first question, it will be remembered that in 1863 President Lincoln, relying upon that provision of the Constitution which declares that the president " shall have power to grant reprieves and pardons for offences against the United States, except in cases of impeachment," granted a full pardon to all who had participated in the rebellion (except certain specified classes) who would take an oath of allegiance. But the president went further, declaring that when a small percentage of the voters, having taken the oath, should establish a state government which should be republican, such should be recognized as the true government of the State, and the State should receive thereunder the benefit of the constitutional provision which declares that " the United States shall guarantee to every State in this Union a republican form of government," the admission of representatives, however, resting with Congress. It will be remembered that, at the time, this proclamation seemed to some radicals an encroachment upon the powers of Congress ; at least Congress, it was argued, ought to have a voice in establishing a " republican government." The successor of Lincoln did not need much persuasion to be convinced that this power of recognition rested with the executive, and he acted accordingly in the cases of Louisiana, Arkansas, and Tennessee. When the Thirty-ninth Congress met in December, 1865, it was argued by Representative Howard, of Michigan, that the president had no right, without the consent of Congress, to recognize a government in a State which was in insurrection against the United States ; but this view was modified in the majority report of the famous committee of fifteen (June, 1866). This report, signed by Fessenden, Stevens, Conkling, and others, said that the president might recognize the people of any State as having resumed relations of loyalty to the Union and act in his military capacity on this hypothesis. He might properly permit the people to assemble, to initiate local governments,

and to execute local laws. But it was not for him to
decide upon the nature or effect of any system of government which the people of these States might see fit to adopt;
this power rested with Congress.[1]   In spite of an able argument contained in a minority report,[2] this theory, that the
proclamations of the president in war times were merely
provisional permission to do certain acts, the validity of
which must be determined by the constitutional government,
was accepted by Congress as a substitute for Johnson's
policy.

The second question as to whether the rebel States were
within or without the Union, a question which Lincoln had
dismissed as an unprofitable abstraction, was taken up and
discussed anew.   It was held by some that these States must
still be in the Union; otherwise the president himself, being
from Tennessee, was a public enemy.   Moreover, throughout the war, in the laying of direct taxes, in the establishment of Federal courts, in submitting the thirteenth amendment, they had been treated as within the Union.   At the
previous session of Congress, Senator Doolittle, of Wis-
consin, had said, " In my opinion the doctrine that these
States are no longer States of the United States is one huge,
infernal, constitutional lie, that would stamp all our conduct
from the beginning as murder, and cover us all with blood."
In December, 1865, Stevens, ignoring the action of the
Federal Congress toward the States which had seceded,
declared that, by the law of nations, the late war between
the two acknowledged belligerents severed the original contract and broke all the ties that bound them together.   It
was, therefore, the right of the victorious party to treat
them as a conquered belligerent, severed from the Union in
fact.   Stevens evidently intended to annex the territory of
these conquered belligerents.   " Since the conquest," he said,
" they have been governed by martial law.   Military rule is

---

[1] Report of Joint Committee on Reconstruction, 39th Cong., 1st
sess., H. Rept. No. 30, p. viii.
[2] Signed by Reverdy Johnson, Rogers, and Grider.   Annual Cyclopaedia, 1866, subject " Public Documents," pp. 650–657.

necessarily despotic, and ought not to exist longer than is absolutely necessary. As there are no symptoms that the people of these provinces will be prepared to participate in constitutional government for some years, I know of no arrangement so proper for them as territorial governments."[1] As early as 1863 Charles Sumner had maintained that the seceding States had committed political suicide, in other words, they had ceased to be "constitutional States." Finally, the majority report of the committee of fifteen (and this was signed by Stevens) said that the so-called Confederate States, "having by treasonable withdrawal from Congress and by flagrant rebellion and war, forfeited all civil and political rights and privileges under the Federal Constitution, could only be restored thereto by the permission and authority of that constitutional power against which they rebelled, and by which they were subdued." No representation of these States was to be allowed until they had made such changes in their organic law as should determine the civil rights and privileges of all citizens in all parts of the republic, should place representation on an equitable basis, should fix a stigma on treason, and repudiate claims for expenses of the rebellion and loss of slaves.[2] This last theory, generally termed the "congressional theory," was practically embodied in the fourteenth amendment. It is sometimes called the theory of "forfeited rights." As contrasted with Sumner's view, it might be termed the theory of "suspended animation." The reader must decide for himself which theory was correct: the "Doolittle," the "conquered territory," the "suicide," or the "suspended animation theory." Perhaps the first three will be found not to differ from one another essentially. Under any one of them Congress could naturally and constitutionally claim the right of guaranteeing "a republican form

---

[1] Cox, Three Decades, p. 371. Cox argued against Stevens's view, saying that there was no authority under the Constitution to hold conquered territory as a province, a view which sounds old-fashioned in 1904.

[2] Report on Reconstruction, p. xxi.

of government" and of providing for the admission of representatives. Such a right did not rest with the president alone. The only question was what should be regarded as "a republican form of government." There was great danger that it would be interpreted by the dominant party as a form of government which would keep in power the Republican party.

The third question as to excluding the rebellious States until suffrage was granted to the negro raised much discussion. Reverdy Johnson argued that if large numbers of negroes were transferred to Massachusetts, that State would exclude them from the suffrage. But Sumner declared: "If negroes had been allowed to vote, there would have been no Secession; if he votes now, there will be peace; without this, you must have a standing army. The ballot box, or the cartridge box—choose ye between them." Hendricks, of Indiana (Democrat), reproached Sumner for trying to establish the ascendancy of the Republican party "regardless of everything;" but the radicals maintained that the freedman in the South must have the ballot because he had shed his blood in the Civil War, and because it would protect his liberty against the old slave-owners.

If the suffrage of the negro sustained the ascendancy of the Republican party, it was, after all, this party which had preserved the Union and abolished slavery. Stevens's sympathy with the freedman went further. Not only must he have the ballot, but the Federal government, by confiscation of southern lands, must grant him fifty acres and a hut. "Unless we give him this," cried Stevens, "we shall receive the censure of mankind, and the curse of Heaven." Finally, on June 13, 1866, Congress passed by joint resolution the fourteenth amendment to the Constitution. It was not so radical as Stevens would have liked to see it, but he voted for it. It made the negro a citizen; forbade the denial of "privileges and immunities;" settled representation on the new basis; denied the right to hold office to certain rebels; declared the validity of the national debt; and while it did not confer the suffrage on the freedman,[1] it placed a penalty on its denial. Though President Johnson, in his message of June 22, doubted the propriety of passing and submitting such an amendment when eleven States were excluded from Congress, it was duly submitted to the governor of each State by Secretary Seward.[2] It was understood that if a " rebel" State ratified this amendment, its representatives would be received by Congress.[3] It was promptly ratified by Tennessee, and in July the representatives of this State were admitted by Congress. When the amendment reached the governor of Louisiana, the legislature was no longer in session, and neither radicals nor conservatives were sufficiently enthusiastic in behalf of the amendment to wish to see an extra session called.[4]

In fact, as far as the radicals were concerned, they had other plans. As these plans form the third question which must be understood before considering the New Orleans riots, let us see what they were.

In the spring of 1866 some thirty or more of the conventionists of 1864, now leaning toward the most radical doctrines, had become so much exasperated at seeing the offices of the State passing into the hands of ex-rebels that they began to meet and to discuss plans for the ousting of the " ins " and for obtaining the recognition of the Federal government in behalf of Unionists. They were much encouraged in this scheme by the attitude of the existing Congress toward the question of reconstruction. At first it was proposed to meet and call a convention to frame a new con-

---

[1] The minority report of the committee of fifteen says that the suffrage was not directly conferred on the negro, for this measure would have been obnoxious to Northern and Western States, and would have prevented them from ratifying the amendment. Annual Cyclopaedia, 1886, p. 654; Report on Reconstruction, pt. ii, p. 9.

[2] An amendment, when passed by Congress, does not require the signature of the president. 3 Dallas, 378.

[3] Burgess says that the president did not view the amendment with favor while it was pending, and it soon became manifest that he was advising its rejection by the States. Reconstruction and the Constitution, p. 80.

[4] The Times, June 27, 1866, objects to the fourteenth amendment because eleven States were excluded.

stitution for "the territory of Louisiana." Such a convention, it was true, might meet with violence at the hands of the ex-rebels; but this result would only show Congress that the president's policy had been a failure, and that rebellion was still rampant in the South. Sober second thought, however, suggested that the admission of a territory would require the signature of the president. This would be refused, of course, and a two-thirds majority for such a purpose might be difficult to obtain.

A simpler method of procedure was to reconvoke the convention of 1864 and to revise the constitution of that year in accordance with radical views, that is, suffrage to the negroes, and a denial of it to ex-rebels. It will be remembered that before the convention of 1864 adjourned it passed a resolution declaring that, " when this Convention adjourns, it shall be at the call of the president, whose duty it shall be to reconvoke the Convention for any cause, or in case the Constitution should not be ratified, for the purpose of taking such measures as may be necessary for the formation of a civil government for the State of Louisiana." This resolution, bitterly opposed at the time by Abell, now offered an opportunity for a coup d'état. It was true that nearly two years had elapsed; the constitution had been adopted and had been in force during that period, and there seemed no good reason for so revolutionary a proceeding. Moreover, the resolution, not having been incorporated in the constitution, had never been passed upon by the people. But the advocates of revocation were reckless. It was widely believed that Congress could be relied upon for support, and if there were any violence on the part of the ex-rebels, Congress would be all the more willing to subject the State to military rule—"a consummation devoutly to be wished." The negroes also, lured on by the promise of the ballot, might be counted on to support the movement. Accordingly, on the 23d of June the following invitation was sent out to the ex-conventionists:—

"New Orleans, June 23rd.
" Sir,
" Several members of the Convention, as well as the Executive, wish you to attend a meeting of the Constitutional Convention of Louisiana at the Mechanics Institute Tuesday 26th at 2 P. M.
John E. Neelis, Sec'y."

In pursuance of this call, between thirty and forty members assembled at the time and place mentioned. The original quorum was seventy-six; but the more cautious members, fearing violence, or regarding the call as illegal, refused to come. Judge Durell, the ex-president of the convention, was not present. When questioned by the Select Committee on the New Orleans Riots,[1] Durell declared that he refused to reconvoke the convention, though pressed to do so, because he thought it would result in a riot. However, he called on General Sheridan, and on June 18 he telegraphed to the radical leaders in Congress, Fessenden, Boutwell, and Stevens, to see if he could get their support in the matter. Sheridan said that it would be impossible for him to protect the negroes at the polls, while the leaders at Washington cautiously refused to answer his telegram.[2] Thus deserted by the Federal authorities, and doubtful as to its legality, Durell refused to further the movement. The radicals, however, found a more compliant agent in R. K. Howell, an associate justice of the state supreme court and a former member of the convention, though he had resigned before the convention closed. At the preliminary meeting of June 26 Howell allowed the minority—only about forty members being present—to elect him president; and on the 8th of July he issued a proclamation reconvoking the convention of 1864 " to revise and amend the Constitution and to consider the adoption of the XIV Amendment." The convention was called to assemble on July 30, in the old Mechanics Institute. Governor Wells, who had given his approval to the preliminary meeting, was now called upon to issue writs of election for the choice of

---

[1] See the report of this committee for mass of testimony on the riots. 39th Cong., 2d sess., H. Rep. No. 16.
[2] This telegram is given in Report on New Orleans Riots, testimony, p. 263.

delegates in those parishes which were outside the Federal lines in 1864.

After Howell's proclamation appeared, he was requested by his adherents to visit Washington and to try to discover what was the attitude of Congress toward the movement. Howell afterwards testified before the committee of investigation that he had the impression that certain congressmen had suggested the calling of the convention and the submission of its work to Congress. There was other testimony that this impression was wide-spread in New Orleans and that it was confirmed by Dr. Dostie, R. King Cutler, and others. On arriving in Washington, however, Howell said he found that this was a mistake, though some members of Congress did tell him: " Well, get before us and we will act; we cannot promise you anything; but if your people adopt a constitution with the principles you mention embodied in it, we will entertain it as favorably as we can as individual members of Congress."[1]   None of the congressmen consulted raised any legal objections to the reconvoking of the convention. Thaddeus Stevens told him that he thought the convention had a right to assemble if it did so peaceably, that the members had a right to do what they pleased if they did not plot treason, and that if they presented a constitution, Congress, he had no doubt, would consider it and the admission of delegates under it; he himself held that " the existing government of Louisiana was a bogus government."[2]   Judge Howell, therefore, received sufficient encouragement at Washington to induce him to persevere in the movement, and on the 24th of July a telegram sent from New Orleans to the Washington correspondent of the New York Times announces: " Howell

---

[1] Report on New Orleans Riots, testimony, p. 56.

[2] The Times, July 18, said that Stevens's words to Howell were: " What! revive that d—— bogus concern of Banks'! Sir, it never was legally born; it was a bastard. I never would have anything to do with it while it was alive, and now that it is dead, it may stay in H—— where it belongs." But Stevens's own testimony does not agree with this. Report on New Orleans Riots, testimony, pp. 489, 490.

has returned with the assurance that Congress will support the Convention."[1]

It had been hoped by the ex-Confederates that Governor Wells would stand by them and refuse to approve the rump convention. It was known that even the radical Thomas J. Durant held that this convention had no legal right to reassemble, and as President Durell himself refused to preside over it, how could Wells decide to take part in such a coup d'état? But this was exactly what the governor had decided to do. He afterwards testified that he thought the convention had a right to meet, and that as he was the creature of the constitution of 1864, he had to obey its mandates.[2] The fact was that the governor had become a convert to the theory of negro suffrage, though one year before he had opposed it; and now that he saw that Congress was likely to win in its contest with the president, he was resolved to be on the winning side. Accordingly, on July 27 he issued a proclamation declaring that as R. K. Howell, president pro tem. of the convention for the revision and amendment of the constitution, had reconvoked said convention in New Orleans on July 30 and had called on him to order an election for the filling of vacancies, the said election should be held on September 3 for the choice of fifty-one delegates. He doubtless anticipated that there would be trouble, but, as we shall see, he intended to keep out of it. The action of the governor met with the bitter disapproval of the other state officials. Protests came from the lieutenant-governor, the attorney-general, the auditor, and the treasurer, while the secretary of state refused to sign the proclamation or attach to it the seal of the State.[3]

It is not surprising that the Democrats should have received with incredulity the early intimations that what they regarded as the defunct convention of 1864 was to be revived. When incredulity gave way to certitude, there were not lacking threats of resistance to such high-handed

---

[1] Report on New Orleans Riots, p. 40.
[2] Report on New Orleans Riots, testimony, p. 440.
[3] Annual Cyclopaedia, 1866, p. 453.

proceedings. Was a small band of thirty or forty men—a
mere fragment of a quorum—to be allowed to upset the
existing government, to debar from the suffrage the great
mass of the property holders of the State, and to extend
that suffrage to the ex-slaves who had never legally enjoyed
it, and who would thereby control the destinies of the State?
The events of the following years were to show that these
were no idle fears. It was a revolution such as the world
had never before witnessed. And what legal basis was
there for such a revolutionary proceeding? It was only a
resolution, passed, indeed, by the former convention, but not
valid except by a strained construction. The constitution
itself provided for its amendment by act of the legislature
and submission to the people. This provision was to be
entirely ignored, and two of the most vital measures concerning the welfare of the State—the disfranchisement of
the ex-Confederates and the enfranchisement of the blacks
—which the former convention had refused to adopt, were
to be incorporated in the organic law of the State. And by
whom was this revolution to be engineered? By a set of
men, many of whom were political adventurers, and none
of whom could claim that they any longer represented their
constituencies. If the Democrats remained supine and suffered themselves to be disfranchised by this " rump," who
knew but that Congress, as was correctly reported, would
recognize the new government and sustain the revolution by
the use of troops, the only way in which it could be sustained? The fourteenth amendment, prescribed by Congress as the condition of restoration, was not so radical a
measure as the one now proposed, for it did not confer the
suffrage on the negro or deny it to the ex-rebel. The new
constitution, it was asserted by the radicals, would be " submitted to the people ;" but it was believed that the " people "
embraced only the blacks and such whites as could prove
that they had taken no part in the rebellion; for only thus
did such a constitution stand any chance of being ratified.
The Democrats were further exasperated by the fact that

some of the leaders of the movement had once been secessionists. Hahn and Howell had held office under the Confederacy, while Cutler had even raised troops for the support of that cause. And now these men were out-heroding
Herod in denunciation of rebels.

One of the chief inciters of trouble was Dr. A. P. Dostie,[1]
a dentist from the North, who had settled in Louisiana, and
who had been auditor of the State under Banks's administration. Dostie had been a consistent Union man, but he
was regarded by the Democrats as a crack-brained fanatic.
At a mass-meeting of the radicals, black and white, held a
few days before July 30, Dostie's speech had been the most
intemperate of all, and only seemed likely to stir up trouble
between the races. The New Orleans Times of August 3
gave a part of this speech " as taken down by a citizen who
is willing to swear that it is correct." It was as follows:
"We have 300,000 black men with white hearts, also
100,000 good and true Union white men who will fight
beside the black race against 300,000 hell-hound rebels; for
now there are but two parties here; there are no ' copperheads ' now. We are 400,000 strong to 300,000, and cannot
only whip, but exterminate, the other party. Judge Abell
with his Grand Jury may indict us. Harry Hays with his
posse comitatus may be expected there; and the police with
more than 1000 men sworn in may interfere with the convention. Therefore let all brave men and not cowards come
here on Monday (July 30th). There will be no such puerile
affair as at Memphis, but if interfered with, the streets will
run with blood. The rebels say they have submitted and
accept the situation, but want you to do the work, and they
will do the voting; and will you throw over them the mantle
of charity and oblivion?" "We will! We will!" was the
unanimous response of the excited throng; to which Dostie
vehemently replied: "No, by God, we won't. We are
bound to have universal suffrage, though you have the

---

[1] Page 29.

traitor Andrew Johnson against you."[1] Ex-Governor Hahn
also spoke, saying, among other things, to the assembled
negroes, "You are as good as any white man."[2] There
was no interference on the part of the Democrats with the
speakers who uttered these sentiments, but such speeches
aroused great indignation and intensified race antipathy.
Little was now needed to precipitate a conflict; and the
ignorant negroes, thus appealed to by white leaders, dreamed
of a future in which they would dominate their ex-masters.

The ex-rebels viewed all these proceedings as actuated,
not by any real desire on the part of the conventionists to
give larger rights to the negro, but by the desire to obtain the
plums of office through negro votes. Most of the conventionists were professional politicians and doubtless had no
great leaning toward the abstract justice of universal
suffrage. But self-interest happily coincided with the glit-
tering generalities of the Declaration of Independence; and
the resolutions passed at the meeting at which Dostie spoke
declared the suffrage to be the right of black and white
alike provided they had been true to the Union.[3]

The success of this new movement, in view of the fact
that the adult negroes were more numerous than the whites
and were eager to side with the radicals, simply meant
negro supremacy, an idea to which the Democrats hoped
never to become accustomed.[4] It meant an overturning
of the whole social order. The situation was still further
aggravated by the fact that under the recent civil rights bill
(to be explained later) any negro or other Union man who
asserted that he could not get justice in the state courts
could have the case brought before United States Commissioner Shannon, and through him transferred to the United

---

[1] The friends of Dostie later denied that he used such incendiary
language, though several witnesses swore that he did. Report on
New Orleans Riots, pp. 312, 313, 350, 476, 481, 482.

[2] Reed, Life of Dostie, p. 294.

[3] Annual Cyclopaedia, 1866, subject "Louisiana," pp. 453-4.

[4] As we have seen above (page 65), the adult negroes were more
numerous than the adult whites in 1860, and the majority of the
negroes over the whites was increased by the fact that more whites
than blacks had fallen in the war.

States courts. Thus the State had lost the power to punish for crime the immense mass of freedmen at a time when recent emancipation and the appeals of white demagogues incited them to unlawful acts.

Mutterings of anger began to be heard among the more reckless citizens, and these increased as the day fixed for the meeting of the convention drew near. The correspondent of the New York Times afterwards testified that the better classes hoped that the convention would pass off quietly, but the rowdies and the men who are apt to meet in hotels and public places thought the members of the convention ought to be hanged, and expressed themselves accordingly.[1] Notices were sent anonymously to some prominent Union men advising them to leave the State. Judge Ezra Heistand, a Union man, received a communication saying: "Beware! Ten days. Duly notified. Begone!" This was signed with some cabalistic characters, and below were rough representations of a pistol, a bowie knife, and a dagger, and enclosed was a bit of floss hemp.[2] This precursor of the Ku Klux Klan was supposed to emanate from an association called the "Thugs."

The city authorities, recognizing that the meeting of this pseudo-convention was fraught with danger for the State and was likely to bring on a riot, made every effort to dissuade the radicals from attempting it. Judge Edmond Abell, himself a member of the convention of 1864, and now judge of the first district court of New Orleans, issued several charges to the grand jury calling attention to the "illegality" of the proposed assembly. The first of these, filed July 3, said to the jury that the constitution of 1864, ratified in September of that year, "is the constitution of the State," and "this constitution makes no provision for the continuance of the convention. . . . any effort upon the part of that defunct body to assemble, for the purpose of altering or amending the constitution, is subversive of good

---

[1] Report on New Orleans Riots, testimony, p. 17.
[2] *Ibid.,* p. 5.

order and dangerous to the peace of the State."[1] This charge was followed on July 23 by another to the same purport though of stronger tone. On August 2 a third charge, explaining that the riot was precipitated by the action of the conventionists, was issued. In the meantime, on July 21, the New Orleans Times announced that on the previous day the respectable portion of the citizens had been startled to learn that Judge Abell had been arrested on a charge of treason. The affidavit charged him " with treason and endangering the liberties of citizens under the Civil Rights Bill as shown in his charge to the Grand Jury." This arrest was denounced by the Times as an outrage.

The United States officer in charge of the department was General P. H. Sheridan, but as he happened to be absent in Texas he was represented in New Orleans by General Absalom Baird. The latter was notified, on July 25, by Mayor Monroe that the proposed convention was an unlawful assemblage, and that the mayor intended to disperse it by arresting the members and holding them responsible to municipal laws, "unless the Convention was sanctioned by the Military." Baird replied that if the convention were legal, it should meet; if illegal, its labors should be regarded as harmless pleasantry to which no one ought to object.[2] Besides, it was not for the mayor to decide whether it was legal or not; this should be left to the United States courts.[3]

Baird's action being unsatisfactory, Lieutenant-Governor Voorhies and the mayor informed the general, on July 28, that, as the governor could not be found, they intended to indict the members through the grand jury of the parish, and process would issue through the sheriff to make the

---

[1] Report on New Orleans Riots, testimony, p. 275.

[2] Report on New Orleans Riots, testimony, p. 442. This dilemma proposed by Baird was much praised by the radicals, but there was another alternative. The convention, though illegal, might be made legal by the sanction of Congress, and this was precisely what the Democrats feared.

[3] In such cases, however, the courts would certainly follow the decision of the legislative department of the government.

arrests. This action Baird refused to permit, saying: " Tell the Sheriff not to do it; with my view of the case, the Convention has a right to meet, and it would be a violation of their rights to arrest the members. If the Sheriff did arrest them, they would undoubtedly, failing to procure redress from the Courts issuing the writs, appeal to me for protection, and, under General Grant's order, I shall feel bound to release them, and possibly to arrest the Sheriff himself." It was, therefore, agreed that the sheriff should serve no writs without the endorsement of Baird.

Both Voorhies and Baird telegraphed to Washington for instructions. Baird, who telegraphed to Secretary Stanton, got no reply, as Stanton did not care to interfere. Voorhies, who telegraphed to President Johnson, received a despatch which read as follows:—

" Washington, July 28.

Sir:

The military will be expected to sustain, not obstruct or interfere with, the proceedings of the courts. A despatch on the subject of convention was sent to Governor Wells this morning.[1]

(Signed) ANDREW JOHNSON."

On Monday, July 30, 1866, the convention was to meet at Mechanics Institute. The hour advertised in the newspapers was 12 o'clock. Mayor Monroe, in the morning, issued a strong proclamation, calling upon the citizens not to disturb the peace and order of the city. He also ordered the police to assemble at headquarters to be ready for any emergency.

Between 10 and 11 o'clock a. m. Lieutenant-Governor Voorhies called on General Baird, taking with him the despatch he had received from the president. As Baird, however, had received no answer to his despatch, he was not willing to permit the issuance of any writs of arrest unless endorsed by him; but he agreed to order up some troops

---

[1] Report on New Orleans Riots, testimony, p. 443. The despatch sent to Wells was published in the New Orleans Times of August 7. It asked Wells by what authority he had called the convention. The governor retorted that it was not he, but Howell, who had convoked it. These communications seemed to have closed the relations between the governor and the president, who were no longer in sympathy with each other.

from Jackson barracks (three miles from Canal Street) to be used in case of a serious disturbance which the civil authorities were not strong enough to quell.[1]   As soon as Voorhies left him—which was about 12 o'clock, says Baird[2] —the latter sent a message to the barracks ordering up the troops, but for some unexplained reason Baird was laboring under the impression that the convention was to meet at 6 p. m., and not at 12 m., though this hour had been advertised in the newspapers.   Hence he did not hasten the coming of the troops until he learned that the convention had already met.   Even then there was unnecessary delay, and the troops did not reach Canal Street until 2:40 p. m., when the riot was practically over.   Had there been no misunderstanding on the part of Baird and his officers, the troops might have arrived in time to prevent some of the worst features of the riot, though this is not certain.[3]   It is clear that both Voorhies and Mayor Monroe expected the cooperation of Baird's troops, and that Baird and his officers were the only persons in New Orleans who had received the impression that the convention was to meet at 6 p. m.

Governor Wells had been in the city since Friday, but since his proclamation he had taken no active part in the proceedings.   He visited his office about the time the convention was to meet; but scenting trouble, he went to see General Sheridan.   Finding that the latter was still in Texas, the governor, though a friend informed him that his son was in the convention and might be dead, retired to his residence and remained there.   He had summoned up

---

[1] According to Voorhies's testimony before the investigating committee, some members of the convention had also requested Baird to bring up troops, but he refused their request on the ground that he did not wish to side with either party.   Baird, however, says, "No request had been made to me for them [troops]—no intimation that their presence would be desired."   Report on New Orleans Riots, testimony, pp. 237, 444.

[2] Voorhies says in his testimony that it was earlier.

[3] Voorhies testified that he sent three notes to Baird, the first as early as 10:30 a. m.; but Baird testified that he received only two, the first arriving about 12:30.   It is impossible to reconcile their testimony.   Report on New Orleans Riots, testimony, p. 237.

a spirit that he had no desire to down. We may well imagine that as he slipped away to his home he muttered the words of Antony: "Now let it work. Mischief, thou art afoot. Take thou what course thou wilt!"

The conventionists met without any opposition at 12 m. They had held a preliminary meeting at 10 a. m. at the custom-house to arrange sureties in case they were arrested. There was no fear among them of a riot; and Dr. Dostie stated to a friend that if there were trouble, he expected the military to be on the ground immediately. When they assembled at Mechanics Institute, prayer was offered by Dr. Horton, but as there was no quorum (only twenty-five being present), there was an adjournment until one o'clock. The sergeant-at-arms was sent out to drum up members who were too timid or were otherwise unwilling to come. Many of the members remained in the hall, but Judge Howell went down to the governor's room, which was in the same building.

Judge Howell had hardly gotten downstairs to the governor's room before a procession of negroes arrived in front of the Mechanics Institute with a United States flag and a drum. As this procession crossed Canal Street a white man jostled one of the negroes in the procession. The negro retorted with a blow, whereupon the white man fired at him a shot from his revolver. The procession, however, moved on. In front of the Institute it halted, and there was much hurrahing. In some way not clear a conflict was precipitated between the blacks and the whites. The testimony of Union men showed that the negroes were to some extent armed, and that the first shot was fired by a negro at a policeman who had arrested a newsboy for stirring up trouble. Soon after, the police, special and regular, who had been massed at headquarters by the mayor, came up in large numbers[1] and charged the procession. The negroes, after hurling brickbats at their opponents, took refuge in the convention hall.

---

[1] Many "specials"—ex-rebels it was said—had been sworn in.

Many of the police, becoming infuriated, fired into the assembly room, and those of the inmates that were armed returned the fire. The Rev. Dr. Horton, waving a white handkerchief, cried to the police: "Gentlemen, I beseech you to stop firing; we are noncombatants. If you want to arrest us, make any arrest you please, we are not prepared to defend ourselves." Some of the police, it is claimed, replied, "We don't want any prisoners; you have all got to die." Dr. Horton was shot and fell, mortally wounded. Dr. Dostie, who was an object of special animosity on account of his inflammatory addresses, was a marked victim. Shot through the spine, and with a sword thrust in the stomach, he died a few days later. There were about one hundred and fifty persons in the hall, mostly negroes. Seizing chairs, they beat back the police three times, and barred the doors. But the police returned to the attack, firing their revolvers as they came. Some of the negroes returned the fire, but most of them leaped from the windows in wild panic. In some cases they were shot as they came down or as they scrambled over the fence at the bottom. The only member of the convention, however, that was killed was a certain John Henderson. Some six or seven hundred shots were fired. Negroes were pursued, and in some cases were killed in the streets. One of them, two miles from the scene, was taken from his shop and wounded in the side, hip, and back. The dead and wounded were piled upon drays and carried off.[1]

While some of the police were firing indiscriminately, others of them arrested ex-Governor Hahn, W. R. Fish, and several more, and escorting them through the excited crowd, saved their lives by shutting them up in the police station. Hahn was bruised and wounded, but not seriously. His life was saved with some difficulty, for the disorderly and ruffianly element of the citizens was abroad, and clamored to get hold of the ex-governor. Many of them were drunk and infuriated. Some of the conventionists

---

[1] Report on New Orleans Riots, passim.

testified that they owed their lives to the exertions of the police who protected them, but others of the police force took no prisoners. Thomas E. Adams, chief of police, testified that he knocked down four or five of his men for acts of brutality. The only man killed on the side of the Democrats was Edgar H. Cenas, a son of Dr. Cenas, who met his death accidentally by the discharge of a policeman's pistol. Ten policemen were wounded slightly, seven of them by pistol shots, a fact which showed that their opponents were armed and prepared to meet violence with violence. On the side of the convention Dr. A. Hartsuff, of the United States army, reported to the investigating committee that he believed ten colored persons had been killed and twenty wounded, but about these he could get no absolute facts. His approved record was as follows:—

	Killed.	Wounded.
Members of the convention	1	8
White citizens loyal	2	9
Colored citizens	34	119
Policemen		10[1]
White citizens disloyal	1	
	38	146

The troops ordered from Jackson barracks arrived about 2:40 p. m. Placing himself at their head, General Baird took possession of the principal streets. The riot was practically over, but the general declared martial law to stamp out any remains of disorder.[2] He exasperated the citizens by patrolling the streets with negro troops, who, it is said, committed many petty outrages. Major-General A. V. Kantz was appointed military governor of the city, and was continued in this office for a while by General Sheridan. Mayor Monroe declared such action superfluous, and said he would not serve under a military governor. But General Kantz was not relieved and the civil officials were not re-

---

[1] The mayor and lieutenant-governor reported to the president that forty-two policemen and several citizens were either killed or wounded.

[2] All the persons arrested by the police were promptly set at liberty.

stored until some weeks later.   Even then, martial law was
"continued and enforced so far as was required for public
peace and protection of property."

When Sheridan returned from Texas, on August 1, he
telegraphed to General Grant, "Everything is now quiet, but
I deem it best to maintain a military supremacy in the city
for a few days."   He condemned the affair of July 30 as
"an absolute massacre," accusing the mayor and the police
of the city of having perpetrated it.   When, on August 4,
President Johnson telegraphed to him for details of the
affair, he gave a brief account, adding that none of the mob
had been indicted, though a number of the conventionists
had been arrested.[1]   He also declared that King Cutler,
Hahn, and others have been "political agitators, and are
bad men."   Of Governor Wells he said, "During the late
troubles he has shown very little of the man."

The universal suffrage men sent up a petition to Congress[2]
in which they called July 30 "the St. Bartholomew day of
New Orleans," and protested "against being left to the
tender mercies of the assassins who use the knife and
pistols."   A long report was also made by a committee of
officers appointed by General Baird.   It naturally upholds
the action of their superior in every particular, and finds
that there was a design on the part of the ex-rebels to crush
the convention "if the occasion offered."[3]

The most elaborate report of the riot was made by the
special committee of Congress in the winter of 1867.   It
contains about six hundred and seventy-three pages giving
the reports of the majority and the minority and the testimony upon which they were based.   One hundred and
ninety-seven witnesses were examined, some favorable and

---

[1] On August 2 General Baird, with the consent of General Sheridan, permitted Sheriff Hays to execute writs of arrest upon members of the convention.   Report on New Orleans Riots, testimony,
p. 448.   They were indicted under an old territorial law for creating a riot, but the cases seem never to have come to a trial.

[2] Annual Cyclopaedia, 1866, subject "Louisiana," p. 458.

[3] Times, October 8, 1866.   That paper condemns it as unjust, being
based on radical testimony.   Blaine praises it as non-political and
trustworthy.

some unfavorable to the convention. The majority of the committee, consisting of Thomas D. Eliot of Massachusetts and Samuel Shellabarger of Ohio, reported that "in our National history, there has been no occasion when a riot has occurred so destitute of justifiable cause, and so fiendish as that which took place in New Orleans." They justify the call of the convention on the ground that this convention in 1864 had provided for a reconvocation in case the State were not readmitted into the Union; while they ignore the fact that the president, who was authorized to recall it, refused to do so. They declare that the riot was prearranged by the mayor, the chief of police, and the lieutenant-governor, and that none of the responsible parties had been punished. They justify the action or want of action of General Baird in not getting up the troops in time. The speeches of the radicals on the Friday preceding they find were earnest and emphatic, but nothing was said that could excite any just apprehension of violence. The report then rebukes President Johnson for saying in a speech at St. Louis on the 8th of September that the reconvoking of the convention could be traced back to the radicals in Congress, "whereas no encouragement had been given by the said radicals." To sustain this position, the majority quoted a part of the testimony of Judge Howell, omitting that portion where he testified that some members of Congress said to him, "If your people adopt a constitution with the principles you mention embodied in it, we will entertain it as favorably as we can as individual members of Congress."[1] They also quoted the general denial of some of the radicals that they had encouraged the movement, but omitted those portions of Thaddeus Stevens's testimony in which he said, "I got one or two letters from him [Flanders of Louisiana], and I may have answered them," and "I recollect perfectly well saying verbally to Judge Howell that I thought they had a right to meet if they did it peaceably; . . . and that if they framed a constitution and presented it to Congress I had no

---

[1] Report on New Orleans Riots, testimony, p. 56.

doubt Congress would consider it, . . . for that I held that
their present government was a bogus government."[1]   The
report of the majority further states that the Democratic
legislature of Louisiana in January, 1866, had proposed to
the people the question of calling a constitutional convention
—a measure not provided for in the constitution of 1864,
and hence as unconstitutional as the recalled convention
in 1866 was alleged to be.[2]   The majority further stated
that, in spite of some testimony to the contrary, it had been
shown that Union men would not be safe in Louisiana if
the military and the Freedmen's Bureau were withdrawn.
Hence they recommended that a " provisional government
be established and maintained by military power until the
time has come when Louisiana is controlled by loyal men
and may be restored to her former practical relations to
the Union, without endangering its security and peace;"
and in accordance with a resolution under which it was appointed, the majority reported a bill providing for such
government.

The minority report of Boyer, of Pennsylvania, contradicted the majority report in nearly every particular.   It
declared that the " rump " convention was illegal; that the
utterances of the orators on the preceding Friday were
inflammatory; that the first shot at Mechanics Institute was
fired by a negro at a policeman; and in extenuation of the
acts of the Democrats it called attention to the murders of
negroes in Philadelphia in former years and to the much
bloodier riots of recent date in New York, resulting in the
wanton murder of several hundred negroes who had committed no offence whatever.   The general conclusions of the
report were as follows :—

---

[1] Report on New Orleans Riots, testimony, pp. 489, 490.
[2] This charge was practically admitted by the minority, though
there was really no ground for it.   The committee seemed to be
ignorant that when state constitutions provide for their revision and
not for their own destruction, the recognized and usual method of
framing a new constitution is not to reassemble a former convention, but to submit the question to the people through the existing
legislature.   Report on New Orleans Riots, testimony, p. 517.

1. The riot of July 30 was a local disturbance, originating in local circumstances of great provocation. It was not an outcropping of the rebellion, nor did it show any indication of a desire to renew hostilities with the Federal government.

2. It would be a monstrous injustice to hold the whole people of the State accountable for the acts of the few engaged in the riot, and to abrogate by act of Congress the civil government of the State now in peaceful and successful operation.

3. The incendiary speeches and revolutionary acts of the conventionists would probably have led to a riot in any city of the Union.

4. "To provoke an attack on the colored population, which was expected to be suppressed by the military before it had seriously endangered the white leaders, appears to have been part of the scheme of the conventionists. This would afford an excuse for congressional investigation, resulting in congressional legislation favoring the ultimate design of the conspirators, viz: the destruction of the existing civil government of Louisiana."

5. In no proper sense is the riot attributable to the government of Louisiana. If there be any members of the government of Louisiana in whose official or personal acts the remote causes of the riot are to be traced, the chief among them are Judge R. K. Howell, who, as usurping president of the minority of an extinct convention, headed the conspiracy to overthrow the state government which he had sworn to support, and Governor Wells, who lent to the conspiracy his official sanction, but on the day of danger deserted his post, without an effort to preserve the public peace. And if there be any members of the Federal government who are indirectly responsible for the bloody result, they are those members of the present Congress, whoever they may be, who encouraged these men by their counsels, and promised to them their individual and official support.[1]

This report of Boyer, while it had absolutely no influence

---

[1] Report on New Orleans Riots, p. 60.

on the radicals in the North, was a strong defence of the anti-conventionists. To the present writer it seems to come much nearer an unprejudiced statement than that of the majority. The two reports, however, illustrate the well-known fact that two persons hearing the same testimony may, by the rejection of certain parts and the acceptance of others, arrive at diametrically opposite conclusions and yet leave their honesty unimpeached.[1] In February, 1867, the report of the committee on the New Orleans riots was ordered by Congress to be printed. Feeling against the Louisianians was strong. No one of the Republicans seems to have considered the minority report worthy of consideration. In a debate in Congress on February 12 Shellabarger enforced his majority report by declaring that though the courts in Louisiana were open, they were under rebel control and authority, and for the purpose rather of protecting and shielding criminals than punishing them, especially when the crime was of a political character. Boyer rose to say that the statement of the gentleman was unfounded in fact, but the words of Shellabarger accorded with the humor of the majority.

A few facts must be clear to the reviewer of the testimony. Judge Howell received encouragement from certain radical congressmen, without which and the presence of Federal troops in New Orleans the convention would not have ventured to meet. The meeting was regarded by the great

---

[1] Subsequent writers have taken sides in the same manner. J. W. Burgess says, "Common sense and common honesty would hold that the convention had been finally dissolved, no matter how the wording of the resolution might be forced in the opposite direction." Reconstruction and the Constitution, p. 93. Blaine, however, says the report of the majority was corroborated by the testimony of the army officers, who were not suspected of partisanship; he condemns the riot, and coolly declares that the new constitution was to be submitted to the vote of the white people. Whatever the convention, therefore, might do would be ineffectual unless approved by the majority of the white voters of the State; hence it could not be claimed that negro suffrage was to be imposed on the State. Blaine herein ignores the fact that it was intended either to submit the constitution to Congress for ratification or to an electorate composed of negroes and Union men. Such a constitution could not be ratified by the white voters. Twenty Years, II, 237, 234.

majority of whites as unlawful and dangerous. The speeches of the orators on the preceding Friday were believed by all Democrats and many Republicans to be incendiary. General Baird made a most unfortunate error in not either bringing up troops or allowing the arrest of the conventionists. Some of the police and some of the citizens of New Orleans behaved with great brutality toward the negroes who assembled to support the convention. Yet neither the majority nor the minority report shows any real appreciation of the natural exasperation felt by the white people of New Orleans when it was found that a handful of men proposed, with the assistance of the Federal government, to establish negro supremacy in their midst by putting the heel of the ex-slave on the neck of his former master.

In about two weeks after the attempted meeting of the convention, affairs in Louisiana had fallen into their usual routine. On August 16 the New Orleans Times said: "The riot has ceased to become food for gossip. The dead body of the Convention of 1864 is lying in the Radical press. The Coroner has been notified, and will bring a disinfectant in his pocket." Unfortunately, however, for the whole South and for Louisiana in particular, President Johnson in the summer of 1866 made his notorious journey through the West—"the swing around the circle"—during which he took occasion to make a series of indignant and undignified speeches. He bitterly attacked the radicals for keeping out of Congress the representatives from the South, and accused them of encouraging the proceedings in Louisiana which resulted in the riot. However true these charges may have been, they only served to intensify the antagonism of the radicals to the presidential policy. The president vented his spleen in vain against Sumner, Stevens, and other extremists; for the fall elections showed only too plainly that the verdict of the people in the States now represented in the Union was overwhelmingly in favor of congressional, rather than presidential, reconstruction.

It was known that the president was opposed to the adoption of amendments by States that were excluded from representation in Congress; it was said that he actually advised southern legislatures to reject the fourteenth amendment. Certainly when these legislatures met in the fall of 1866 and the winter of 1867, they with one accord and by large majorities rejected that amendment.[1] The New Orleans Times argued that to adopt the amendments when representation was denied was to bow to the will of the radicals, and to barter honor, faith, and manhood for political rights and advantages.[2] But the attitude of the South was regarded by Congress as a defiance to that body, to be answered by sharp measures of repression. The fourteenth amendment was regarded as an olive branch, rejected by a stiff-necked people determined to persecute Union men and freedmen and to force[3] their way into Congress on their own terms.

The Louisianians were indignant that the radical press of New Orleans continued to defend the conventionists and to assert that Union men were not safe in Louisiana. The New Orleans Times pointed to the fact that while the radicals were saying that Union men were in danger of their lives in Louisiana, between five and ten thousand Union soldiers had settled in Louisiana. The same newspaper complained that any instance of violence in the South was seized upon by the radicals of the North as justification for extreme and unjust propositions of reconstruction,[4]

---

[1] The Louisiana legislature rejected it unanimously February 9, 1867. Governor Wells approved the rejection on the ground that the amendment was not radical enough.

[2] Times, February 1, 1867.

[3] J. R. G. Pitkin, of Louisiana, who was a secessionist in 1860, and wore the gray, was now making speeches in Philadelphia in which he declared, " The meeting of the Convention was made a pretext on the part of the Rebels to slay not only the members of that body, but all the Union men of the City." Warmoth was making similar speeches in the North. Times, October 1, 1866.

[4] W. A. Dunning calls attention to the fact that acts of violence had always been more common in the South than in the North, but that the latter section viewed them improperly as a recrudescence of rebellion to be repressed by Federal legislation. Essays on the Civil War and Reconstruction, p. 140.

though these accounts were frequently from irresponsible sources. On such reports grave senators based plans of settlement of national troubles. "But," continues the Times, "the unsettled state of our political affairs, the uncertainty of our civil condition, the discontent, and with the more sensitive and excitable, the despair as to our future, are the principal sources of such disorders as may arise in the South. Citizens, whose influence, authority, and example are very great, are prevented by their uncertain status from controlling the thoughtless and the reckless. Men who would be powerful agents in restoring good feeling and an earnest love of the Union, are driven by remorseless ostracism into indifference to public concerns and patriotic duty; into engrossment in private and selfish affairs. They are in danger of rapidly gliding into the temper of foreigners who come here to make money. There is another consideration, in view of which the reported instances of lawlessness and disloyalty in the South, upon which our sectional enemies dwell with such indignant emphasis, ought to be regarded with little significance. It is this: We boldly affirm that so radical, comprehensive, and violent revolution in the political and social condition of a people was never before attended by so little of social disorder."[1]

About the same time[2] General P. G. T. Beauregard, a beloved son of Louisiana, and representative of the best sentiment of the State, wrote a letter to the Times saying: "The South will not and should not accept the Amendments [sic] even if presented as a finality. We feel we are now at the mercy of the North. I believe the South should remain passive spectators of the struggle for power going on at the North, relying on the sober second thought and the sense of justice of both parties to protect the South." It was also held that the South should maintain by its firmness and consistency the policy of President Johnson, now regarded as the staunch friend of that section. Perhaps also

[1] Times, January 3, 1867.
[2] Times, January 11, 1867.

the Supreme Court, which had just declared the test oath
for lawyers practising in Federal courts to be unconstitutional,[1] would, as soon as a case came before it, pronounce
other reconstruction acts to be of the same character.[2] To
stand firm, therefore, "were wisdom in the scorn of
consequence."[3]

Why, it may be asked, did not Louisiana accept the status
quo and, like Tennessee, admit the negro to the suffrage?
One important reason is that in Tennessee the negroes were
in the minority, while in Louisiana they were in the
majority. Hence negro suffrage in Louisiana, where practically all negroes had been won over to the Republican side,
meant to hand over the State to the lawless class, who could
enact laws to bring about miscegenation, mixed schools, and,
in general, the social equality for which the negro organs
were clamoring.[4]

The only thing that embarrassed the radicals in Congress
in the determination to force negro suffrage on the ex-rebel
States was that in many of the Northern and Western
States the suffrage was granted only to whites,[5] even where
the negroes were in the minority. Was it fair, therefore,
to compel those Southern States to adopt it where the
negroes were in the majority—either actually, or by the

---

[1] Ex parte Milligan, 4 Wallace, 2–142.

[2] Times, March 6, 1867.

[3] Blaine says: "Governor Parsons of Alabama telegraphed him
[President Johnson] indicating that the rejection of the Fourteenth
Amendment might be reconsidered by the Alabama Legislature, if
in consequence thereof an enabling Act could be passed by Congress
for the admission of the state to representation. Johnson promptly
replied on the same day: 'What possible good can be obtained by
reconsidering the constitutional amendment? . . . There should be
no faltering on the part of those who are honest in a determination to sustain the several co-ordinate Departments of the Government in accordance with its original design.'" Twenty Years, II,
249–250.

[4] New Orleans Tribune, April 11 and 14, 1867. Yet Blaine says,
"The madness of this course on the part of Southern leaders was
scarcely less than the madness of original secession." Twenty Years,
II, 248.

[5] In five New England States negroes were allowed to vote;
New York and Connecticut permitted negroes with certain property
or other qualifications to vote; but in every other Northern State the
suffrage was restricted to white men. Blaine, Twenty Years, II, 244.

disfranchisement of ex-rebels—and thus transfer political power to the hands of the ignorant and landless classes? The radicals, however, facing this question, found an easy answer. Civil rights might be obtained in the North for the negro without the suffrage; in the South the ballot was the only means of protecting those rights. True, the smouldering rage of the South might break forth in revolutionary form, but the military rule was at hand to crush any such outburst. The South must submit even though she found herself confronted with a condition of things anomalous in the history of the world. In Rome, slaves when freed were still, though they might be equal in race, subject to the authority of their former masters. Here an inferior race was suddenly, by the accident of a civil war, to be lifted to a dizzy height of political power. By their numbers, as well as by the disfranchisement of the ex-rebels, they were to be made the ruling class, dictating laws to their former masters.[1]

---

[1] Full social rights and privileges may exist for a time without political rights as in the case of women, but full political rights will almost certainly be followed by social rights. It is inevitable where the class raised to political equality is in the majority that the legislative power will enable such a class to dictate the terms of social equality. It was this instinctive knowledge which made the whites determined to overthrow negro domination.

CHAPTER VIII.

THE RECONSTRUCTION ACTS, 1866–1867.

In the winter of 1866–67 the Republicans in Congress, flushed with their success at the polls in the preceding autumn, decided to carry out a radical program of reconstruction in the South. They entered upon the accomplishment of their plans with the greater enthusiasm because of the fact that their plans were known to be particularly objectionable to the president, whom it was now their aim to humiliate. As Thaddeus Stevens expressed it: "Though the President is Commander-in-chief, Congress is his commander; and, God willing, he shall obey. He and his minions shall learn that this is not a Government of king and satraps, but a Government of the people, and that Congress is the people."[1] If they needed further justification of their determination to subject the South to a Cromwellian method of reconstruction, they could point to the reports, appearing in radical newspapers of that section, telling of the oppression by the Democrats of the freedmen and their allies, the loyal whites. Such reports supplemented the majority report of the committee on the New Orleans riots, which was placed before Congress in February, 1867.[2]

Already on December 5, 1866, Sumner had offered a series of resolutions in the Senate, which were ordered to

---

[1] Annual Cyclopaedia, 1867, subject "Congress," p. 206. The president, on the other hand, insisted that the constitution is the organic law of the people, even against Congress. Ibid., p. 654.

[2] While the Republicans had a sufficient majority in Congress to pass measures over the president's veto, the radical Stevens was much disgruntled at the lack of unanimity in the House toward the measures he advocated. He derided the "Babel which has been produced by the intermingling of secessionists, rebels, pardoned traitors, hissing Copperheads, and apostate Republicans." Annual Cyclopaedia, 1867, subject "Congress," p. 205.

be printed.   They defined in clear-cut terms what was to be
the policy of Congress: (1) Executive reconstruction is
usurpation.   Reconstruction must be conducted by Congress.   (2) New governments in the South must be
fashioned according to the requirements of a Christian com-
monwealth, so that order, tranquility, education, human
rights, shall prevail within their borders.   (3) In determin-
ing what is a republican form of government, Congress must
follow implicitly the definition supplied by the Declaration
of Independence; and in the practical application of this
definition it must, after excluding all disloyal persons, take
care that new governments shall be founded on the two
fundamental truths therein contained: (a) that all men are
equal in rights, and (b) that all just governments stand only
on the consent of the governed.[1]   In explanation of the fact
that the consent of the disloyal was not necessary, Stevens
explained that disloyal persons were malefactors.   As the
disloyal "malefactors" might prove to be more numerous
in some Southern States than the loyalists, it was, of course,
necessary to guard against opposition in carrying out this
program by subjecting the South to military rule.

Some members of Congress maintained that it was wrong
thus to make negro suffrage the test of true republicanism
in the South and not in the North, Le Blond, of Ohio,
suggesting that as his State did not give suffrage to negroes,
it should be put out of the Union.   Boutwell, of Massachusetts, however, answered this pertinent question by
declaring that though Congress was not able to make Ohio
truly republican, it should exercise that power wherever it
could.   Thus the South could become a model after which
the North might fashion herself.   The Union Democrats
ingeniously insinuated that the maintenance of a republican
form of government in the South had been confused by the
radicals with the maintenance of the Republican party in
power.   This insinuation was either ignored or answered to
the effect that the Republican party, in supporting the

---

[1] There was a fine irony in quoting the father of Democracy
against the Democrats of the South.

Union, had stood for republican government, while the Southern Democrats, in attempting its overthrow, no longer represented anything but treason and the suppression of equal rights.[1] Moreover, if negro suffrage was to be enforced in the South, it was only because that section had rejected the fourteenth amendment.

In accordance with Sumner's resolutions, and in spite of the able veto messages of President Johnson, the famous— or in the eyes of the Democrats the infamous—acts of reconstruction were passed by Congress in the spring of 1867. The first, under date of March 2, was, in substance, as follows: As no legal state governments or adequate protection of property existed in ten of the Southern States, these States should be divided into military districts, subject to the military authority of the United States, and under command of an officer of the army appointed by the president. This commanding officer should protect property and life and punish insurrection or disorder, using for this purpose the existing civil courts or, at his discretion, military tribunals.[2] It was further provided that when any one of these States should have framed a new constitution in a convention composed of delegates elected by voters without distinction of color or race, except such as had been disfranchised for participation in rebellion or for felony, and when this constitution should provide that the elective franchise should be enjoyed by all having the qualifications given above, and when such constitution should have been

---

[1] It was especially distasteful to Stevens that in South Carolina 200,000 whites should rule 400,000 blacks.

[2] In his veto the president called attention to the fact that in the recent Milligan case the Supreme Court had decided that martial law cannot exist where the courts are open and in the proper exercise of their jurisdiction. Annual Cyclopaedia, 1867, subject "Public Documents," p. 655. But Stevens denounced this decision as infamous, "dangerous to the lives and liberties of the loyal men of the country," and urged that on account of the decision the reconstruction act should be immediately passed. Ibid., p. 210. Perhaps Stevens also held that the Milligan case did not apply to the South because there were no lawful governments there, or at least only provisional ones. By others it has been held that the Milligan case only decided that the president had no right to establish such military tribunals.

approved by the majority of voters and by Congress, and when the legislature of such State should have adopted the fourteenth amendment and the said amendment should have become a part of the Constitution of the United States, then the said State should be entitled to representation in Congress: provided that no person excluded from holding office by said fourteenth amendment should be a member of the convention or vote for any member. Finally, until representation in Congress should be granted to the rebel States, their existing civil governments should be deemed provisional and subject to modification or removal by the Federal government. A few weeks later, on March 23, for fear that the rebel States might not accept these drastic measures, preferring to remain without representation in Congress, a still more strenuous act was passed. This supplementary act took the initiative out of the power of the State and placed it in the hands of the commanding general in each district. It declared that before September 1 of the current year each general in his district must hold a registration of persons qualified to vote (of undoubted loyalty), and then proceed to carry out the provisions of the preceding act.

When this act was put in force, however, it was found necessary to legislate still further against the obstacles which the president and his legal advisers were placing in the way of the " thorough " process of government instituted by the radical Congress. Accordingly, by a supplementary act of July 19, it was provided among other things: first, that in the removal of state officers the commanding general should be subject to the disapproval, not of the president, but only of the general of the armies of the United States, thereby placing Grant above his commander-in-chief, Johnson; second, that the oath of a person swearing that he was entitled to register should be rejected by the board if it thought proper, while if any persons qualified to register should fail to do so, their names should be placed on the registration list by the board, a provision which made the board absolute master of the situation since in its discretion it could go behind the solemn oath of the would-be voter and exclude him, while registering others who had not applied; third, that no pardon or amnesty of the president should entitle any one to vote who was previously disqualified, and that no district commander should be bound in his action by any opinion of any civil officer of the United States—a provision which was added because the attorney-general of the United States had given the president two opinions on the first act which promised to interfere seriously with its execution.

Having thus nullified the effect of executive pardon as well as of any other act of interference on the part of the president or his civil advisers, Congress felt that its hands were free to work its will on the South. It would, moreover, cap the climax of its power by the impeachment of a president who had vetoed these bills, and who, in its eyes, had been guilty of other crimes and misdemeanors. Rebellion in the executive chair and rebellion in the South should be crushed at the same time.[1]

Let us briefly consider how these laws affected the people of Louisiana. During the winter of 1867 the General Assembly had been encouraged by the firm attitude of the president to resist the measures of reconstruction proposed by Congress. It was held that the president was right in declaring that the Congress at Washington, as long as the South was unrepresented, was no real Congress; it was merely a rump parliament. When the fourteenth amendment was brought before the legislative body for ratification, the members were not pleased to learn from the governor's message that he regarded the amendment as an inadequate measure, and that he should be satisfied only with the granting of equal rights to all. The legislature, as we have seen, promptly rejected the amendment by a unanimous vote (February 9), and suggested that Governor Wells be impeached. In view of the threatening attitude

---

[1] On March 2, the same day on which the reconstruction bill was passed, the judiciary committee made a preliminary report which led to the impeachment of the president.

of Congress, the New Orleans Times declared the rejection of the amendment to be "an heroic act."

The passage of the first reconstruction act three weeks later was not unexpected, and was received with calmness by the Democrats and with satisfaction by the governor and those who sympathized with him. Wells immediately declared that an election for aldermen in New Orleans should be subject to the provisions of the new act. The Times denied the right of the governor to interfere, saying that such action belonged to the military officials. The commanding general, Sheridan, took up the matter, and decided that on account of the troublous condition of affairs the election should be postponed.

The Times of March 17, echoed by the country papers, advised the people of the State to accept as gracefully as they could all the provisions of the reconstruction program; only in this way would they escape military rule and a possible confiscation of property.[1] As negro suffrage was now seen to be inevitable, Duncan F. Kenner, a prominent politician of the State, issued an appeal to the people not to remain inactive, as some proposed, but to accept the negro as a voter, and try to influence him to vote in the interests of the South. A few days later this appeal was followed by an open letter from that distinguished son of Louisiana, General P. G. T. Beauregard, also counselling submission and taking what eventually proved to be a very optimistic view of the situation. "If the suffrage of the negro," he said, "is properly handled and directed, we shall defeat our adversaries with their own weapons. The negro is Southern born. With a little education and a property qualification, he can be made to take an interest in the affairs of the South, and in its prosperity. He will side with the whites." About the same time, March 18, General James Longstreet, the distinguished Confederate leader, who had taken up his residence in New Orleans, published

---

[1] Thaddeus Stevens favored confiscation and criticised the president for restoring confiscated property. *Annual Cyclopaedia*, 1867, subject "Congress," p. 235.

two open letters in which, also, submission to congressional legislation was urged. " We are a conquered people," he said. " Accept therefore, the terms offered by the conqueror. Our people desire that Constitutional Government should be reestablished, and the only means to accomplish this is to comply with the requirements of the recent congressional legislation." He added that all should return to their allegiance in good faith, or leave the country.

So far Longstreet's utterances received the approval of prominent Confederates; but in the following June the Times accused him of having given " his adhesion to a party whose whole policy seemed to be one of vindictive persecution and abuse of his [Longstreet's] late Confederates in arms." Longstreet answered rather tartly that " the war was made upon republican issues, and it seemed fair that the settlement should be made accordingly." This confusion of the Republican party with the radicals then in control was sharply attacked by the Times, which pronounced Longstreet's position to be a false one, and added that the general was already claimed as a convert by a portion of the Republican party, and was spoken of as a possible United States senator.[1] Longstreet, now alienated from his old friends, permitted without a protest a radical newspaper of New Orleans to say of him: " The great crimes of his life have been partially atoned for by the sincerest repentance that has yet been brought to light."[2] Among the prominent Confederates, however, Longstreet seems to have been alone in " going over to the enemy."

---

[1] Times, June 8, 1867.

[2] The Republican, August 9, 1867. His conversion was rewarded with the office of surveyor of customs (1867–1873). Longstreet, in June, 1867, wrote to General Lee asking his approval of his (Longstreet's) position; but Lee answered: " I cannot think the course pursued by the dominant political party the best for the interests of the country, and therefore cannot say so, . . . This is the reason why I could not comply with the request in your letter." Jones, Reminiscences of Lee, p. 228. Longstreet's wife, in her account of this period, said that to stand up against public opinion in New Orleans " was the noblest act of her husband's life." " By accepting Federal office, he lost a good business in cotton and insurance." Perhaps there is room for an honest difference of opinion.

His defection aroused much indignation; his desertion of his people seemed so much the worse that it came in their critical hour of distress, when wise and faithful leaders were sorely needed.

Two events soon came to modify the earlier optimistic views of the ex-Confederates. The first was that Sheridan began almost immediately to show the mailed hand. On March 27 he removed from office Attorney-General A. S. Herron, Mayor John T. Monroe, and Judge Edmund Abell, appointing in their places B. F. Lynch, Edward Heath, and W. W. Howe, who were all believed to hold radical views. Before the indignation caused by this legal but drastic measure had subsided, Sheridan ordered his registration appointees to exclude from registration all those about whose rights there was any doubt. The result, according to the Times,[1] was that more than one half the white citizens qualified under the law to register were refused the privilege, under one pretext or another, while every negro was immediately accepted. " Such a miserable farce," added that journal, " such trampling on all law, decency, and right, will arouse further hostility." The second fact that now became patent was that the negroes now registered would vote, not with their old masters, but with the party which had conferred on them the suffrage. By July 26 the number of blacks registered was 78,230, while the number of whites was only 41,166. Moreover, the negroes had already been organized against the whites in reconstruction clubs, loyal leagues, lodges, and " Companies of the Grand Army."[2]

Democratic optimism now changed to pessimism. The white radicals were triumphant; the negroes were jubilant. Now, at last, they believed that they had reached the promised land. They were to vote, to hold office, to make laws. Nay, more: " We want," said the negro organ, " to

---

[1] April 21, 1867.

[2] The New Orleans Republican, November 17, 1867, announced that the Republican party in Louisiana had 94 clubs and 57,300 members. The Loyal League, which was merely a branch of the Union League of the North, was elaborately organized, and held the negroes to a stern discipline.

ride in any conveyance, to travel on steamboats, eat in any steamboat, dine at any restaurant, or educate our children at any school."[1]   On July 4 the orator of the day, J. R. G. Pitkin, encouraged them to believe that their dream would be realized; for after commending negro suffrage, he added, "But if my colored brother and myself touch elbows at the polls, why should not his child and mine stand side by side in the school room?"   Such utterances confirmed the Democrats in their belief that political equality was the first step toward social equality.

A system of "star" cars, by which the blacks were separated from the whites, existed in New Orleans at this time, and on May 5 the presidents of the street railways called on General Sheridan to know if they could obtain his assistance in confining the negroes to the "star" cars. Sheridan refused to issue any instructions on the subject. Two days later some negroes forced their way into the cars for whites, and nearly precipitated a riot. Two weeks later the Times announced that the system of "star" cars had been abandoned because neither Sheridan nor the mayor would protect the drivers in enforcing it. The former, it was said, refused to act because he was unwilling to enforce the rules against his own negro troops. After this small triumph, the negroes began to demand mixed schools and a share of public offices. Those Republicans who, like Hahn and Cutler, did not immediately respond to these demands were bitterly denounced by the negroes for wishing to get into office by negro votes, while refusing offices to their constituents.

The Democrats were now destitute of hope. It looked as if the State was surely to be handed over to the blacks, registered in large numbers and controlled by radical leaders. The first step, it was believed, would be that bugbear of the South—mixed schools, to be followed, perhaps, by a law authorizing the intermarriage of the two races. To add insult to injury, the negro journal, The Tribune,[2] gloated

[1] Tribune, April 14, 1867.
[2] April 17, 1867.

over the discomfiture of the Democrats, declaring in one of its leading articles that the whites were now subservient to the ex-slaves. "It is certainly a great triumph," it said, "for us to see proud planters, haughty chevaliers, humiliating themselves to the point of flattering their former slaves and crouching to their very feet. The deeper their bow, the more their detestation and desire for revenge are growing in their bosoms." Such utterances, though no facts to support them were given, naturally widened the breach between the two races. They excited all the more indignation because the negro, whatever his acts, was safe from prosecution in the civil courts. Through the action of the civil rights act and the Freedmen's Bureau he was now under the aegis of the Federal government, while the white Democrat felt he had little chance of justice when haled before a military commission or one of the bureau courts,[1] for these courts, intended for the protection of the negro, were now to exercise their jurisdiction at the discretion of the Federal authorities.[2]

One incident, however, at this time came to gratify the sorely tried Democrats. By order of June 3 Sheridan removed from office Governor Wells, as "an impediment to the faithful execution of the Act of March 2nd," and appointed in his place Thomas J. Durant. On the same day he telegraphed to Secretary Stanton that Wells was a political trickster and a dishonest man, and that his conduct had been "as sinuous as the mark left in the dust by the movement of a snake." As this was also the Democratic estimate of the governor's character, there was no little rejoicing over his downfall, and the Times cleverly punned: "All's well that ends *Wells.*" Lieutenant-Governor Voorhies, a staunch Democrat, was not disturbed for a year longer. If the

---

[1] In 1866 the bureau courts had been given up except in parts of Virginia, Louisiana, and Texas. Dunning, Civil War and Reconstruction, p. 141.

[2] The Times of April 13, 1867, said, "J. W. Walker, having killed a negro in St. John the Baptist Parish, and the civil authorities having, it is believed, connived at his escape, he will be tried before a military commission in New Orleans."

powers of his office had not been merely nominal, he would have done more to aid the ex-rebels. As much as he could, he exerted himself to mitigate the severity of Reconstruction. For reasons best known to himself, Durant refused to accept the office of governor, and Sheridan appointed B. F. Flanders. His duties, under Sheridan's dictatorship, seem to have been merely nominal. At first Wells refused to vacate his office, and appealed to President Johnson, saying that the quarrel between him and Sheridan was merely personal.[1] Sheridan promptly sent General Forsyth to oust Wells and install Flanders. A week later, Stanbery, attorney-general of the United States, gave his opinion that the commanding general had no right to remove state officials without a trial; but, as we have seen, the supplementary act of July 19 instructed district commanders to pay no attention to the opinions of any civil officers of the United States.

Thus confirmed in his action, Sheridan, on the first of August, dismissed the board of aldermen and assistant aldermen of New Orleans, on the ground that they impeded the execution of the reconstruction acts and had brought the credit of the city into a disorganized condition.[2] Their places were filled by men some of whom were known to possess business capacity and integrity. Others of the new appointees, however, were negroes—a recognition on Sheridan's part of the colored element in the city which numbered about sixty thousand. In the following September this council appointed four assistant recorders, three of whom were colored, and two city physicians, both of whom were colored.[3] Such a departure from the old order of things excited some indignation among the whites, and gratified the blacks proportionately.[4]

On the 17th of August the district commander ordered

---

[1] It concerned the appointment of levee commissioners.
[2] There was much fiscal confusion in New Orleans, the city paper money amounting to three and a half million dollars.
[3] Times, September 12, 1867.
[4] In spite of disparity in numbers, Sheridan had registered about an equal number of blacks and whites in the city, that is, 14,845 whites, and 14,805 blacks.

that an election should take place on September 27 and 28,
to determine whether a constitutional convention should be
called. The number of registered voters was declared to be
127,639;[1] and these were to vote on the same date for
98 members to constitute the convention in case the
majority of the voters decided that the said convention
should be held. It was further provided that to make the
election valid, the votes cast must constitute a majority of
those registered.

A few days later the New Orleans papers announced that
General Sheridan had been relieved from his command by
President Johnson, and that his place would be filled by
General Winfield S. Hancock.[2] Before his departure from
the fifth district on September 5, Sheridan wrote to Grant
that the work of reconstruction in Louisiana had met with
no opposition from the people, but was opposed by the
press and by office-seekers. As far as the press was concerned, this statement was subsequently denied by the
Picayune and the Times, which declared that they differed
from Sheridan, but that they had urged the people to
submit. Commenting on his departure, however, the Republican said that he ought to have turned out more rebels,
and that he had left the city in a deplorable condition,
financial, political, and sanitary. The same paper now accused the Democratic papers of keeping severely silent on
the subject of voting, while a few months before they had
urged their people to register. This accusation seems to
have been just. General Wade Hampton, Ben Hill, and
other prominent Southerners, seeing how the reconstruction
laws were being administered, had already begun to advise
opposition to every organization under these laws, and the

----

[1] Of this number 82,907 were blacks.
[2] The president's dislike of Sheridan was well known, and his
action in this case offended General Grant, who admired Sheridan
greatly. As Hancock was in accord with the president's views, his
appointment was received in the North with marked disapproval.
Hancock did not assume charge until November 29, the temporary
appointees being General Charles Griffin, and after his death General Joseph A. Mower.

Democratic newspapers began to hope that enough of those who had registered would stay at home on election day to prevent the Republicans from getting the necessary "majority of registered voters."

The Times of September 1 even ventured to issue a warning to the negroes who, by the enforcement of the reconstruction acts, had now been put in control of the State. "In a few years," it said, "the white vote in the State will more than double that of the colored, and the sins which the colored man now commits against equal rights and manhood suffrage will be remembered against him." The negroes, however, trusting to a continuance of military rule and the supremacy of the Republican party, recked little of such warnings. Their opportunity of obtaining a share in the government and all other rights had come; and whether their old masters were disfranchised or not, they were eager to seize it.

CHAPTER IX.

RESTORATION OF LOUISIANA TO THE UNION.

The election to decide the question of holding a constitutional convention and to choose the delegates for the same took place on the appointed days, September 27 and 28. It passed off quietly except for a small riot in Jefferson City. The negroes, who never before in Louisiana had been legally entitled to vote, came out in large numbers, but the white citizens, especially in New Orleans, generally abstained from voting, with the forlorn hope that this action would defeat the plans of the Republicans, which required the majority of the registered voters to vote. In this they were disappointed. The registered voters, as we have seen, amounted to 127,639, of whom 82,907 were blacks. The vote for the convention was 75,083, with only 4006 against it.[1] Of the 98 delegates elected, 49 were whites and 49 were negroes, a fair division previously agreed upon. All but 2 were Republicans.

On November 23 the convention met in the hall of the Mechanics Institute; but there was no repetition of the scenes which marked the opening of the rump convention of 1866. The Democrats bided their time, hoping that once the State was restored to the Union and the Federal troops were withdrawn, it would be possible for them again to get possession of the government. They little dreamed how long they would have to wait. The assembly was declared by the Republican to be a truly representative body. " The Convention of 1861," it added, " had taken the State out of the Union; this one would restore it." Many of the negro members were free men of color, of better character

---

[1] The Times claimed that 13,000 voters had been disfranchised by the construction put upon the act of Congress. Cox estimates the number at 40,000. Three Decades, p. 547.

and of more intelligence than were to be found in subsequent political bodies in Louisiana; others had once tilled the soil as slaves. As president the convention chose Judge J. G. Taliaferro[1] of Catahoula parish, and then entered upon a session which lasted till March 9 of the following year, nearly three and one half months.

At first there was no great harmony among the delegates. Dr. G. M. Wickliffe, a dentist from Clinton, Louisiana, who had once edited an anti-abolition journal, but who had now swung around and, like most converts, held extreme views, moved in the early days of the convention that all subordinate officers of this assembly should be drawn equally from the two races. This motion was defeated, 47 to 38, by the efforts of the more conservative Republicans, who declared that such action would place race above merit. Equal rights to all (Unionists), with no favoritism even to the negro, was their shibboleth. They were supported by the Republican, which declared Wickliffe to be a demagogue, and condemned him and the organ of the negroes, the Tribune, for trying to create distinction between the races. If special favors were granted to negroes because they were negroes, the conservatives of the North would be prejudiced against the constitution about to be framed; and such action might seem to justify the contention of the friends of the administration that Louisiana had become a negro colony, and that the whole South was to be Africanized.

When about this time Ohio voted down a proposition to grant the suffrage to the few negroes in that State,[2] the Republican enraged the Tribune by saying that the defeat of the measure in Ohio was due to the political conduct of the

---

[1] As Taliaferro had opposed immediate secession in the convention of 1861, the Republican described him now as the old grayhaired Union hero of secession—the one wise man in an age of madness.

[2] The Picayune, December 8, 1867, with evident satisfaction, announced that the three States of Ohio, Kansas, and Minnesota had recently rejected negro suffrage, the vote in Ohio being 255,-340 to 215,937; in Kansas, 16,114 to 7591, and in Minnesota 28,759 to 5114. In 1868 Minnesota gave a majority for negro suffrage, but in 1870 the State contained only 246 adult negro men.

enfranchised negroes in Louisiana, and that unless the latter changed their conduct, the Republicans as a party would be defeated and the suffrage of the negroes would be lost.[1] The more radical negroes, however, could not see how their conduct in Louisiana could affect distant Ohio. They knew that they numbered twice as many voters as the whites, and they argued that they should have at least half of the offices. Had not the two races equal representation in the convention? Was not this cry of saving the Republican party merely a skillfully devised excuse for filling all the offices with white Republicans? If this were to be the only result of the disfranchisement of the Democrats and the giving of the ballot to the negro, that is, to hand over the spoils to the Republican whites, the Tribune was prepared to enter a protest. Its attitude might have found favor with those who wished to use the negro vote had not the ablest leader of the colored element in the convention, Pinckney Benton Stewart Pinchback[2]—himself a chocolate-hued orator of no mean ability, and destined to hold high office in the State— now opposed Wickliffe, and taken sides with the Republican. Offices must be awarded with reference not to race but to education and general ability.

This contention having been settled on safe lines, the convention proceeded to frame such a constitution as would meet with the approval of the dominant party in Congress. It was to be based on the general principle that loyal Republicans should be protected for all time against the ex-rebels, who had tried to break up the Union, and who had not repented of their wicked folly. This view was expressed by the Republican as follows: "As for us, we would rather see another war, another revolution, had rather see every rebel from the Potomac to the Gulf proscribed, disen- franchised, their property confiscated, and every mother's son of them stripped naked and sent out into the world as

---

[1] Times, October 16, 1867.
[2] Pinchback was the son of a white man, who had carefully edu- cated him in Cincinnati. He was born in Macon, Georgia, in 1837. In 1867 he was made inspector of customs in New Orleans.

they were born than the right of suffrage taken away from the loyal people of the South."[1]   This journal did not add, but it was clearly understood, that unrepentant rebels, while not permitted to vote or hold office, should be duly taxed for the support of Republican government.

In the meantime, the Tribune continued to air its grievances.   The Times, on January 5, 1868, with great gusto, quoted " this organ of the black and tan Convention " as declaring: " The Republican party in Louisiana is headed by men, who for the most part are devoid of honesty and decency, and we think it right that the country should know it.   The active portion of the party in Louisiana is composed largely of white adventurers, who are striving to be elected to office by black votes. . . . Some of these intend, if elected, to give a share of office to colored men.   We admit that, but they will choose only docile tools, not citizens who have manhood."   " The white adventurers," or " carpet-baggers," as they now began to be called by the Democratic papers, did not enjoy these attacks, for such a defection boded ill for their future supremacy.   They showed a bitter feeling against Dr. Roudanez, the negro proprietor of the Tribune, for his failure to support the Republican party.[2]

While this controversy over party loyalty was going on, the convention was discussing the provisions of the new constitution.   While so doing, however, it was found necessary to make arrangements for raising a revenue and paying the expenses of the members.   The Democratic legislature had adjourned in the preceding March, and as yet there was no Republican legislature to take its place.   The state treasury was declared by the governor to be bankrupt; there was no money to pay the state debt or the salaries of the state

---

[1] Republican, December 3, 1867.
[2] The Tribune was not a financial success.   Roudanez made a public statement saying that he had sunk $35,500 in the paper in order to keep up an honest organ of the radical party in Louisiana. It was finally suspended in April, 1868.   The Tribune seems to have been revived later, for it is mentioned as appearing in 1869 while the committee on Louisiana elections was meeting.   41st Cong., 2d sess., H. Mis. Doc. No. 154, pt. I, p. 768.

officers. The levees were out of repair; many plantations had been overflowed; the negroes were discontented, and unwilling to work in times of such political upheaval; and the crops were almost a failure. Accordingly, the convention whose function was to frame a constitution degenerated for the time being into a legislature, and passed a stringent law laying a tax of one mill on all property for expenses of the convention, with a penalty of twenty-five per cent. for default. It also decreed that warrants issued by the convention to pay the mileage and the per diems of members should be received for taxes.

The Times protested against this assumption of the taxing power, but the state auditor recognized the authority of the convention. It was feared by the conventionists that there would be resistance to the payment of this tax, and that General Hancock, who had taken command of the fifth district on November 29, and who had already shown a strong leaning toward the president's interpretation of the reconstruction acts, might support the resistance. The commanding general, who had restored some officials removed by his predecessor, General Mower, and who had revoked Sheridan's order permitting negroes, contrary to state law, to sit on juries,[1] now announced that in civil cases the administration of justice belonged to the regular courts, and not to the commanding general. "Arbitrary power," he added, "such as I have been urged to assume, has no existence here. It is not found in the Laws of Louisiana or of Texas; it cannot be derived from any acts of Congress; it is restrained by a Constitution, and prohibited from action in many particulars." While disclaiming judicial functions in civil cases, however, Hancock added that it would be improper for him to anticipate any illegal interference on the part of the courts, but that whenever a case arose for the interposition of the powers vested in him by the acts of

---

[1] In the United States district court Judge Durell decided that his juries should be drawn without distinction of color, but in the state courts Judge W. W. Howe, a prominent Republican, sided with Hancock.

Congress, he would preserve law and order. This Delphic utterance left the convention in some doubt as to its position; and on January 9 Judge Taliaferro told the convention that unless Hancock would prevent the interference of the courts, the mill tax could not be collected. This fear, however, was groundless, and though the tax was collected with some difficulty, there seems to have been no actual resistance.

On March 9, 1868, the convention, having completed the constitution, adjourned. The Rev. Josiah Fisk, who was invited to close the proceedings with prayer, pleased his hearers with a quasi-political invocation, saying, among other things: "Bless the President of these United States. Enable him to pause in his career of vice and folly. May he cease from doing evil, and learn to do right!" The constitution on which Fisk called down the blessing of heaven, though it was longer by six pages than that of 1864, filled only about twenty-seven pages—just half the length of the organic law which closed the period of reconstruction in 1879. The chief provisions which differentiated it from the constitution of 1864 were as follows.

First, as it was intended to furnish to the negro that equality with the loyal whites which the organic law of 1864 had fought shy of, it recited portions of the Declaration of Independence, with slight modifications of language suitable to the existing circumstances, and with a practical application of principles which would have shocked the author of that immortal document. Thus, after declaring that "all men are created free and equal," the constitution provided that all persons should enjoy equal rights and privileges upon any conveyance of a public character. All places of business or of public entertainment, or for which any license is required, should be deemed places of a public character, and should be opened to the accommodation and patronage of all persons without discrimination on account of race or color. This article, proposed by Pinchback, was adopted by a vote of 58 to 16.

Second, in order to prevent future secession, it was provided that all persons born or naturalized in the United
States and resident for one year in Louisiana were citizens
of the State, and that allegiance to the United States was
paramount to the allegiance owed to the State.

Third, representation in both houses was to be in proportion to the total population, instead of in proportion to
the number of qualified voters, as in 1864.

Fourth, no public schools or institutions of learning should
be established exclusively for any race. By a special clause,
the University of Louisiana, in all its departments, was
thrown open to both races.

Fifth, and most important of all, was the new suffrage
law, the most stringent, perhaps, in its disfranchising clauses
to be found in the constitutions of all the Southern States.[1]
It permitted every adult male citizen of the United States,
resident in Louisiana for one year, to vote, except (a) persons convicted of crime or under interdict; (b) those who
had held any office for one year or more under the so-called
Confederate States; (c) registered enemies of the United
States; (d) leaders of guerilla bands during the rebellion;
(e) those who, in the advocacy of treason, wrote or published newspaper articles or preached sermons during the
rebellion; (f) those who voted for or signed the ordinance
of secession in any State. As a premium on perjury, it
was added that no one thus excepted should vote or hold
office in the State until he signed a certificate acknowledg-
ing the rebellion to have been morally and politically wrong
and that he regretted any aid or comfort given thereto. He
could be excused, however, from furnishing this certificate
if, prior to January 1, 1868, he had favored the execution
of the reconstruction acts, and openly and actively assisted
the loyal men of the State in their efforts to restore Louisiana to her place in the Union. This severe measure,
which seemed to disfranchise certain classes of unrepentant
rebels forever, was passed by a vote of 44 to 30. A number

---

[1] Dunning, Civil War and Reconstruction, p. 197.

of negroes voted against it; among others, Pinchback, who said that he did so because he firmly believed that two thirds of the colored men of the State did not desire disfranchisement to such an extent.[1]   Somewhat later he signed the constitution, but, with three other members, filed a protest against this clause, saying, " We are now, and ever have been, advocates of universal suffrage, it being one of the fundamental principles of the Radical Republican party."[2]   Verily, the radicals were out-heroding Herod.

Sixth, an oath was prescribed, even for members of the legislature, that they should accept the civil and political equality of all men, and should agree not to attempt to deprive any person of such equality on account of race, color, etc.

Seventh, all the labor laws passed by the Democratic legislature of 1865 were declared to be null and void.

Eighth, in case the constitution was not adopted, the convention might be recalled by a majority of the members. The constitution was finally signed by eighty-five members. Several members were absent, and five who were present[3] refused to attach their signatures, chiefly because of the disfranchising and civil rights clauses.

The days appointed for taking the popular vote on the constitution were April 16 and 17, 1868. Before these dates came around, however, General Hancock, who had won great popularity among the Democrats by his conservative course, was removed from office at his own request. The occasion was this: he had removed a city recorder, and when the city council provided for the election of another, he removed those who had so voted—two whites and seven negroes. General Grant was applied to, and as he resented the president's removal of Sheridan and the appointment of Hancock, he now suspended Hancock's order, asked for a full report, and finally restored the deposed members. Whereupon General Hancock, feeling that he could no

---

[1] Journal of Convention, 1867–8, p. 259.
[2] Journal of Convention, 1867–8, p. 293.
[3] These were Cooley, Crawford, Dearing, Ferguson, and Harrison.

longer occupy his position with dignity, asked to be relieved.[1] His request was granted, and General J. J. Reynolds took his place for a few days. Reynolds's successor was Major-General R. C. Buchanan, who had been an assistant commissioner of the Freedmen's Bureau. Verily the road to reconstruction which the State had to travel was hard and uncertain. The uncompromising and radical Sheridan had been removed by Johnson; the liberal and magnanimous Hancock was persona non grata to Grant. Government from a distance is generally bad government, and especially bad when no consistent policy is followed.

Louisiana, which in the eyes of Congress had not been restored to her proper relations with the Union, was now to have the remarkable experience of voting for state officers on the same days on which she voted for or against a constitution the acceptance of which by Congress was to restore her to a place in the Union. But Congress was in a hurry, and there was nothing to do but to submit to the anomaly. To facilitate matters still more, General Buchanan, on March 25, 1868, issued an order that a recent act of Congress (of March 12) should apply in the approaching election, namely, that the said election should be decided by the majority of the votes cast, without reference to the number registered.[2] He also ordered that no negroes should be discharged for voting the Republican ticket, and that all unfairness at the polls would be prevented by the presence of the military. The election passed off quietly. The constitution was ratified by a vote of 51,737 to 39,076. At the same time, H. C. Warmoth, who had claimed an election as delegate from the territory of Louisiana in 1865, was chosen governor over J. G. Taliaferro by a vote of 64,941

The Times fully approved the course of Hancock, but in January, 1868, forty-three members of the convention had signed a petition asking Congress to remove him as an " impediment to reconstruction."

[2] This was to prevent the stay-at-homes from defeating the constitution as had happened in Alabama on February 4. Congress made the act of March 11 retroactive, and held that the constitution of Alabama was legally ratified. Burgess, Reconstruction and the Constitution, p. 153.

to 38,046.[1]   The other officers of the State were: lieutenant-governor, Oscar J. Dunn (colored); secretary of state, George E. Bovee; attorney-general, Simeon Belden; auditor, G. M. Wickliffe; treasurer, Antoine Dubuclet; and superintendent of education, Rev. T. W. Conway.

In the neighboring State of Mississippi, two months later, the Democrats were so well organized, and persuaded so large a number of negroes to vote against the reconstruction constitution, that they succeeded in defeating the adoption of that instrument by a vote of 7629.   In Louisiana, however, at the spring election, the Democrats discussed the matter, and concluded that it would not be worth while to nominate a full state ticket in opposition to the two Republican factions, though they managed to elect a minority of the members of the General Assembly.   In New Orleans, moreover, J. W. Conway, a Democrat, was elected mayor. The incumbent, Heath, denied that municipal elections were authorized by the election ordinance of the constitution, and refused to yield the office to Conway.   He was promptly arrested by General Buchanan, and compelled to surrender the keys.   He then brought an action of quo warranto against Conway.   It was of no effect.   General Grant having approved Buchanan's action, the court was informed that a decision in favor of the plaintiff would be of no avail, and proceedings on the case were dropped.

General Buchanan now proposed to withhold his consent to the meeting of the legislature until the new constitution had been accepted by Congress.   On the 25th of June, however, Congress passed an act admitting North Carolina, South Carolina, Louisiana, Georgia, Alabama, and Florida to representation, in view of the fact that they had framed and adopted "Constitutions of State Governments which

---

[1] Albert Voorhies, Democratic lieutenant-governor of the State since 1866, was succeeded by a negro house-painter, Oscar J. Dunn. B. F. Flanders, appointed governor by Sheridan, had resigned on January 2, 1868, and had been succeeded by Joshua Baker, a Union man from Attakapas, who now gave place to Warmoth.

are republican."[1] In accordance with the orders from General Grant, Buchanan now removed Governor Baker and Lieutenant-Governor Voorhies, and placed in office H. C. Warmoth and Oscar J. Dunn.

Two days later, June 29, 1868, the new legislature met in New Orleans. About one half the members were negroes; the Republicans had a majority of 20 to 16 in the senate and 56 to 45 in the lower house. At the organization of the two houses an effort was made to exclude most of the Democrats by forcing them to subscribe to the iron-clad oath of 1862,[2] as well as to the oath required of members of the General Assembly as laid down in the constitution just adopted. This position was taken by the president of the senate, Oscar J. Dunn, and by the temporary chairman of the lower house, R. H. Isabelle, who, like Dunn, was a negro. They explained their attitude by declaring that the State being still under military law as well as under reconstruction laws, they deemed it necessary for members to take both the test oath and the oath of the new constitution. This action of the presiding officers caused great indignation among the Democratic members,[3] partly because it was the attitude of two negroes at the time when their race had just been raised to high office in the State, and partly because General Grant, who had been telegraphed to a few days before for a decision on the question, had informed Dunn through General Buchanan that only the oath of 1868

---

[1] Tennessee and Arkansas had already been admitted. Texas, Mississippi, and Virginia were still "without." In discussing the admission act of June 25, Burgess says: "It was utter self-stultification for Congress to take the ground that the Johnson "State" Governments were unrepublican because they did not enfranchise all adult males of whatever race, color, . . . and then proceed to create new 'State' governments in their places upon the basis of a minority of the already duly qualified and registered voters." It was "a high political crime." Reconstruction and the Constitution, p. 154.

[2] This oath required of persons accepting office under the United States government that they should swear that they had never borne arms against the United States, aided its enemies, or supported the Confederacy.

[3] The Picayune criticised Dunn's action as "grotesquely impudent and exquisitely absurd."

should be required. When Dunn showed a disposition to reject Grant's view of the matter, a great crowd assembled once more around the doors of the Mechanics Institute to insist on the admission of the Democrats; and for a time it looked as if the scenes of July, 1866, were to be reenacted. The whole police force, with a regiment of artillery, was called out to prevent disorder. Luckily the General Assembly reconsidered its illegal action, and, " induced by a due respect for the General commanding the armies of the United States," decided to admit the Democratic members under the milder oath. The incident, however, was a bad augury for the future relations between the two races. It showed a disposition on the part of the negroes and their white allies to adopt a more radical platform in their treatment of the whites than General Grant himself would authorize, and forecasted a determination to legislate wholly with reference to their own interests.

The first act of the legislature was to pass the fourteenth amendment as required in the act of reconstruction. The next was to seek representation in Congress by the election of two senators. Accordingly, William Pitt Kellogg and John S. Harris were elected, and took their seats on July 18, 1868.[1] They were the first senators admitted from Louisiana since John Slidell and Judah P. Benjamin resigned in 1861. As soon as he was inaugurated, Warmoth informed General Buchanan of the ratification of the fourteenth amendment, and that officer immediately gave orders declaring that military law no longer existed in Louisiana; the civil law was once more supreme. All civil officers acting under authority from military headquarters were ordered to transfer their offices, with the records of the same, to their duly elected successors. The military forces, however, were not withdrawn from the State, but were to stand ready to preserve the peace whenever proper application was made by the civil authorities, or whenever so ordered by the commanding general.

---

[1] The representatives to the lower house of Congress now admitted were J. Hale Sypher, J. H. Menard (colored), Michael Vidal, John P. Newsham, and W. Jasper Blackburn.

CHAPTER X.

PARTY ORGANIZATION.

Louisiana now seemed to be in a state of peace and order, but it was only the calm which precedes the storm. The anomalous condition of political affairs could not continue; friction between the property owners and the irresponsible legislature was sure to come. Warmoth knew this, and his only hope was to keep enough of the Federal troops at hand to support him in his precarious position. It was not to be expected that the conduct of the Democrats, especially in those country parishes where the negroes were in the great majority, would be so circumspect as not to give the radicals many an opportunity to appeal to the Federal government for aid in keeping down Democrats and guaranteeing "life, liberty, and the pursuit of happiness" to white and black Republicans. Moreover, the order of the Knights of the White Camelia, which had been established in Louisiana during the preceding year, was now to be organized in a thorough manner, and was to spread over the whole southern part of the State. Its history will be given later.

When Warmoth's inaugural message appeared, it was approved by the Democratic papers as conservative in character and more moderate in tone than could have been expected. It naturally declared for "equality before the law and enjoyment of every political right by all citizens, regardless of race or previous condition." It added, however, with a cautious forecast of the future, that while the majority had adopted the constitution, there was still "a minority not wanting in intelligence and virtue that was opposed to such equality." "So let our course be moderate and discreet," argued the governor; "it is better that our legislation should fall behind than outstrip the popular wishes and demands. Let us try to bring back the era of good feeling.

I believe this epoch has the smiles of Providence. Cursed
for sins with war, scourged with epidemic, our crops
blighted for a succession of years; our fair State overflowed
by the torrents of the Mississippi; commerce paralyzed and
people impoverished; the event of my inauguration is
welcomed by the full restoration of civil government and
re-admission into the Union, the fairest prospects of crops,
receding floods, and improving credit. Let us vie with each
other in seeing who of us shall receive most blessings for
good and faithful services rendered the State."

The approval of the governor's attitude, however, did not
last long. Some lawlessness began to crop out in the country parishes as the result of the strained relations between
the races, or perhaps as a natural result of the political upheaval. The Picayune maintained that the lawbreakers
were deserters from the Confederate army, or jayhawkers,
now pretending to be Union men. The governor sent a report to President Johnson declaring that one hundred and
fifty men had been murdered in Louisiana in six weeks; a
statement which the Picayune promptly pronounced to be
false. The outrages, it said, of which Warmoth wrote
really numbered only three, and these were personal, not
political.[1] Senator Jewell, a Democrat from Orleans, attacked Warmoth's character in the legislature, saying that
he had been sent out of Vicksburg by Grant for conduct
unbecoming an officer and a gentleman, and dismissed from
the staff of General Banks for non-observance of the truth,
and that he had now set himself up in Louisiana as a dictator
and a maligner of the best portion of the people. Jewell
was answered by a Republican, who said that these charges
were but the shafts of malice.[2]

---

[1] Forty-two officers of the Freedmen's Bureau reported only fourteen deaths, black and white, in the parishes included in Warmoth's
report. Picayune, August 8, 1868.

[2] Henry Clay Warmoth was at this time twenty-six years old. He
was born in McLeansboro, Illinois, May 9, 1842. He was admitted
to the bar in 1861, and became district attorney of a judicial district of Missouri in 1862; but resigned to enter the army. He was
appointed lieutenant-colonel, and took part in the assaults on Vicksburg in May, 1862. He was for a time judge of the military court

In the General Assembly some attempts were made to pass laws which lacked the moderation advocated in the governor's inaugural. For instance, in July there was pending in the senate a printing bill providing for the payment of certain items at a price six times greater than had ever been paid before for similar work. This bill was so bad that a Republican senator of full African blood, from Lafourche, spoke against it, and the price was reduced. Worse, however, than any form of plunder was the threat of "mixed schools," a measure which in Louisiana, as in other Southern States, was regarded as the opening wedge to social equality, and hence as a dire insult to the old aristocratic population. On August 11 the Picayune announced that T. W. Conway,[1] the state superintendent of education, who was known to be a fanatic on this subject and had proved himself to be a meddlesome political agitator, had drawn up a bill to be submitted to the legislature. This bill, carrying out a provision of the new constitution, placed under state control all institutions established by the State or incorporated by the legislature, and declared that children of all colors between the ages of six and twenty-one were to be admitted to the public schools. But for fear that this mingling of the two races might be obviated by the refusal of the whites to allow their children to attend "mixed" schools, the bill further provided that "all children between eight and fourteen years, shall attend school at least six months in each year; and if the parents or guardians, on being admonished, do not cause them so to attend, a justice of the peace may fine them to the extent of $25 for the first offence, and $50 for subsequent ones; and after three such admonitions, the State board is authorized to

---

of the Department of the Gulf. Judge Howe informs me that Warmoth claimed that he was dismissed from the army when he was very young because he made a speech criticising General Grant for his treatment of General McClellan. After a visit to Washington, however, Warmoth was reinstated. Judge Howe says also that Pinchback was a professional gambler, used to get drunk, and was a rascal generally.

[1] T. W. Conway was an ex-army chaplain, and is not to be confounded with J. R. Conway, mayor of New Orleans.

take such children or wards and give them instruction at
least five months in each year, in such school or place of
correction as shall be provided by the board for that purpose, at the expense of the parents, if they are able to
bear it." The Picayune predicted that if this bill with
its drastic compulsory feature passed, it would stir up
civil war. Perhaps as a result of this prediction, the bill
did not become a law; and when in the following year it
was passed, it was shorn of its compulsory provision. The
bare threat of compulsory mixed schools, however, showed
the animus of the radicals in the legislature, and aroused
intense antagonism toward men of the type of Conway and
Pitkin, who seemed to long for the day when white and
black children should sit on the same school bench.

In September both houses of the General Assembly passed
a " social equality bill " punishing by a fine of not less than
one hundred dollars any hotel keeper, steamboat master,
and the like who should refuse to give equal accommoda-
tions to whites and blacks; but the bill was promptly vetoed
by the governor on the ground that a law of this nature
would really injure the cause of the negro. The veto was
sustained in the lower house, and Warmoth was publicly
thanked for his action by the Picayune.[1]

There was great dissatisfaction, however, over an act of
the legislature authorizing the governor to appoint five police
commissioners for New Orleans, Jefferson City, and St.
Bernard parish. These commissioners, three of whom were
negroes, were vested with large powers; and they soon contrived to make the so-called " Metropolitan Police Bill " a
most unpopular measure. They were empowered to appoint or remove the police force of the city, to assess the
various municipal corporations for the sums necessary to

[1] Picayune, September 29, 1868. Pinchback had opposed the civil
rights provision in the constitutional convention when it was first
proposed, saying: " Social equality, like water, must be left to find
its own level, and no legislation can affect it. Any attempt to legislate on it will be the death blow of our people. The national civil
rights bill is imperative." For some reason, however, Pinchback
changed his mind, and the provision on this subject finally adopted
in the constitution was proposed by him.

carry out the law, to lease and purchase property for the purposes of the bill, and to pass enactments pertaining to its functions.[1] The city council, having decided that this act was illegal and that the police appointed under it were incapable, organized the police under the old law, but General Steedman, superintendent of the police force, refused to allow the authority of the commissioners to be superseded.[2] Finally, on October 28, the governor wrote to General L. H. Rousseau,[3] the commanding general, that, Congress having prohibited the organization of the militia in Louisiana, he required him to keep the peace in Orleans, Jefferson, and St. Bernard.[4] Rousseau agreed to support the police force organized under General Steedman.

On November 4 the election for presidential electors took place. In order to understand the success of the Democrats in that election it will be necessary to review briefly the organization of the party during the spring and summer preceding. Encouraged by the fact that Hancock had shown himself favorable to fair treatment of the Democrats, and by the fact that the Tribune, the negro organ, had refused to support Warmoth for governor, the Democrats began to bestir themselves in the early spring. At first it was proposed to put up a state ticket in opposition to Warmoth and Taliaferro, but the Democratic leaders decided that it was not worth while. If, they said, the constitution is defeated, there will be no offices to fill; if it is ratified, the Republicans will naturally elect their candidates.[5]

---

[1] Picayune, August 19, 1868.

[2] Annual Cyclopaedia, 1868, subject " Louisiana," p. 440.

[3] General Rousseau had supplanted Buchanan, September 15.

[4] Picayune, October 28, 1868. The Democrats offered to make Steedman superintendent of the new police bill, but he refused to accept, though he was a Democrat. By an act of March 5, 1869, the mayor of New Orleans was made dependent entirely on the metropolitan police. Acts of Legislature, 1869, p. 61. The same year the Metropolitan Police bill was amended and reenacted, ibid., p. 92. This quarrel over police was explained before the committee on Louisiana elections, 41st Cong., 2d sess., H. Mis. Doc. No. 154, pt. I, p. 760.

[5] This policy was not followed by Mississippi, which in the following June had the ephemeral satisfaction of defeating both the radical state ticket and the constitution. The victory, however, only deferred for a year the reconstruction of the State.

So Colonel T. L. Macon, chairman of the central Democratic committee, advised that only local nominations be made for Congress, parish offices, the legislature, and the bench. Between the two gubernatorial candidates, Warmoth, "the adventurer," and Taliaferro, an honest Union citizen of Louisiana, he advised the conservatives who cared to vote to support Taliaferro. How many of them did so is not known.

While, however, no attempt was made to carry the gubernatorial election, the Democrats decided to organize and to try to carry the State for Democracy in the presidential election to be held in November. Resolutions were adopted declaring that the people of Louisiana were threatened with the consummation of a policy involving their degradation and ruin, promising the destruction of their material interests with the overthrow of all constitutional safeguards, and aiming at the perversion of every social, educational, and governmental institution. The organization of the party effected during the summer of 1868 was the most thorough that the State has ever seen. Old Democrats now living still speak with admiration and pride of the work accomplished at that time. One of the leaders has told the writer that before the summer was over he could sit in his office in New Orleans and in twenty minutes he could assemble three thousand Democrats on Canal Street.

The Republicans maintained that every negro was naturally a Republican, and could become a Democrat only through intimidation or violence. This theory turned out to be false. Doubtless many negroes did change sides as the result of intimidation and violence; for the Democrats, where it was safe, did not hesitate to use these weapons. But if the newspapers of the time and living witnesses may be believed, a large number of negroes, having no political convictions, and being densely ignorant, were easily organized into Democratic clubs.[1] Others, more intelligent, were

---

[1] For instance, James A. Pugh, of Morehouse, testified that a negro said to him: "We are all democrats; we have been deceived

unwilling to become the tools of Republican adventurers from the North seeking office through the negro vote, and refused to array themselves against the property owners of the State. Certainly the Democrats had no difficulty in obtaining negro political speakers to address meetings of their own people, though such speakers were often exposed to violence and were denounced by the radicals as "Judases, Cains, Benedict Arnolds, and traitors to their race."[1] One negro driving a carriage in a Democratic procession was actually killed.

In the month of May the Picayune urged the Democrats to lose no opportunity to win over the blacks. It commended heartily the people of Caddo parish, who had helped the anti-radical negroes to form a club, had promised to protect the club from radical violence, and had offered to give the members preference in employment and advice in perplexities.[2] The Opelousas Courier criticized the Picayune for wanting to induce negroes to join Democratic clubs; as for itself, it did not want negro suffrage in any shape, for or against the Democrats. The Picayune, however, insisted that the industrious negroes could and should be induced to abandon the radical party. "We don't blame," it said, "those negroes who vote the Republican ticket: 'they know not what they do.'"

The policy of the Picayune found favor. In New Orleans at least one colored club—called the "Constitution

---

by the radical party; I have strained these old eyes of mine nearly out looking down the road for the drove of mules that were to be divided amongst us. We were promised forty acres of land and a mule and three hundred dollars if we would vote for the convention. We did it, but the mules have not come, and now we are democrats, and do not want to vote the radical ticket." Report on Contested Elections, pt. I, p. 292.

[1] Picayune, September 11, 1868.

[2] In Rapides parish planters held a meeting and resolved: "We will ever hold in high esteem the freedmen among us who came out boldly in the recent political excitement, and ranged themselves on our side, and when we have favor to render they shall not be forgotten." Report on Contested Elections, pt. II, p. 149. Wm. Norman (colored) testified, "I think it was the kindness of the whites toward the colored people that made them vote the democratic ticket." Ibid., p. 177.

Club No. 1 "—paraded the streets.   Moreover, colored
orators, who had joined the Democratic party, were
promptly enlisted as speakers to convert their brethren to
Democratic principles.   Some of them spoke from the same
platforms as the white orators.   The white radicals were
enraged at this successful attempt to split the African vote,
supposedly solid for them; and when Willis Rollins, a
loud-mouthed negro orator from one of the country
parishes, was brought to New Orleans and began to make
violent speeches against the radicals, his life was in danger.
There was a riot on Canal Street, and some three hundred
black and white radicals, catching sight of Rollins, fell upon
him and beat him until he was rescued by some friendly
Democrats.   When the frightened darky had been hurried
off to the police station for safety, Governor Warmoth
addressed the mob on Canal Street, and counselling moderation and the privilege of free speech for all, persuaded them
to disperse.   A week later, Rollins, with several other
negroes, addressed a crowded meeting in Lafayette Square;
but while he had a marvellous flow of language, what he
said was for the most part abusive nonsense, and the Democratic leaders concluded that though the negroes were
flattered to see one of their own race on the same platform
with " white folks," his speeches really did more harm than
good.[1]   The Democratic cause was really aided, however,
by the defection of a negro preacher in the adjoining State
of Mississippi.   In August this man published a statement
in which he said, " I leave the Republican party, believing it
to be ruinous to the Union, an enemy to the black race, and
the upbuilder of tyranny in our beloved Union."   This
statement, published in the New Orleans papers, may well
have influenced those of the blacks who were wavering in
their allegiance to their northern friends.

The Tribune, as we have seen,[2] disappointed at the non-
recognition of the best class of negroes, or at least asserting

[1] Personal testimony of Col. T. L. Macon.
[2] Page 196.

this as a grievance, inveighed against the Republican leaders in Louisiana as "devoid of honesty and decency." But the Tribune, of course, had no intention at the time of deserting the Republican ranks; it was simply attacking the radical faction. Many of the negroes, however, were too ignorant to make distinctions; and, dissatisfied with the party in power, they believed that there was little hope from the Republicans, and that the Democrats, in recognition of negro aid at the ballot box, would give the negro a fair chance. They listened to able addresses from men like General J. B. Steedman, the Federal collector of internal revenue in New Orleans, who, though a Democrat, won the confidence of the colored voters by telling them that he had served in the Federal army and had commanded five thousand negro troops at Nashville. Steedman told them frankly that if a Democratic president was elected, the question of negro suffrage would probably be decided by a vote of the entire people, or perhaps by a decision of the Supreme Court. If negro suffrage was decided to be constitutional, he said, he did not believe a respectable man in Louisiana would attempt to deprive the negro of his vote. At the same time he told the negroes that the radicals were using them as tools with which to get into office, and cared nothing for their general welfare. Steedman could also point to the fact that General Rousseau, the commanding general of the department, was a Democrat, and that there was in New Orleans a Democratic club of ex-Federal soldiers and army and navy officers numbering more than two hundred members.[1]

The Democrats, however, were well aware that to obtain a victory in November for Seymour and Blair they could not depend on gentle suasion. They remembered that in the preceding spring the radicals had adopted the constitution by a vote of 51,737 to 39,076. If they would change the minority into a majority, they must register a large

---

[1] Report on Contested Elections, pt. II, pp. 756–768. Steedman's testimony is very enlightening.

number of Democrats, and at the same time intimidate as many negroes as possible to vote the Democratic ticket or to remain away from the polls. As far as possible no intimidation was to be used, for they knew that the state administration, if defeated, would be only too happy to raise the cry of fraud, and to persuade Congress to reverse the returns.

The whole State was alive to the issue, and for some months before the election the Democrats seem to have been confident of victory. New Orleans teemed with political clubs, both Democratic and Republican. Among the most conspicuous Democratic organizations were the Seymour Tigers, the Swamp Fox Rangers, the Seymour Infantas, and the Innocents. This last-named association, whose name was supposed to be derived from that of a republican club in Sicily, numbered twelve hundred members, a mixed crowd of Spaniards, Italians, Sicilians, Portuguese, Maltese, and Americans. The radicals declared that many outrages were committed by these " Sicilian cut-throats," and that they had instituted a reign of terror in St. Bernard parish. Certainly there was almost sure to be a fracas whenever they paraded in New Orleans.[1] They sallied forth from the Orleans Ball Room, where it was said they would consume a hogshead of wine and innumerable cigars. The radical clubs were equally active in parading the streets, and it was reported that the leader of a negro Republican club was heard to say that he wanted nothing better than to meet a Democratic parade; " he would bore right in." Every effort was made by the radicals to encourage the negroes to claim full equality with the whites—both political and social. Campaign documents were sent down from the North to incite the negroes to vote the Republican ticket. Some of these were illustrated, and contained easy catechisms for

---

[1] General Hatch, assistant commissioner of the Freedmen's Bureau, reported that during one month, in the parishes adjacent to New Orleans, there were two hundred and ninety-seven negroes killed, fifty wounded, and one hundred and forty-two maltreated. Report on Contested Elections, pt. I, p. 32.

the darkies, thus: "Who set you free?" "The Radicals." "Who fought the battles of Slavery?" "The Democrats." Social equality was advocated from the stump. An orator named Vidal in one of the country parishes was heard declaring to a crowd of negroes that he was "raised" in France, where social equality of races existed. He told the negresses present that in that country they would be received like white women. He added that as the negroes were in the majority in Louisiana, they should control everything.[1]

A potent factor in the organization of the Democratic party in Louisiana was the secret association. In 1867–8 an association called the "Knights of the White Camelia" sprang up like magic in southern Louisiana, whence it spread under the same or similar names through Alabama and other neighboring States. It attracted numbers by its secrecy and held them by a binding oath. Its cardinal doctrines were white supremacy and opposition to every effort of the radicals directed toward miscegenation. While its adherents vehemently denied that it was political in character and even voted down on one occasion a proposal to make it such, its opposition to negro rule naturally took a quasi-political character, and helped to consolidate the ranks of the Democratic party.

In Franklin, St. Mary's parish, it was organized as the White Man's or Caucasian Club as early as May 22, 1867. Its founder, it is said, was Judge Alcibiade de Blanc, of that parish. In New Orleans, which was to be the headquarters of the association, its formal organization dated from May 23, 1867, but there was no convention of the order in that city until 1868. Then the Federal organization was completed, a constitution was framed, and the knights began to extend their influence throughout the other Southern States.[2] The preamble of their manual de-

---

[1] Report on Contested Elections, pt. II, p. 51.
[2] See for the rise of the Knights of the White Camelia, Fleming, Documentary History of Reconstruction, II, 349 ff., and Brown, The Lower South, pp. 209–10.

clares that " there is a fact which stands beyond denial—
it is that the Radical Party, the freedmen, and the colored
population of the whole republic have coalesced against the
white race."

The ceremonial provided for the introduction of members into the association was as elaborate as those in use
among the Greek-letter societies of our colleges. The
novitiate was required to swear a solemn oath that at all
times he would maintain and defend the superiority of the
white race on this continent, and at all times observe a
marked difference between the white and the negro or
African race; that he would do all in his power to prevent
the political affairs of this country, in whole or in part, from
passing into the hands of the negro or other inferior race;
that he would never fail to cast his vote against a person
opposed to these principles who might be a candidate for
any office; that he would never marry any woman not belonging to the white race; that he would obey the orders
of those who by the statutes of the society had the right to
give orders; that he would, at all times, even at the peril
of his life, respond to a sign of distress or cry of alarm
coming from any fellow member of the order; that he
would defend or protect them, and do all in his power to
assist them through life; that he would never reveal to any
one without authority the existence of the order, its signs
of recognition, its pass words, its signals of alarm, or the
names of its members; that he would cherish the principles
of the order, and use his influence and power to instil them
in the hearts of others. When this oath had been duly
sworn, the grand commander said, " By virtue of the power
in me vested, I now pronounce you ' Knight of the White
Camelia.' " Following this ceremonial, the knight was instructed in the signs of the order. The sign of recognition
was made by carelessly drawing the index finger of the
left hand across the left eye. The signal given by a knight
in distress was " ih! ih!" The signal of alarm was four
knocks—first, one; then two, rapidly; and then one.[1] The

---

[1] Report on Contested Elections, pt. II, pp. 402 ff.

questions and answers to insure recognition were as follows:
Q. "Where were you born?" A. "On Mount Caucasus."
Q. "Are you free?" A. "I am." Q. "Were your ances-
tors free?" A. "They were." Q. "Are you attached to
any order?" A. "I am." Q. "To what order?" A. "To
the Order of the White Camelia." Q. "Where does it
grow?" A. "On Mount Caucasus."

The leading men of the State very generally joined this
order, though the principles which it inculcated were already so deeply implanted in the breasts of the southern
whites that it seems useless to have framed them into a
constitution. In fact, one of the knights afterwards testified before a congressional committee that such an organization was both useless and absurd.[1] However, at the time
the object of the order was very generally interpreted by
the members to be the securing of white supremacy by an
appeal to race pride. It was a protest against social equality
and miscegenation as taught by the radicals in the North
and as embodied in some of their legislative acts in the
South. The social and the political are so closely connected
that such an organization, as was said above, could not but
help to strengthen the ranks of the Democratic party.[2]
While it did not attempt to defraud the negro of his ballot,[3]
its members were constantly warned that negro clubs had
been formed all over the South by the radicals in open and
sworn hostility to the whites, and that those negroes who

---

[1] Testimony of J. H. Boatner. Report on Contested Elections, pt.
I, p. 290.

[2] The chief of the knights in Alabama told W. G. Brown that
no act of violence was committed by his circle, but they sent out
silent squads to intimidate negroes and carpet-baggers. Lower
South, p. 213. The writer cannot discover that the association in
Louisiana, as such, took any part in politics.

[3] Colonel Zacharie says that spies got into the order in New
Orleans, and that little or nothing was done there by the Knights
of the White Camelia. This is true, for Warmoth states that he
had detectives who were members of the Knights of the White
Camelia in good standing, and who gave him information. One
was an ex-officer in the United States army. Report on Contested
Elections, pt. II, pp. 454, 527, 529.

had remained true to the whites should be generously dealt with and kindly remembered.[1]

It was but natural, also, that the widespread organization known as the Ku Klux Klan, which had been established first in Tennessee in 1866, should extend its operations to Louisiana. The Ku Klux was quite distinct in its methods, if not in its objects, from the Knights of the White Camelia, and the latter generally denied that the Klan existed in Louisiana. It seems true that as an organization it did not exist, but the testimony of many witnesses shows that reckless bands of whites did disguise themselves, and, adopting the methods of the order as it existed in other States, did range some of the country parishes at night, intimidating the ignorant, superstitious darkies, and endeavoring to frighten away the more extreme of the radical whites.

The aim of the Ku Klux, like that of the Knights of the White Camelia, was to maintain white supremacy and to resist with all their might the influence of the Loyal League, by which, as we have seen, the negroes were held under strict discipline and sworn to vote the radical ticket.[2] As the Loyal League had its constitution, its ritual, its catechism, so had the Ku Klux Klan. This remarkable organization had its first home in Pulaski, Tennessee, where it was formed in 1866 by a band of young men who had served to-

---

[1] The congressional committeemen sometimes amused themselves by asking ignorant negroes about the Knights of the White Camelia. A Democratic negro named Everett was questioned as follows:—
Q. "Are you a member of the Knights of the White Camelia?"
A. "I don't understand that name."
Q. "You know what a Camelia is, don't you?"
A. "No, sir."
Q. "Did you ever see a flower called the White Camelia?"
A. "I don't know what kind of word that is. I knew a girl of that name once. That is, she was 'Melia'."
Q. "But she was a black Camelia, wasn't she?"
A. "No, sir, pretty near white."
[2] The Union League, according to Professor Fleming, was largely responsible for creating the conditions which led to the Ku Klux movement, and the Klan had much to do with the breaking up of the organization of the League. Documentary History of Reconstruction, II, 4.

gether in the Confederate army.[1]   Its original object seems to have been social rather than political; it resembled a college fraternity, with initiation ceremonies and good fellowship. The order became so popular that it spread into other Southern States, where branch dens were established with more or less connection with the headquarters in Tennessee. Its very secrecy exercised a charm over its members. As the Union League began to spread through the South, and it became necessary to control thieving freedmen and their associates the carpet-baggers, the order changed from a social club to a vigilance committee, or band of " regulators." It soon absorbed the patrols who had been so commonly employed in the South to keep the negroes in order on the plantations.

In the spring of 1867 the various " dens " were requested to send delegates to a convention in Nashville, Tennessee. Here a constitution was drawn up which provided for a central administration and supervision over subordinate " dens." This " prescript," as it was termed, did not state the objects of the order, but was simply designed to bring all branches into better discipline and to prevent the disorder and violence to which such an association was liable. In 1869 a revised constitution was issued in which the principles of the order were clearly stated. The Klan was declared to be " an institution of chivalry, humanity, mercy, and patriotism." Its objects were declared to be (a) to protect the weak, the innocent, and the defenceless from the wrongs and outrages of the lawless, the violent, and the brutal; (b) to defend the Constitution of the United States and all laws passed in conformity with it; (c) to aid in the execution of all constitutional laws, and to protect the people from unlawful seizure and from trial except by their peers and the law of the land. The accompanying creed

---

[1] Thomas Dixon is doubtless right in saying that the name was derived from *" Kuklos "* (Gr. *Circle*), to which *Klan* was added; the Kuklos being changed into the fantastic *Kuklux*.   Metropolitan Magazine, September, 1905. See also Lester and Wilson, Ku Klux Klan, p. 55. Brown, The Lower South (1902), p. 200, gives the same derivation.

reverently acknowledges the majesty and supremacy of the Divine Being as well as the relation of the people to the United States government, the supremacy of the Constitution, the constitutional laws, and the union of the States. The " Empire " of the order was declared to include all the States of the ex-Confederacy as well as Kentucky and Missouri.   The officers were to be known as the grand wizard of the empire and his ten genii; a grand dragon of the realm and his eight hydras; a grand titan of the dominion and his six furies; a grand giant of the province and his four goblins; a grand cyclops of the den and his two night hawks; a grand magi (sic), a grand monk, and others.   The body politic was designated as " the Ghouls."   The candidate for membership was put through a catechism resembling in many respects the ritual of the Knights of the White Camelia.   He must swear that he was not a member of the radical Republican party, of the Loyal League, or of the Grand Army of the Republic; that he was opposed to the principles of the radical party and to negro equality; and that he favored the reenfranchisement of white men and a white man's government in the South.

The order, which was now highly centralized, was presided over by the grand wizard, General N. B. Forest, the brilliant Confederate leader.   Its " invisible empire " was to prove more than a match for the visible Union League.   It was found very difficult, however, to control the lawless elements which began to insinuate themselves into the order. From the extermination of the so-called " Tories " of the mountain districts, who committed outrages on the Confederate sympathizers, the more reckless dens of the association passed to the commission of outrages on their own account.   Even private quarrels were settled through the instrumentality of the K. K. K., and persons having no connection with the order used its name and disguise to cover their crimes.   As a result, in March, 1869, a decree of the grand wizard disbanded the order. and declared that all papers and property of the dens should be destroyed.   This decree never reached some of the dens, and the operations of the scattered clans, relieved from central control, became more violent than before. Spurious dens were established, and the better class of whites repudiated the lawless conduct of the midnight bands who, disguised as ghosts, whipped and even killed those who had aroused their enmity. It was maintained that these lawless bands, bent on plunder and outrage, were often radicals.[1]

In 1871 two drastic laws or force bills against the order were passed by Congress. It was only natural that the later discreditable history of the order should lead to the general belief in the North that from the beginning the society had warred against law and order. Its original aims and objects, which were justified by the disorganization of the South in politics and the social unheaval accomplished by the reconstruction acts and the supremacy of negro rule, were obscured by the lawless acts of its more reckless elements. Such secret organizations, whatever good they may accomplish, bear within themselves the seeds of their own destruction. They become a cloak for the deeds of desperate men; and the better elements of society, in self-protection, find it necessary to disown or destroy what they have founded.

The organization has been compared by one writer[2] to the famous Carbonari, who worked for the liberation of Italy in the early nineteenth century; by another to "that secret movement by which, under the very noses of French garrisons, Stein and Scharnhorst organized the great German struggle for liberty." "It was a magnificent conception," says Thomas Dixon,[3] "and in a sense deserved success. It differed from all other attempts at revolution in the caution and skill with which it required to be conducted. It was a movement made in the face of the enemy, and an enemy of overwhelming strength. Should it succeed, it would be the most brilliant revolution ever accomplished. Should

[1] Brown, The Lower South, p. 209.
[2] Garner, Reconstruction in Mississippi, p. 353.
[3] In Metropolitan Magazine, September, 1905.

it fail—well, those who engaged in it, felt that they had nothing more to lose."[1]

The evidence of the existence of Ku Klux methods in Louisiana, though not of any organization connected with the parent association, is found abundantly in the reports of the congressional committee. A merchant of Sabine parish testified that there were some K. K. K. in his parish. They did not attack negroes, but only white hog-stealers. When they became reckless and attacked good citizens in order to steal their horses, the honest folks of the parish rose up against them. "They passed as spirits," testified an old negro of De Soto parish, "and pretended to raise the dead rebel soldiers. . . . They charged right through the grave-yard on horseback. . . . They would come round and tell a man 'Hold my head till I fix my backbone right'; and the colored people didn't know whether they were ghosts or not, because one of them went to a man's house and called for a drink of water. He drew three buckets of water and carried to him, and he drank every drop of it."[2] If one of these sheeted visitors was asked why he drank so much, he would answer: "If you were dead and in hell as long as I have been, you would drink a sight of water," or, "That's the first drink I have had since I was killed at the battle of Shiloh." In Franklin, Sabine, Washington, Claiborne, Morehouse, and Tangipahoa parishes the K. K. K. were abroad more than once, and in the latter parish they killed one John Kemp and wounded another man. In Morehouse parish the K. K. K. sent warnings to objectionable radicals in the following form:—

---

[1] When Congress (in 1870–1871) sent committees to investigate the Ku Klux Klan, "to the majority, 'Ku Klux' meant simply outlaws; the minority thought that the first Ku Klux in history were the disguised men who, against the law, threw the tea overboard in Boston Harbor." Brown, The Lower South, p. 222.

[2] Report on Contested Elections, pt. I, p. 153. They had large leather sacks concealed under their disguises.

"OLD GRAVE YARD,
"The Hour of Midnight.
"W. A. Moulton:
"The time has come. Nine (9) is left you. The time is yours! Improve it! Or suffer the penalty! The pale faces are against you. Depart, ye cursed. We cannot live together Nine days!
K. K. K."

Prominent men in Louisiana, when examined before the congressional committee in 1868, denied that there was any connection between the Ku Klux Klan and the Knights of the White Camelia; they were proud of their membership in the latter, and generally condemned the excesses attributed to the former association. Yet the two orders were so similar in their objects that it was only natural that the knights should be accused of acts of violence and intimidation perpetrated by the K. K. K. Color was lent to this accusation by the fact that some reckless individuals joined the knights to secure the protection of that organization, and then disguised themselves like the Ku Kluxes and committed outrages.[1] The better class of whites deplored these outrages, and this feeling was expressed in the following editorial:—

"STOP THEM!

"We understand that outrages are occasionally perpetrated under the name of Ku Klux Klan. We really believe that the principles of that organization are truly set forth in the article we publish to-day on the first page, and if we are correct in our opinion, the organization is such a one as the times and the circumstances in which the people of the South are placed call for. It is an organization that is intended, in the absence of law and order, to protect ourselves, our families, and our property, and eventually to insure us the possession of our inherent and constitutional rights. We cannot believe that the men who, some nights since, went to Cardell's and abused negroes and robbed them of their watches were the Ku Kluxes. . . . These were a set of violent men that took upon themselves the name of Ku Klux and under that name were doing a great deal of injury to the good citizens who were doing their best to prevent it."[2]

It was only natural that in the excited state of public sentiment in the North all outrages in the South should be regarded as political and should be exaggerated in number

[1] Testimony of R. P. Webb, Report on Contested Elections, pt. I, pp. 725 ff.
[2] Franklin Sun, October 3, 1868.

and in degree. Rhodes, in his recent history of this period, recognizes this tendency to exaggeration on the part of the North, and then falls into a similar exaggeration by declaring that the Ku Klux Klan was not responsible for the disorder and lawlessness in the South, and that "Godkin showed a true appreciation of the state of Southern society when he wrote, 'the South before the War was one vast Ku-Klux-Klan.' Gentlemen used the revolver, and the poor whites the bowie knife as the final argument in a controversy."[1] It is certainly true that before the war, as well as at the present time, the Southerners have recourse far less frequently than the Northerners to the courts for redress of grievances, especially where the honor is touched, but it is simply gross exaggeration to assert that the disorder under the Ku Klux régime in 1867–1870 was the normal condition of the South before the Civil War. The candid student of southern life before the great conflict will enter a strong protest against Rhodes's approval of Godkin's judgment on this point.

[1] Rhodes, History of United States, VI, 184.

CHAPTER XI.

For two months previous to the presidential election of 1868 there was much excitement in Louisiana, and there were constant reports of outrages or "massacres" in the country parishes and even in New Orleans. Although great numbers of the more timid negroes were frightened by bands of disguised whites in some of the parishes into voting the Democratic ticket or into staying away from the polls altogether, while others were intimidated by the processions of the Innocents, the Rangers, and other Democratic clubs, there were great numbers who were aroused by their radical white leaders to assert their legal rights against the whites and even to commit acts of aggression. This was especially the case when the blacks were assembled in large crowds and were excited by reports of attacks on their own race. Many of them who individually would have been fearful of opposing their old masters, to whom they felt they owed a kind of natural obedience, were, when congregated, capable of acts of extreme violence, which in all cases brought down upon them the swift vengeance of the whites. To the carpet-baggers and other white leaders, who had come down from the North and were hopeful of using the negroes for their own ends, it seemed eminently proper that the negroes, if threatened or attacked, should repel violence with violence. To the Southerners the sight of their ex-slaves, excited by strangers to take up arms for any reason against their former owners, seemed nothing less than a servile insurrection, the fear of which had hung over the South like a dark cloud in the days of slavery. When the blacks, therefore, appeared in arms, all thoughts of politics were dropped, and the ensuing conflict, which in the

North was reported as "a political massacre," became in reality a race war. Even southern Republicans, and there were many such, joined the Democrats in stamping out "the negro uprising."

Several of these so-called massacres occurred in Louisiana during the month of October, 1868; and both the northern Republican papers and the speeches of congressmen rang with the oppression of Union men in the South, and with the necessity of military rule to guard the rights of "loyal citizens." The most important of these conflicts between the whites and the blacks took place in the parishes of Bossier, St. Landry, St. Bernard, and Orleans. With the sworn testimony of the participants on both sides before us,[1] it is extremely difficult, if not impossible, to obtain an accurate account of the occasion and the results of these conflicts. The testimony is distorted by the usual passion and exaggeration which characterize such affairs.

There were in Bossier parish two so-called riots. The first was at Bossier Point, where some two hundred negroes armed themselves for the purpose, it was believed, of seizing by violence the lands of the planters. The whites promptly put down the uprising, and eighteen of the negroes, having been tried by juries of whites and blacks, were sent to the penitentiary for exciting a riot. It was believed by the whites that in this affair the blacks had been egged on by the agents of the Freedmen's Bureau at Shreveport, but there was no evidence to corroborate this belief. About the middle of October of the same year there was a much more serious trouble in the same parish. Bossier, being on the border of Arkansas, was the scene of an active trade with that State and with Texas. There were engaged in this trade many reckless characters, who, moving from State to State, could not easily be held responsible for their acts. One of these Arkansas traders, passing by Shady Grove plantation, not far from the border of Caddo parish, asked some negroes whether they were radicals; and when a

[1] Report on Contested Elections, passim.

radical was pointed out, he fired a pistol at him, but failed to hit him. The white man was immediately seized by the negroes and bound; but when some other whites arrived on the scene, the prisoner was surrendered to them. However, about a hundred men came down from Arkansas to investigate the affair, and in the mêlée which followed several negroes were killed. A little later the negroes arrested two respectable white men on the charge that they had been concerned in the previous shooting of the blacks; and when a rumour spread that these two prisoners were to be rescued by the whites, the negroes killed them both. The news of this action aroused much indignation; the whites began to assemble from all directions, and to shoot down negroes wherever they could be found. Some of the blacks took refuge in the swamps, and did not reappear for a month. How many were killed it is impossible to say; the Democrats said forty at most, the Republicans declared that one hundred and twenty were killed and a large number wounded.

On September 28 of the same year (1868) another serious riot occurred at the town of Opelousas, in St. Landry parish. It continued for nearly two weeks, during which time, according to the testimony of the radicals, two or three hundred negroes were killed, while the Democrats asserted that the number did not exceed twenty-five or thirty. The cause of the trouble seems to have been as follows. Several political meetings of negroes were held at Opelousas, and at these, excited speakers declared that in the neighboring town of Washington many of the negroes had been inveigled into a Democratic club, that efforts must be made to bring them back into the Republican party, and that this must be done at the point of the bayonet or, if necessary, by the burning of the town. These speeches aroused the whites of Opelousas, and a number of Seymour Knights went over to Washington to attend the subsequent meetings of the negroes and to discover if violence were really meditated. These men addressed the negroes, warning them of the danger of their proposed action. Nearly two thousand negroes are said to have been present. The next event was the appearance of an article in a Republican paper of Opelousas, written by a Republican from Ohio who had settled in Opelousas and was teaching a negro school. The writer gave what was regarded by the Democrats as a distorted account of the action of the Seymour Knights in going to Washington, whereupon the school teacher was visited by a committee of three and given a severe whipping. A report spread that he had been killed, and the negroes, at the suggestion of a free man of color, gathered from the neighboring plantations and marched on Opelousas. The citizens, having armed themselves, went out to meet them. Most of the negroes were turned back without difficulty, but with one squad of twenty-three there was a conflict. The negro leader was armed, and when he was told not to fire, he answered that arms had been brought, and that he intended to use them. Thereupon one of the negroes fired a load of buckshot at the whites, who responded with a fusillade. Three whites were wounded and four negroes were killed. The blacks having finally made submission, some ten or twelve of them were put in the Opelousas jail, only to be taken out that night and shot. Great excitement followed, and other negroes were killed in the surrounding country—the Republicans claimed to the number of two hundred, and the Democrats to the number of thirty.

About a month after the Bossier riots (October 25, 1868) a deplorable trouble broke out in St. Bernard parish, just below New Orleans. In this parish there were three hundred and twenty-five Democrats registered and seven hundred Republicans, mostly negroes. The latter, having the upper hand, were for a time very unmanageable. There was much speaking by P. B. S. Pinchback and other Republican leaders, who, the Democrats asserted, made incendiary speeches to the negroes. On the night of October 25 a large band of negroes surrounded the house of Pablo Filio, who kept a grocery, and was a well-known Democrat. The house was closed, and when they demanded drink, they were refused. Who fired the first shot is disputed, but the negroes riddled the house with bullets, killed Filio, and fired several shots at his fleeing wife and children. They then pillaged the house and retired. This outrage excited great indignation, and a body of Innocents went down from New Orleans to avenge Filio's death. They seized a quantity of goods found in negro cabins, and killed a number of the blacks. Sixty negroes, charged with complicity in the crime, were arrested and put in jail. Here they remained for nearly two months, when the Freedmen's Bureau, finding that there were no specific charges against them, had them released. Later they were again arrested by order of the judge of the parish and put in jail, but no further record of them is obtainable. The judiciary in times of such confusion appears to have been powerless. On election day the sheriff of the parish, who was a Democrat, took upon himself to open the polls, and as no Republican commissioners appeared, the Democrats carried matters to suit themselves.[1] In New Orleans for several weeks preceding the election there were many acts of violence, chiefly as the result of conflicts between the Democratic and Republican clubs which were constantly parading the streets. One night, in front of Dumonteil's confectionery, a negro procession caused some trouble, and was stampeded by shots fired from the gallery of this shop. Just before election day an appeal was issued by the Republican state campaign committee urging all Republicans to go to the polls and do their duty manfully, though it was admitted that there was danger of outrage and violence. On the other hand, the central committee of the Democratic club issued a notice guaranteeing

---

[1] The testimony of Oliver Taylor, a Democratic negro, is delightful reading. It shows what preparation the average negro had for the exercise of the suffrage, and also the feelings of many negroes toward their old masters. In his testimony Taylor stated that he had persuaded one hundred negroes in St. Bernard to vote the Democratic ticket. Report on Contested Elections, pt. II, pp. 376–382.

protection to all who wished to vote. However, there appeared in the newspapers a mysterious proclamation, signed by " The Council of Seven," and headed " A White Man's Government or no Government," which declared that none but the blue-blooded should be allowed to vote. The Republicans said that this emanated from the Knights of the White Camelia or the Ku Klux Klan, while the Picayune promptly declared that it was a forgery gotten up by the radicals to invalidate the election. The Democrats, in a quiet election, were sure of a large majority, and did not wish the election put aside on a charge of intimidation. However this may be, the Republicans, asserting that they feared violence, did not turn out in large numbers. Of the forty clerks and commissioners of election appointed by them only three appeared. Warmoth himself admitted that he advised Republicans to stay away from the polls.

The election turned out just as both parties expected. The negroes for the most part stayed away from the polls, or if they voted at all, voted the Democratic ticket. The result was that the Seymour and Blair electors received 80,225 votes and the Grant and Colfax electors only 33,225. The Republicans published the returns showing that in seventeen parishes, where no disturbances had occurred, the Republican votes in 1867 was 28,509 in a total registration of 39,812, and that in 1868 it was 25,088 in a total registration of 43,348. In sixteen other parishes, where disturbances had taken place, there was a tremendous falling off in the Republican vote. The registration increased from 63,441 in 1867 to 73,783 in 1868, but at the same time the Republican vote fell off from 28,737 to 6047. This great diminution was of course attributed to the violence and intimidation by the Democrats, and to these causes much of it was certainly due; but it is also certain that a large number of negroes were persuaded without any threats of violence to cast their fortunes with the rehabilitated Democratic party. Warmoth showed that he had received in the spring of 1868 64,901 votes and Taliaferro 38,046, and the

Republicans spoke as if he had received a Republican majority of 26,000; but it will be remembered that the Democrats had no organization at that time, and that those who voted for Taliaferro, who was a native Republican, regarded him only as "the lesser of two evils." Hence this vote was not a fair test of the Democratic strength in the fall of 1868.

INDEX.